TUR

STORIES OI

BY DEREK HARRISON

For Lee,
who does so much for others,
and who knows —
Derek 8/10/16

Published by Starry Night Publishing.Com
Rochester, New York

What I really need is to get clear about what I must do, not what I must know, except insofar as knowledge must precede every act.

-- Soren Kierkegaard

Contents

Preface 7
Chapter One 11
PEACE TREES........ 23
Chapter Two 51
TUESDAY'S JAIL 63
Chapter Three 91
THE CAVE........ 103
Chapter Four 129
REFUGEE LUNCH........ 145
Chapter Five........ 169
BUILDING BLOCKS 187
Chapter Six 215
STREET DRUGS 229
Chapter Seven 263
TEA DRIVING........ 275
Chapter Eight 305
LITTLE THINGS 317
Chapter Nine 349
An Acknowledgement 367
About the Author: 369

Preface

We are living in troubled times. At least, that is what we are constantly being told: times that are uncertain and frightening, threatening, dangerous, often even deadly. We need, though, to think about what we mean when we say that. For one thing, the point has been made so often–a commonplace now of political or social conversations – that it is in danger of losing its force and becoming little more than a way to get attention. In any case there is nothing new being said by the observation. Times have *always* been troubled for some people somewhere, while being not so difficult, or even enviously easy, for other people in other places.

Suffering is highly personal. We may feel genuine compassion for the difficulties of people far away from us, or because of their particular tragic circumstances when they are close to home, but we truly suffer only when hard times arrive at our own doors. And they sometimes do.

At such times, it is natural for us to put up our defenses. We try automatically to preserve whatever is left to us, while at the same time we grow increasingly worried and pessimistic. We are likely to blame whomever or whatever is nearest to our problems or is most vulnerable. We become fearful, and we are inclined to turn that fear into its natural vent, anger. We may take refuge in fantasy, using one or another kind of entertainment to provide a momentary stay against the real threats to our well-being.

All of these reactions are understandable. In the end, we are humans, moving through our lives with all the frailties that go with the remarkable condition of humanity. For all of our differences, one thing held in common is that all of us are trying to find our way in a world that sometimes allows us to float contentedly on a sea of calm water and at other times tosses us about in storms that threaten us with drowning. At best we have a limited knowledge on how to navigate either kind of sea. And so we become naturally uneasy and ever more defensive.

There is another kind of reaction. It is to move not away from troubles and fears, but toward them. This book is about people who do that. Not that they are always moving in a direct line toward their own difficulties; that might suggest a dangerous degree of self-absorption, or even masochism. No, these people are finding satisfaction in helping others who are experiencing difficulties of their own. At some point, the persons featured in this book have figured out there is nothing to be gained from hand-wringing; hands have better uses. They also have grown weary of hearing the endless predictions of doom that some people, for reasons only they can understand, so much enjoy. By their actions, they seem to be saying that even if we *are* doomed, there is still much to do and also some satisfaction to be gained from the doing. Above all, they are not waiting for someone else to do something.

There is no sense of elitism that might lessen the value of either their attitudes or their actions; these people are not inherently special. There is certainly no indication of *noblesse oblige* in their personal philosophies, because they are not the highborn who have come to bestow benevolence on the downtrodden. There is enough in their actions and in the places where I found them to make them at least distinctive, but they are not all that extraordinary in their common concern for others. That is the word to note: common. Helping one another, in one way or another, is what almost everyone does almost every day, dozens or even hundreds of times. It may be nothing more than holding a door or smiling or offering a compliment or encouraging someone in difficulty -- actions so common that we are only vaguely aware that we are doing them. It is better that way: those many small acts of kindness are less to be valued if they require recognition, by others or by ourselves.

Then again, maybe they should receive recognition. Our entertainments and our news media offer constant examples of the worst of human behavior. We understand that: bad behavior and bad news are far more entertaining in their pandering appeal to the back side of our world view, and good news is quickly boring. The net effect, however, is to have us forget that most of human behavior is not bad. It is neutral or it is good, even if there is no particular appeal in presenting it.

This, then, is not a book for the eternally pessimistic; nay-sayers should read no further. It is also not recommended reading for the self-righteous, the naïve, the hopelessly idealistic, or persons incapable of finding some humor even in troubling situations. On the other hand, there may be something here for those who believe that we *can* make small improvements in the human condition when we put our minds and bodies to the task. That is true for everyone, at any time.

****

This is a work of non-fiction. The various narratives correspond to actual events as closely as notes, journals, pictures and memory allow. The same can be said for the people found here. In most cases their names and some of their descriptions or characteristics have been changed, for obvious reasons of privacy.

Above all, it should be stressed that these people and the work they did or are still doing represent only a tiny fraction of the many people and the many kinds of work being done by millions who have decided to move against suffering in their own places and in their own ways. Outside of these pages, they will likely never be recognized for what they achieved. They would be the first to admit that their efforts were only marginally effective, usually short-term in their material benefits, and to some degree even self-serving. For all of that, they provide a sampling of good news that can be stored away for encouragement when the world seems to have become so filled with trouble that all effort seems hopeless.

It is to these people that this book is dedicated.

Chapter One

Breaking down a door is a lot harder than it looks in the movies. It is noisier, too, especially when you are doing it at 6:15 in the morning. Still worse, doing it in an inner-city neighborhood where old frame houses stand close to one another and neighbors are tuned to the kind of noises that can threaten a fragile peace.

It was not just all the thumping and banging that was making me nervous. We were trying to break through the back door of a drug house.

First, Ken raised a bent leg and put his hand on my arm for support, as though he had in mind to karate-kick his way in. Thinking better of that, he went instead for the run-and-smash technique, right shoulder crashing against the door in a passable imitation of a determined cop on a drug raid. Except that in this case it was just the opposite, since Ken was the occupant of the place, and the police -- at least for the moment -- were nowhere around.

With an almost human indifference, the door remained exactly as it was, except for giving out a dull thud as Ken bounced back, bumping into me and rubbing his shoulder.

"Sorry, Uncle Derek."

"How about the front door?" I suggested, since I was not doing much else to help.

"No key. Landlord probably nailed it up anyway."

"A window?"

"Naw, they're all stuck tight."

Ken was in hyper mode, enjoying the chance to get rid of some excess energy and not wanting to waste time with talk. He spun around and began searching the back entryway, looking for any kind of tool. A set of wooden stairs, grey paint worn at their edges, led to the apartment above. They were empty of anything looking like a suitable tool. Two black garbage bags in a corner of the landing looked even less promising.

"Wait here a minute," he said. He was back in something more than a minute, carrying a short piece of iron pipe. One end had a rusted corner fitting from which a couple of short pieces extended. The appearance was that of a crude medieval mace.

It took two sharp blows with the heavy end to destroy the thin door panel to the right of the knob, and in the immediate silence that followed we could hear splintered pieces of wood skittering across the kitchen floor inside. Reaching in, Ken felt around, pulled his hand back, and then bent and stuck his whole head inside.

His voice came back distorted by the narrow opening.

"Gawda bawd crossit."

"What?"

He pulled his head back. "The landlord's got a board nailed across the door."

It took several minutes of pounding and prying to undo what the landlord had meant as security. At one point, Ken stepped back and called into the darkness of the stairs leading to the second floor.

"It's me, Ken. Just gettin' in my place."

A timely announcement, and thoughtful too, since the upstairs tenants were probably about ten seconds away from dialing 911. The last thing we needed at the moment was a visit from the police, and I suffered a quick mental flash of a squad car pulling quietly into the driveway. Still, I thought, it is not illegal to break into your own apartment. Unless maybe Ken hasn't been paying the rent.

"You paid the rent this month?" I asked.

"Sure." He laughed. "It doesn't matter. The landlord's a friend of mine."

"Well, hurry up anyway."

Tina and I had picked Ken up in the jail lobby at exactly 6:00 a. m., standard release time. He had been arrested on a weapons charge, and we had visited him the day before. That was Tina's doing. I went along partly because she, slightly insecure about going into the jail alone, had asked me to. More importantly, it was a chance to see Ken after what had been a long disappearance. At least we finally know where to find him now, Tina and I agreed.

When he saw the two of us sitting at the table, his face registered something between happiness and embarrassment. My first thought was that he looked even thinner than usual, his cheekbones prominent over a narrow jaw, and drawn. He must have read my mind.

"Yeah," he said as he sat down across from us, hands extended flat on the table. "I'm not eatin' real good these days."

"You always did like giving me something to worry about," I said. Close up, I could see that the lid above his left eye was swollen, with tiny purple veins that gave the impression of poorly-applied makeup. The eye itself was half shut. He put one finger up to the lower lid, gingerly.

"I totaled my car, on 490." He gave me a rueful look, like a teenager explaining to a parent. Then, seeing that I didn't respond, he let out a little laugh, a defensive snort.

"You know I never could go slow. But I walked away from it."

"Doesn't matter," I said." It's just good to see you again. You've been kinda hard to find these days."

"Yeah. Sorry, but you know..."

"It's okay."

As it turned out, Tina and I had not been Ken's only visitors, just the most recent ones. It took her several days to arrange our visit, and by the time we got in to see him he had been visited by an assistant to the mayor, a newspaper editor, and a local state congressman who claimed that Ken had been an inspiration to him. Others, too, Ken was happy to tell us. The deputies must have been wondering if they were running a jail or an embassy.

A welcome constant in our relationship -- along with a total lack of pretense or deference -- was that Ken and I could always find things to laugh about. So it was not long before we got right back to old times, which are always the better times. It was as though nothing had changed and we were again laughing it up on my back porch rather than sitting at a jailhouse table with a couple of deputies watching us.

Tina was inclined to be more serious, interrupting to press Ken about where he planned to go after his release. She tapped her index finger on the table like a mother dealing with a stubborn child.

"I dunno," Ken waved his hand in a dismissive circle.

"But you can't just, you know. You need --"

"I'll get somebody to pick me up." It clearly wasn't the two of us he had in mind.

"Who?"

"Maybe the woman I'm with now." Turning to me, "Man, she's like..." He grimaced and made a smothering motion with his hands, palms down. I got the point, though I was not sure which woman he was referring to.

"But where are you going to live?" Tina pressed. "You can't -- you don't want to go back *there*."

"Well, maybe I can-"

"Maybe you can come to my place for the weekend," Tina finished for him. "You know you've gotta get out of the city, do some serious thinking about where you're going from here."

Ken looked at me doubtfully, or looking for help. Tina kicked me under the table, a blow that glanced painlessly off my ankle but carried the point.

"Why not?" I said. "She's right, and you need a change."

It took more of that to persuade him, the two of us drifting from one memory or mutual friend to another and Tina forcing us back to the issue. In the end, he gave in.

"Okay, it's your place for the weekend, anyway," he said to Tina. Then to both of us, "You'll be here in the morning?"

"Right on time."

"But we've gotta go by my place first. I need some of my clothes and some other stuff, if I'm staying over."

"That's fine," Tina nodded twice.

"There's a couple little problems, though." He widened his eyes slightly, and the familiar double row of furrows crossed his brow.

"Like what?" I asked.

"Like some guys broke in my place while I've been gone."

"How do you know that?"

"The word gets around fast in here."

"That's not a big problem, a break-in."

"No. But the place is gonna be pretty messy. Not just from the break-in, but... you know."

He was referring to the murder that had taken place in his apartment just three days before. The front page story in the morning paper was headlined: "Man Shot Dead in Activist's House." Since Ken's picture accompanied the story, anyone's first thought could have been that he was the victim.

My phone rang more than once that day. No, I told the callers, the dead guy was a customer, or maybe a friend. Seems like some kind of lover's quarrel. About the only good news was that Ken couldn't possibly have had any role in it, since he was safely in jail.

"What were they doing in your place anyway?" Tina wanted to know.

"They're, you know, *friends* of mine. So to speak."

"High," Tina said flatly.

Ken ignored that. "They were arguing. She said he was two-timing her."

"Was he?" Tina asked.

"What?"

"Was he two-timing her?"

"Yeah, probably."

"Okay," I cut in. "That stuff doesn't matter now. We can handle whatever shape your place is in."

"There's gonna be blood and stuff. You know what happened, right?"

"Not exactly."

"Well, they were arguing for a while, and then he stuck a shotgun in his mouth and dared her to pull the trigger. She did. So it'll be messy."

The three of us took a moment to imagine just what "messy" might include in that scenario. "At least that's what I heard," he added, as if by questioning his own version of the homicide he might distract us from our private visions of the details.

Impatient then, or disgusted, Tina puffed her cheeks and shot out a quick burst of air." Okay, but we're not gonna be hanging around."

"Also," Ken paused and then went on, "you need to know that there's some guys looking for me right now."

"What's their problem?"

"I, uh, owe them some money."

"How much?" I wanted to know, as though the amount somehow mattered.

"One, two thousand. In between." He shrugged.

"Right. So we'll just get your stuff and get out of there."

"One more thing." Ken lowered his voice. "There's some stuff in the apartment that... shouldn't see the light of day."

"Don't you be bringin' any of that crack to *my* house," Tina demanded, a little too loudly.

Ken's eyes darted to the nearest deputy as he lowered his hands to the table in a shushing movement.

"Don't worry. Anyway, it's hidden. *Nobody* can find it."

"Just clothes," Tina said.

"OK, and my toothbrush and stuff. Oh yeah, I want to bring a couple of my lamps."

"Lamps?" Tina's voice rose again.

"Forget it," I said to both of them. My look told Tina: don't push it. We left just after that. We picked him up the next morning at 6:00, and we drove through the empty morning streets to his apartment...

Finally the back door was free. It swung in, pushing pieces of wood to the side with a rasping sound. Ken went in first. With table and countertops clean and almost bare, the kitchen at least looked normal enough. But the portable phone, sitting on the counter, did not. It was streaked with dried blood, mostly on the handle but also on the earpiece and on some of the buttons, as though it had been finger-painted for an avant-garde art show. Or a still-life: smeared phone on Formica.

"Aw, God, look at the phone," Ken said. None of us touched it.

The living room was obviously the crime scene, with the chalk outline of a body still partly visible on the floor in front of a blood-stained sofa. Someone had pushed the sofa out at an awkward angle from the wall and thrown two of its beige cushions, also spotted with blood, onto the floor. A crumpled sleeping bag hung like a limp body over the left armrest.

Ken kicked one of the pillows, in a motion wanting somehow to undo what had happened in his living room." It's soaked," he said. Then he picked up the sleeping bag, turning the top back to inspect the fabric inside. "Jesus, there's *brain* matter in here!"

"Ken, put that down," I demanded.

He dropped it, though reluctantly. "Jason was a good guy," he said softly. In spite of myself, I pictured Hamlet holding Yorick's skull. Alas, poor Jason.

We followed him into the single bedroom. Drawers had been pulled open, clothes and shoes were scattered on the floor.

"They got everything," he said. "TV, VCR, my camera. And the stereo." Then he scanned the bookshelf and spoke for the first time with real anguish. "They got the Youth Day videos too." He ran his hands through the top drawer, scattering socks. "My Rolex is gone. That means I know who did it. I'll kill the fuckers."

"Yeah, but later," I said. "Let's just get your stuff and get out of here."

We pulled slacks from hangers and draped shirts and suits over our arms. Stepping around the splintered wood in the kitchen, we began carrying the clothes out to Tina's car.

The neighborhood, happily, was still lifeless, except for the thud of a car door and the grinding of a starter motor somewhere down the street. An early June sun was warming the air, throwing tree-shadows in fine definition onto the driveway. Tina was in the house, gathering, while Ken and I were moving in the driveway, facing the street with loaded and outstretched arms, when the car appeared.

It was a giant black roach, slow, silent, oddly low to the ground. As if that was not enough, its threat was magnified by windows so heavily tinted that it was impossible to see inside. It crept into our field of vision at a walking pace, and by the time we saw it the distance was less than 20 yards.

In a time like that the mind can run well ahead of the events. My first thought was that somebody must be making a hackneyed mob movie, since the real world does not include cars that look like that.

The second thought was an expectation: the side window would roll slowly down, and the film cliché would be completed by the barrel of a machine pistol leveling itself at us.

Immediately after that was the image of the two of us trying to squirm under the rocker panel of Tina's car.

Action lagged behind, or indecision: we stared blankly at the car and turned our heads slowly to match its movement. In a moment it was directly in front of us, slowing without stopping.

"You know somebody here?" I asked.

"Yeah. They're the guys I was telling you about. Don't worry, they won't do anything with a white guy standing beside me."

"Maybe you should go over there and tell them I'm with the FBI."

There was no need for that. In a few more slow seconds, the roach was past us. Nothing had been said, no machine pistol had been aimed. At the near intersection, it turned slowly to the right and was gone. Not being given time for a proper scare was, in the aftermath, something of a disappointment.

I started to ask Ken why any right-living underworld types were not still in bed. But I didn't, since he had already told me: the word gets around fast.

So that question went unasked, and that was probably just as well. The better question was, why I wasn't home in bed myself? Or more pointedly, how does it happen that a middle-aged academic, whose normal life is one of classes and meetings and students and books, ends up breaking into a drug house and being threatened by a gangster car?

That is not necessarily a long story, but it *is* complicated, in the way of any story with lots of very different people and events in it.

Taken by itself, no one experience has any particular value or significance. Its importance, its meaning in any kind of larger scheme, can be understood only in relation to other events whose own uniqueness elevates them above the normal hum-drum of life, fixing attention on them like a rare coin among a handful of bus tokens. And while the drone of normality makes certain events stand out, it can also lure a person to wonder how they connect, how they relate to each other.

Here's a thought experiment. Imagine yourself riding an interstate bus through a mid-western night. It is cramped and you can't sleep, so you find yourself spending a lot of the time staring out the window into the dark. Murky shapes and scattered lights move across the glass as though inches from your eyes, the nearer ones -- fence posts and telephone poles --quickly, and the farther ones -- silos, cellphone towers -- more slowly, less distinctly. Every so often you become aware that there is a town coming up: a few more lights dot the window, some intersections and the shapes of low buildings glide past.

Then you are at the bus station, which is little more than the parking lot behind a drugstore or dry-cleaners. A few people stand in small groups beneath your window. You watch these people handing over some luggage, saying their goodbyes, turning to climb inside and to become for a few hours a fragment of your own journey. Maybe you even talk to one of them as the bus hums its way through the night, hoping when he sits beside you that your new companion is not a reformed alcoholic on his way to a revival meeting. Whether or not, it turns out that his story has some interest, if you listen carefully, because no story is ever the same. Lives often touch each other in ways like that, and then they detach again.

Later, when you've returned to staring out into the night, you may feel the impulse to make some imperfect sense of it all. Why did we have this particular conversation in this specific place? Has this person just played some walk-on role whose purpose will become clear at some other time? Is there some pattern here, a collection of connections? For some people, believers in the fixed philosophies of western determinism or eastern karma, the answer is yes. It has all been worked out ahead of time. At best we are just pushed along, like flotsam in sluggish water.

That is much oversimplified. It is more arguable that some experiences really have no meaning, while others have a great deal of it. Those are the ones that are important because they change you. They move you in a direction that you would not have taken without them. The past and the present are connected to the future in a continuity of becoming, even if we rarely take the time to notice. At a minimum, we take life as a series of experiences, overlapping and entangling, causing and being caused, leading on to other experiences most of which are entirely unpredictable and, unless you take that quiet time to sort them out, seemingly without meaning.

Even when you do take the time, you can find yourself caught and pulled by the tides of a maddening yin and yang. The idea that great effort can accomplish wonders is countered by accepting that our successes are mostly accidental. The inflexibility of causes and their effects finds its counterpoint in the doctrine of random and senseless change. And then you begin to ask yourself if life really *is* without purpose, or is it driven instead by some stern and stubborn hand? At the end of that swim, like a person awakening from a long coma, you discover that you never left the shore.

Does anyone's life have a clear meaning? On the one hand, it seems best to leave the matter alone. Just live. On the other hand, the question nags, especially for the philosophically-minded. In the end, though, it is the wrong question. The first and final question of philosophy is not about the meaning of life; rather, it asks each of us to consider how a life can be lived *well*. That is the question that echoes down through the centuries. In western philosophy it was posed first by Socrates. Still today it challenges anyone who takes any amount of time to question personal values and goals in general, or ways of acting in particular.

So instead of worrying about life's meaning, it can be more illuminating to focus on life's direction. For anyone who has lived into adulthood, direction is something that can be traced and thought about. A life's direction does not happen all by itself. It is the result of linkages -- some random and some arranged -- that together create for us the possibility of living well. It is those that need to be explored and explained.

One of the ways to do that is to concentrate on those experiences that seem to be the shaping ones -- by writing them down at the time, keeping faith with as many of the people and events, the details and perceptions and thought as you can remember. Sometime after you can go back and work them into something worth reading.

That is the trick, as any writer knows: worth reading. It may be that the material has a slight interest for at least some readers, but how best to present it? The problem is that we live in an age of instant messages, sound bites and angry diatribes, communication stumbling over itself in haste and confusion. That is exactly the reason to consider going in the opposite direction: all the way back to some of the principles of classical literature.

One of these is the idea of the unities, which were intended to foster discipline and concentration, as well as to preserve a sense of realism. One of these is unity of action: for the sake of sustaining attention, the work should focus on only one main action, not several. Another is unity of place, which advised that probability is better served if the action does not move around anymore than is necessary.

Unity of time is the obvious third: it requires that the action should be concentrated roughly within the amount of time, maybe no more than a few hours, needed to experience the literary work. That was also meant to serve the cause of realism. Unity of time makes sense in the context of the other two, but it does not fully address how time is to be used in the telling of a story.

Is it really necessary to follow a strict chronology in a narrative? The ancients apparently did not think so. As far back as the first great epic poems, we find the technique of *in medias res*, the starting of a story literally "in the middle of things," then back-filling as needed while the main action goes forward. It is an easy way to secure early interest: what exactly is going on here?

So in the best classical tradition, we will let this story, these stories, make use of the unities, and let them begin somewhere near the middle. There may be a familiar challenge to the reader in that, but because it is familiar, it is not challenge enough. Does a story have to be told entirely in the past, or in the present? Could part of it be in one time frame, other parts in another? Time should not dictate the way a story is told; it should be used for best effect.

One last bit of advice from the classic writers: put away what you have written, not for months but for years, and then see what you think of it. The results can be discomfiting. Did I really think *that*? If I did, I do not now, so get rid of it before someone actually reads this. At the very least, couldn't there have been a better way to write it? Revisions are almost always more gracious with greater distance from the original. But – and this is fundamental -- let the facts remain as they were. The story-teller who is concerned more with the truth and less with public acceptance prizes accuracy over popularity.

So much for theory. Trying to keep all that in mind, we can begin to explore the connections and, as part of that process, single out whatever is there of value. The attentive reader should have a role to play in that.

PEACE TREES

"If you think in terms...
of ten years, plant trees;
if in terms of 100 years,
teach the people.

-- Confucius

Let us therefore see what qualifications
a member of the contemplated peace brigade
should possess.

-- Mahatma Gandhi

Gentry hoists her bucket up onto her head and holds it with both hands, elbows out to the side. She is standing on a slope, so one of her legs is straight, the other angled behind her for balance.

"Big smile, okay?"

She smiles, wide. My picture will show a tall, angular woman in her late thirties, dressed in a black tee-shirt and very dirty jeans. Her thin face, itself not entirely clean, is brightened by the smile and by an off-white scarf tied loosely around her neck. Wisps of greying hair poke from beneath her baseball cap.

Behind her on the hillside, some full-grown trees, a few skinny ones, and some clumps of low ferns are growing amid short grasses. On her left a shovel leans against a split boulder and a red bucket is poised to slide away. At her feet are hundreds of unplanted baby pine trees, each wrapped in a little black plastic bag. Twelve more of those pine trees are in the square bucket she is holding on her head.

"Wait till I put my camera away," I tell her. "I'll walk up with you."

"Sure."

She puts her bucket down while I go over to the fence post where we have all hung our small backpacks. I put my camera into my pack and poke around for the bottle of insect repellant. The liquid feels cold on my hands and arms.

"Want some of this for your arms, Gentry?"

"That's okay."

"How about a hunk of bread?"

"Yeah, I'll have some."

"It's a little hard. It's the stuff we got yesterday."

"Thanks."

Now and then we buy these small, misshapen loaves at a local bakery, the front room of a tin-roofed stucco house, as we ride up here in the morning. Before I hand the bread to Gentry, I turn it over to look at the browned backside.

"You were riding up front yesterday, weren't you?" I ask.

"Uh huh. Why?"

"Then you missed all the fun with this bread. First, Toni found a rock in her loaf, and -- "

"A *rock*?"

"Yeah, you know, a stone. Anyway, I'd just taken a bite out of mine, but then I turned it over to check it out. There was a fly stuck on the bottom."

"You ate a *fly*?"

"Nope, just missed it where I'd bitten. Actually, I think I might have eaten one of the wings."

Gentry laughs and breaks her loaf into several pieces. She turns each piece over and looks at it carefully before she pops it into her mouth.

"I'm glad I was riding up front."

"We were thinking it sort of looked like raisin bread."

While we talk, I pack twelve trees into my own bucket. Its plastic is ripped in several places, so the trees are inclined to fall out of one side or the other. A few days ago, Gentry had the idea to wrap tape around all our buckets to hold the four sides together. But the tape on mine has already gotten dirty and fallen partly off, hanging now like floppy ears.

“Okay, I’m ready, more or less,” I tell her.

Gentry puts her bucket back on her head. I have to carry mine in front of myself to hold it together. We start up the hill toward the planting area, first splashing through the stream where we sometimes wash the mud off our hands. There is typhoid in Ocatal, the town where we’re staying, so no one drinks this stream water.

Nine of us are living for a month in Ocatal, a small town near the border between Nicaragua and Honduras. We have volunteered to help with a reforestation project, replacing trees cut years ago when the dictator Anastasio Somoza was ravaging Nicaragua’s resources in any way he could.

“How many trees did we do yesterday, Gentry?”

“Four hundred and fifty-six.”

“So how many altogether?”

“Three thousand, nine hundred and something. I forget.”

Gentry is our unofficial tree accountant. Our Nicaraguan forestry supervisors want exact totals each day, I suppose for purposes of reporting back to the government in Managua.

“Are we going to hit five thousand, you think?”

“Yeah,” she says, “We should do it now. Easy.”

That five thousand is an arbitrary number. We originally had in mind to plant ten thousand. But things move a little more lowly in Central America. Sometimes Pablo brings up only one load in the truck, other times we have enough trees but not enough help. Still, we like the idea of a goal, and each afternoon we ask Gentry to go over the figures for us. At one point I set a record by planting 120 trees in one day, and then Bob surpassed that. But no one is competing. We are just all trying to do as much as we can while we are here.

We stop at a barb-wire fence and put our buckets down. I spread the wire for Gentry and she bends and climbs through, keeping her back low to keep from getting snagged. After she has pulled her bucket under the lowest wire, she parts two of the higher ones for me.

Now the path follows the fence on up the hill, which has been planted here and there with plantain trees whose large green leaves spread out like limpy ferns. We are both panting fairly hard from the climb. Three of the Nicaraguans we work with, one of them an older woman who is barefoot beneath a long, puce-colored skirt, pass us on their way down. They look at me and say something, then start to laugh. Gentry's Spanish is not great, but it's a lot better than mine.

"What did they say?"

"I heard them say '*cumpleanos*', so I think they were talking about your birthday yesterday, laughing about you being forty-five."

"Yeah, that seems to amuse them."

"Well, forty-five is getting up there in their world."

"Don't remind me."

My birthday turned out to be one of the best ever. First, my eight American *companeros* broke into a chorus of "Happy Birthday" while we were waiting for the truck, sitting on the concrete steps of the forestry compound at 6:30 in the morning. Then they did it again, with some tentative help from the Nicaraguans, while we were planting on a brush-covered hillside later in the morning. Their song came floating down the hill to me, caught on the warm wind from the north. Then I was feted with song again in the evening, during a little party on the porch of the old wooden dormitory. Our treats were a bottle of rum, although we had no ice or anything to mix it with, and one of the cans of sardines from my backpack.

Most of us have brought various snacks, which we've been sharing and trying to stretch out for the duration of our time here. There is almost no snack food for sale in Ocatal, and certainly nothing of the kind of junk food snacks available in the states. For some reason, my sardines have made quite a splash, and about once a week I open a tin and pass little hunks of the fish around on crackers. We joke about how quickly we all began to fantasize down here about our favorite rich foods, chocolate sundaes and jelly donuts. At the moment, my own breakfast fantasy is of two or three waffles dripping with syrup.

Our diet here is mostly rice and beans, three times a day, although a late lunch and small dinner usually include a little bit of meat and a coleslaw salad for variety. When they are available, we buy soft drinks or beer to wash it all down. While our diet is nutritionally sound, there must not be enough calories in it, because some of us are losing weight steadily. We call it the third world diet, maybe an idea for a new kind of tourism: live in a remote Central American town and plant trees to lose weight.

Now the path and the barb-wire stop, although the reason for that is not clear. Gentry and I are on a ridge, looking into a long valley that stretches to another ridge farther north. Over that ridge is Honduras, home of the Contra camps with their estimated 10,000 fighters. We are in Nicaragua's northernmost area, the war zone, and at this moment we are only three kilometers from that Honduras border.

Having climbed steadily now for fifteen minutes, we find ourselves winded, so we stop to take in the view to the north. In the distance, the mountains appear to become less jagged, as though smoothed by a gentler hand. They are blue-green and hazy in the morning light, disappearing at the horizon into low-lying clouds. The valley below us is broken into little hills and occasional arroyos; in places it is spotted with open brown areas between clumps of trees, like a child's version of cubism.

A fine morning mist is blowing towards us from across that far ridge, the moisture beginning to dampen our clothes. Our boots are already soaked from the morning's wet grass and that stream, and they will not dry out until late in the day, after we return to our dormitory. But the hot Central American sun will dry our clothes as soon as this mist blows past.

"How's Sharon this morning?" I ask Gentry.

"Umm, maybe a little better. She had a bad night."

Sharon has been sick for much of our time in Nicaragua. In fact, we have all been sick in one way or another, but Sharon has had serious attacks of vomiting and diarrhea that have kept her behind, in town, a number of times. In spite of purifying our water and sharing our medications, sickness remains a major concern, especially with such limited medical help available in this far northern province. It is also a regular topic of conversation.

"Is she taking anything?"

"She's got a few of her own pills left, but they aren't helping all that much. Plus she's got that stuff Sybil uses."

"Actually, I'm more worried about Brian right now," I say. "Have you noticed him lately?"

"Like what?"

"Like he's lost his sense of humor, maybe. Seems like he's quit eating, or even talking much."

"Maybe he's just tired and wants out of here. Do you?"

"Yeah, sometimes."

"It's your first time in the third world, right?"

"Uh huh."

"It's always toughest the first time," she says with a shake of the head that is meant to be sympathetic.

"What about you, Gentry? You feeling okay?"

"Oh, I'm good, real good."

"You're not, you liar. You look like hell. You've still got the runs, don't you?"

"Sort of."

Gentry is a granola, a health freak who refuses to take medication and relies instead on eating garlic and using herbal treatments, none of which seem to be working. Toni and I have been trying for days now to get her to take some of our strong prescription stuff, even just a little to get her through the rest of the month. But she refuses, with talk about insults to Mother Earth and remedies I have never heard of. So I press her.

"When did you eat last?"

"I just had some of your bread, didn't I?"

"You know what I mean, a complete meal."

"Yesterday."

"Don't lie to me. You weren't even at dinner."

"Well, the day before, then." She gives me a mocking smile and then looks up at the sky for the help she knows is there.

"That's not good enough, Gentry. You've gotta eat if you want to keep working. You want to plant trees or be in bed like Sharon? Tonight Toni is going to sit on you and I'm going to stuff three of my pills down your throat. We'll plug you up so tight you won't shit for a week."

That little scene makes us both smile for a moment. "We'll see. Anyway, let's plant some trees."

Scattered across a broad hillside, a few of our group are on their knees, setting the little pine trees in small holes. Brian's cowboy scarf makes a bright red patch against the green moss and ferns. Jack is standing nearby, stretching his back. His tee-shirt says "Let's samba, not bomba." Farther up the hill, young Nicaraguans of both sexes are digging the holes with wide-bladed picks. Ahead of them, Jose Santos slashes down ferns with a machete, clearing away undergrowth so the tiny pines will have some light to grow by. Two of the teenage Nicaraguan girls working to our left wear camouflage outfits.

Jack watches us approach with our buckets. As we come near, we hear a single gunshot far off in the valley below.

"The Contras!" he screams, arms flailing and eyes wide. "They're coming!" Jack loves to tease about Contra attacks. The rifle shot was probably from a Nicaraguan soldier shooting at a tin can. The soldiers guard the bridges on the main highway we use out of town, looking bored as we drive past.

"Yeah, this is it!" Bob calls back to him from across the grass. "Where do we hide?" He looks around at the little ferns and the few scraggly trees on the hillside.

"We've got to run for it," Jack says, now almost calmly.

"This way." Bob points dramatically toward the north.

"Not that way! That's Honduras!"

"Oh, right, I forgot." He is obviously laughing at himself. "So maybe we can get around behind them?"

Jack shakes his head and goes back to planting.

Joking about Contra attacks is a natural way to deal with our real worries. The Nicaraguan government has assured us that, although we are working in the war zone, the particular area we are in is militarily "secure," as they always like to put it. The Sandinista government soldiers that we see carrying their AK-47's around Ocatal are evidence of that, and we understand that Ocatal itself has not been attacked in several years. But if it is so secure, we've wondered, why do we have an armed guard 24 hours a day at the forestry compound where we stay? And what good would he do anyway, since he just sits by the front gate? The fence around the several acres of property is nothing more than a few strands of wire.

What really gets our attention is that Ocatal and its garrison soldiers are twelve kilometers south of where we are at the moment. They would be no help at all if a band of Contras came across the border we are working along. We have also been told that several reforestation workers have been killed by the Contras in recent times, including the forestry director for this region. He was shot, so it is claimed, in the truck we use every day. I notice that his replacement carries a mean-looking .45 automatic tucked in his belt, just over the left hip.

But we are starting to realize that life in a war zone can breed its own special kind of mischief. Like the rumor a few days ago that five Contras had been spotted near town, at the nursery from which our pine trees come. Why, Gentry wanted to know, would a bunch of Contras be wandering around a nursery, and I wondered the same thing. That story was later explained as a practical joke on us gringos. As for the shooting of the forestry director, I am still looking for bullet holes in the truck. Maybe it was some other truck.

Who knows? It is because we do not have a clear sense of our risks here that we tend toward worn-out jokes and feigned optimism. Still, nobody laughed the other day as we listened for maybe five minutes to machine-gun fire somewhere to the northwest. It sounded awfully close. For our Nicaraguan co-workers the sounds of gunfire are normal, but even they stopped to listen, speaking quietly among themselves. One of the young women looked at me with a weak smile and pretended to wipe worried sweat from her forehead. Another remarked that their soldiers can't afford to waste that much ammunition shooting at rocks.

Of course the Nicaraguan workers are in more danger than we are, since no well-informed Contra would deliberately shoot a North American. The government of the United States is *paying* them to wage war on Nicaragua, the idea being to restore some sort of right-wing, pro-US government. So we just keep hoping that all the Contras are well-informed, and we say that we will all start yelling "*Norde Americanos*" if they actually appear one of these days. In the end, that day of all the shooting, we just went back to work. There was a welcome quiet when the shooting stopped.

Whatever the real risks, it is a new experience for all of us to go to sleep at night to the sound of gunfire, even if it is just soldiers across town at the army quarters, practicing. But we are never really sure just what it is. I'm glad I slept through a mortar attack on a nearby communal farm last week.

Gentry and I have put down our buckets and are moving among the holes that have been dug ahead of us. I watch as she pulls the wrapper off one of the *pinos*, being careful to keep the ball of dirt around its delicate roots. She kneels to plant it, reaching for some loose dirt to create a little half-basin on the downhill side of the planting. We have been taught this procedure by the Nicaraguan forestry people, who are concerned that the trees be able to trap and hold enough rain water as it runs down the hillsides. I can hear her murmur something as she rises from her kneeling position.

"What are you telling it?"

"Just to be healthy and strong, to grow. You know, sort of a prayer."

"You tell every tree?"

"Sure. These little babies need lots of help."

She moves a few yards to the next hole, which has been dug beside a rotting tree trunk. Thinking I might know what will happen next, I watch from where I am kneeling as she places her tree and uses her bare hands to form another little catch basin. In a flash she is on her feet, wildly slapping her arms and hands, making little whimpers of pain and anger. Her arms are alive with tiny red ants, so small and so close to the dirt in color that they aren't noticed until it is too late. Their bites make your skin feel like it is on fire. Finally she stops slapping herself and notices that I'm watching her. And apparently grinning.

"What are you laughing about?"

"'Cause the fire ants got you. They're just around old tree trunks, I think. That's where they got me, twice."

"Why didn't you tell me?"

"You don't listen to me anyway."

"Jerk. It hurts."

"It'll stop in a minute. Rub some dirt on your arms."

"What's that supposed to do?"

“Nothing really. I just said that.”
“Not funny.”
Sybil is looking up at us from way down the hill, an empty bucket in her hand. She is wearing her usual oversized man’s work shirt, and her baggy jeans are tucked into heavy grey socks above her boots. When she sees us looking down at her, she waves. Her voice is surprisingly strong in the morning air.

“Whan that Aprill with his shoures soote -- “
In unison, Gentry and I shout back down to her:
“The droghte of March hath perced to the roote,
And bathed every veyne in swich licour -- “

“Of which vertu engendered is the flour,” Sybil shouts back to us. Then she stops and waves her arms in a way that indicates she can’t remember the next lines. Gentry and I pick it up again:

“Whan Zephirus eek with his sweete breeth
Inspired hath in every holt and heeth
The tendre croppes -- “

Now all three of us are going again, and we chant together the remainder of the first 18 lines of Chaucer’s *Canterbury Tales*, our voices echoing across the valley. In some college literature courses, memorizing those lines and reciting them correctly in Middle English was a standard assignment. I don’t recall just how this routine got started. Probably Sybil was connecting our little pine trees to the roots of Chaucer’s crops and flowers. Now we throw our lines back and forth every few days. As we recite, getting more enthusiastic, some of the Nicaraguan workers stand to watch and listen. The heavily-Germanic sound of Chaucer’s English must be unlike anything they have ever heard before. A few of them clap when we finish, even if they don’t know what for.
Gentry and I go back to planting the rest of our trees. We move farther up and along the hill, looking for the holes that have been dug in careful triangulations to allow for adequate growing distance between the trees. Kneel, plant, make the little basin, move on.

Sometimes it is difficult to keep our balance on the steeper slopes, where we have to be careful not to let our buckets slip away from us when we set them down. We work slowly.

I can tell that Gentry is tired, and so am I. The tree-planting itself is easy enough, but the long hike up to the planting areas is strenuous. We struggle at times to keep our footing. The buckets get heavier. The altitude makes it difficult to get our breath. Most of the time, these days, my legs feel like rubber, or like they have gone out on strike.

Part of the problem is that my legs haven't recovered from the race last weekend. That was a weekend of festivities to celebrate the ninth anniversary of the Sandinistas' triumph over Somoza. Because the Contras have a history of stepping up their attacks during the several days of celebration, we were not allowed to work here, so close to the border. As we came down from the planting area the afternoon before the celebrations began, we saw that some tents and howitzers had been placed along the logging roads, facing north.

Nobody minded being grounded: it was a chance to get off the mountains and rest a little. More than that, we were interested in seeing how the Nicaraguans would celebrate their revolution, their equivalent of our Fourth of July. For them the date is July 17th, the day eight years ago when Somoza fled the country and ended a 45-year family dictatorship. The call it "*el dia de alegria*," the day of happiness.

The main event was the military parade, followed by the usual patriotic speeches. Along with hundreds of townspeople, we squeezed with our cameras onto the sidewalks of the main street as the army marched through the town square and past the bullet-pocked building with its large, iconic mural of Che Quevara. The building's two stories make it one of Ocatal's more impressive structures. Now it's remembered as the building in which U. S. Marines were garrisoned decades ago when Auguste Sandino was waging the guerrilla warfare that would make him the symbol and the namesake of the Nicaraguan struggle for liberation.

We watched as the soldiers passed under the red, white and blue Pepsi sign of the *Comedor Occidental*, then marched toward the wooden reviewing stand. There, behind a row of chairs, a white backdrop was adorned with a red and black 8, replacing the 7's that we've seen painted on many of Ocatal's buildings. Beside that, a familiar slogan: "*con el frente al frente*," going forward with the front. And more defiantly: "*aqui no se rinde nadia*," here no one surrenders.

Children walked in their own formation ahead of the soldiers, two of them holding aloft the *rojo y negra*, the red and black flag of Nicaragua.

We mingled with the crowds along the sidewalks and pressed against the buildings, making what we could of the speeches and taking our pictures. Taller, whiter and obviously foreigners, we might have felt out of place, or even, as Americans, unwanted. As it was, we attracted no special attention. The mood was too festive, the energies of the crowd directed toward celebrating.

The next day, we were invited to join in a celebration race. Jack and I accepted. Fairly casual joggers in our normal lives, we were not at all sure we could complete the hilly, seven-mile course in Central American heat and humidity. Most of the other runners were young boys or Nicaraguan soldiers who ran in their heavy, black army boots. Some of the boys wore sneakers or street shoes, and a few ran barefoot.

Jack and I were not just the only *gringo*s in the group, but also by far the oldest of the runners. That difference became obvious in the first mile, when we found ourselves running dead last, the rest of the pack already past the town's paving-stone streets and onto the dirt roads. We got a few smiles from onlookers, along with some laughter. A few people clapped. We'd agreed to pace ourselves carefully, and that began to pay off by the third mile as we started to pass over-heated soldiers who had slowed to a walk, heads down, on the longer hills.

For a while the route seemed to go mostly up, but finally it flattened and then dropped. The Rio Coco's brown waters appeared at the bottom of a hill around mile four. For a moment Jack and I thought we had made a wrong turn: the road ran straight into the water.

"Did we miss something?" I panted.

"I don't think so. It's the only road."

"So where's the bridge?"

"I dunno. But look over there."

Across the river, a Red Cross emergency van was waiting, maybe for one of us to have a heart attack.

"Let's go," Jack said.

At mid-stream the water came to above our knees. We found ourselves struggling to keep our balance on the slippery rocks, more feeling our way across than running or even walking. The Red Cross people passed out cups of water as we splashed up the bank on the other side and asked if we were okay. Jack told them we were fine, just a little old. We dumped some of their water over our heads and ran the rest of the race with river water squishing out of very heavy shoes.

Our pace, as it turned out, was perfect. We turned onto Ocatal's main street to the cheers of onlookers, and a dozen children ran the final blocks with us, jumping and squealing. Out of a field of thirty runners, the middle-aged *gringos* came in tied at fifteenth and became, at least for the moment, local heroes. Apparently the Nicaraguans had had even less faith in us than we had had in ourselves. Jack, with his excellent Spanish, was interviewed on the local radio station, using the chance to speak of our solidarity with the people of Nicaragua. It seemed to us that we had done more to build international relations between our country and theirs in one hour of running than in weeks of tree-planting.

Sometimes we wonder about just why we are doing these things, running races and chanting Chaucer while we plant trees on a remote Central American mountainside. Right now Gentry and I are talking about that.

"Because we're all a little crazy, I guess." She laughs and brushes a bug off her cheek with the back of her wrist, the one part of her that's not dirty.

"What's this trip costing you?" I ask her.

"I don't know exactly. The plane fares, the room and board -- maybe $1000 altogether. You?"

"The same, I guess. So you're right. We must be a little crazy to pay that kind of money to plant trees in a war zone. But aside from that, why are you here, Gentry?"

"What do you think? Because I support the revolution."

We all know something of the history. It is the history of a revolution that was slow in coming. Nicaragua won independence from Spain in 1821. Before long it, like other countries in the region, fell victim to the doctrine of Manifest Destiny.

The middle of the nineteenth century was especially interesting. Acting on behalf of several large banks and with a nod from the government of the United States, William Walker led a small private army into Central America. Over the course of several expeditions, he made himself, variously, president of Nicaragua, Honduras and El Salvador. He instituted slavery at one point; at home he was welcomed as a hero. His activities were the first in a series of invasions and expropriations and forced treaties, as US corporations gradually took control of governments and treasuries, above all of land and resources. Banana republics were born as more than metaphor.

The Nicaraguan revolution is the result of the long civil war between the guerrilla army of the leftist Sandinista National Liberation Front, aided by Cuba and the USSR, and the right wing dictatorship of the Somoza family, supported for many years by the United States. Nicaragua became another cold war proxy battlefield, but this one a lot closer to home. When in 1979 the Sandinistas finally drove Somoza and his last supporters out of Nicaragua, many of his soldiers fled to Honduras, where our government formed them into the Contras. That word means "counter" in Spanish; the Contras have been trained by the United States as counter-revolutionaries, their purpose to reverse the Sandinista victory and return the country to, among other things, a source of inexpensive fruit, coffee and raw materials for the United States.

The situation has become a giant headache for conservatives at home, who worry that other countries might follow Nicaragua's example. It is a Central American domino theory. But for many others, Nicaragua has become the symbol of a people's struggle to control their own national destiny, not unlike our own colonial fight for independence from England. And not just for some Americans, like those of us who are here planting trees.

In fact, least of all for Americans. These trees we are planting were donated by Sweden. We've talked with Germans who are here to build a clinic and met Basques working on a new school. Other European countries have donated time and resources in other ways.

The whole thing reminds me a little of the Spanish civil war in the 30s, when thousands of people went to Spain to fight fascism. Of course that is not exactly the impression people are being given by the media at home, where the picture of Nicaragua is painted in the colors of terrorism and communism and the Contras, predictably, are the "freedom fighters."

Once you are here, though, you quickly get a different story. We've been given tours -- both here and earlier in Managua -- that obviously are designed to showcase the progress of the revolution. A new school, large windows and wooden frame rising above concrete block half-walls, was utilitarian in its furnishings but certainly a first for peasant children. At a collective farm, sleepy at mid-afternoon, we admired modest new housing for the workers. We are told that land ownership has become a combination of private and cooperative: a compromise in the name of profit. Altogether 1500 former estates totaling two million acres were taken from the Somoza families and cronies. Almost as a symbol, a pig lay in the sun in front of one house, a cat asleep on its back.

At a day-care center we looked into a bomb shelter, which had been dug into the earth and covered with a roof of logs and plastic. Half-filled with muddy water, it seemed to be a victim more of rain than of bombardment. Other tours have included a rebuilt factory now making prosthetic limbs, a hospital for the war-wounded, a water project half-finished and waiting for funds that have to be used instead to fight the contra war.

Like the tours, meetings are laced with statistics showing the improvements in Nicaraguan life since the triumph over Somoza: the number of new clinics and schools, the improvement in literacy, the vaccination programs, the amount of land given to the peasants, the houses built.

The speakers refer often to what they call the new government's "inheritance" from the Somoza regime: 1. 6 billion in foreign debt, the destruction of factories and infrastructure, an agricultural sector ruined by the civil war. Above all -- the theme is consistent -- we hear about the financial burden of fighting the counter-revolution. We've been told again and again that we need to carry this information back to our own country. Their assumption, however naive, is that Americans will change their government's policy once they understand what's really going on in Nicaragua.

Taken together, it is an impressive picture. That it is one-sided is to be expected. I think now and then of the phrase "revolutionary tourists" -- used to describe visitors to the new Soviet Russia in the 1920s and 1930s -- and of the repressive measures the Sandinistas have taken against the country's internal opposition to their revolution. Insofar as we are not here as tourists, those thoughts are unfair. Still, some measure of doubt is the legitimate province of any good philosophy. The Greek work *skeptikos*, from which our word for doubt comes, does not mean doubter; it means seeker. Seeker of truth, that is. It should apply in this situation as well. In any event, it prompts me to some teasing.

"So you support the revolution, huh? It's more like you're just into their propaganda."

Gentry jerks her head at me angrily, and then sees that I am laughing at her.

"I'm serious," she says. "We're all here to support their revolution, right? What about you?" She picks up another tree and absent-mindedly begins peeling away the black plastic.

"Sure. The revolution's fine with me. I guess I'm as much into the environmental part of this as all the other stuff. I figure the world needs trees, and I don't care all that much where they get planted. This trip seemed like a chance to make a political statement and plant some trees at the same time, okay? Actually, I didn't know all that much about this whole business before I came down here. But I'm learning."

"Like what are you learning?"

"That people will believe, they'll work for a better life if they think there's a chance to get it. I like all the building going on around here. It's fun to watch people build stuff. It seems like they get really excited. Maybe it gives them a sense of, you know, dignity. They can plan, sort of look forward, and then see some results."

"And leave something for their kids," Gentry adds.

"Yeah, that too. These people have a lot of courage. Living with this war all the time, all around them. It must be a hard life, and I don't know if I could do it. But they still seem to be optimistic. When you build something, you're optimistic."

"Hope," she says." I guess we're all learning. It sure helps to be here. It's pretty hard to figure out where you stand on something like this when all you get at home is a half-minute on the news now and then."

"A friend of mine at home actually asked me if I was coming down here to work for the Contras or the Sandinistas."

Gentry laughs and shakes her head in disbelief. "Some friends you got."

"How much did you know before you got here, Gentry?"

"Lots. I knew lots. That's why I came. I've got friends who have been here before. One of them's in Estili with the literacy crusade right now."

"So what do you think, now that you've been here yourself?"

"I think the same as they do. This revolution's going to work, one way or another, in spite of everything our government is doing to stop it." She waves her hand south, toward Ocatal. "You've seen the schools and all that stuff. "That'll pay off later."

"For now, anything's an improvement over two generations of the Somozas."

"Yeah. This country can only go up. But Somoza couldn't have stayed in power so long and done the things he did to these people without help from our government. So in a way we're all responsible for what's happened down here."

"Isn't this whole scene a little weird when you think about it? We pay taxes at home to support the Contras and then we come down here to help the Nicaraguans."

"So who pays taxes?"

"You don't?"

"Let's just say there are people who don't pay taxes, just for that reason. I know a few of them."

"What about the IRS?"

"Well, in the first place these people don't make all that much money. Not a lot to worry about there."

Gentry does not seem to worry too much about anything. Living so closely with her and the others under these conditions, I've noticed that laid-back attitude a lot. It is beginning to infect me.

When I first saw Gentry, she was lying flat out on the floor of the Mexico City airport, her head against a backpack, cap down over her eyes, her long legs stretched out alongside a shiny new shovel. We had been instructed to assemble at the Mexico City airport, since direct flights between the U. S. and Managua have fallen victim to an embargo. While most of us spent that time talking and fussing over our plane tickets and our gear, Gentry slept on the tile floor, content inside some little world of her own.

Right now her only worry seems to be finding more holes for the few trees we still have in our buckets. We move along the hillside, finding tiny pines that have already been planted by others. Eventually we have to go over the top of the ridge to find some empty holes. These are on a slope so steep that it is going to be impossible to wriggle down it, plant trees, and hang on to our buckets all at the same time.

"Let's do it together," Gentry suggests. "How many trees do you have left?"

"Three."

"I've got four. One of us can climb down there and the other can send the trees down."

"Okay, I'll go."

Finding footholds and handholds wherever I can, I edge along the slope. Above me, Gentry hands the trees down. When I am too far to reach, she tosses them gently. The little black bags look like hand grenades flying toward me. One of them drops from my fingers. As I catch it again my thumb pokes through the thin plastic. Luckily the bag doesn't tear much and the root system stays intact.

My left foot loses its tentative hold and I slide a few yards down the slope, then have to scramble back up to where I am again within reach. There is another empty hole to my left. I squirm over to it, and Gentry follows me from above, throwing down another tree.

In a few minutes, the seven we had left are planted and I can climb back up. We go over the ridge and notice that the others have already gone back.

"Guess that's it for now," Gentry says. "The best thing is going back down."

Walking down to where the truck stops is easy, all downhill and with empty buckets. We walk in silence, tired. Under her breath, Gentry starts to hum the Sandinista "hymno." It is a kind of national anthem whose rhythm and melody remind me every time of a football fight song. The words speak of marching together to advance the revolution, winning or dying to free their country.

She is humming or maybe singing it so quietly I can barely hear her, and I wonder if she even knows that she is doing it.

"*Adelante marchemos companeros*
Avencemos a la revolucion,
Nuestro pueblo el el dueno de
Su historia..."

Let's march forward, friends, let's advance the revolution. Our country is the dream of its history... I like to hear the Nicaraguans sing it in the old flatbed truck as we go back to town. They sing a little self-consciously in front of us, and their voices are blown away by the wind and the highway sounds.

Eventually Gentry stops humming and we walk down in silence. There is a perfect stillness all around us. It is the stillness of mountains that are, for the moment, at peace.

"It's hard to remember there's a war going on in this country," she says.

"I wonder if these people even understand what their war's all about."

"It's always the same. War's about money. Maybe not always money directly, but in the form of land, resources, whatever."

"Yeah, that's what Socrates said. In this case, it's about economic systems."

"In other words, money."

"I read their new constitution, the one somebody was passing around. It definitely says they want to set up a mixed economy. Some private ownership, some socialism, or whatever you want to call it."

"And that's what they've got. You saw it -- all those stores and restaurants we've been in are *privately* owned. Hardly socialism."

"Back home they make it sound like it's total Marxism down here, everybody dressed in Mao jackets."

The image of Nicaraguans walking around in Mao jackets gets us both laughing.

"Anyway," she says, "I'm not that much into the bullshit and the rhetoric either. I just want to help the kids. That's what matters if this country is ever going to get anywhere. You notice anything about the kids here?"

I have noticed lots about the children we see around Ocatal. They stand and watch quietly as the tall Americans walk by. They smile shyly when we wave, and sometimes they wave back, little hands flexing their forefingers. There is a gentleness about the children that puzzles me, since even the littlest ones must have some idea of the danger and stress that have been part of life in Nicaragua for so long.

"I think they look fairly happy, considering," I say to her instead. "But then kids can take a lot."

"How about that little bunch in the street yesterday?"

Maybe because there were five of them, they had put together the courage to come up to us, or maybe they wanted a better look. Two of the littlest ones could have been brothers: they had wide, flat noses beneath short brown hair cut in bangs, and wide brown eyes. The smaller of the two wore only a shirt, no pants. The third boy was taller. He stood with shoulders back and hands slightly raised, as though ready to defend the two girls. His red hair and blue eyes pointed back, possibly, to one of those periods when our marines were stationed here.

The girls presented a contrast. The thin one wore a pretty blue dress with ruffled sleeves and embroidered flowers running down the front. She stood with hands raised and clasped under her chin, and her worried eyes avoided ours. The other was round-faced and smiled with baby teeth. Over her skirt she wore a sleeveless tee-shirt, full of holes.

"It was a mixed bunch, if the clothes tell you anything. But if you didn't know better, those big bellies on three of them --.

"Yeah, malnutrition. Still, they're healthier than they used to be, for sure. But their diet's still way off. And they need lots of medical care. They also need to learn how to read and write."

"Teaching people to read and write doesn't seem all that revolutionary, does it? Maybe it's just the word revolution. It scares a lot of people. You think of Molotov cocktails and wild, bearded guys running around."

"Uh huh. We watch too many movies. Revolution's a pretty gradual process, if this is any example."

Gentry has been slowing the pace. Now she stops completely and stares off toward the southeast. The sun, stronger now, brightens one side of her face, giving it a pink glow. Except for the calling of some birds, it is still total silence around us. At first I think she is looking at something in particular, but all I notice is a thin slip of smoke from over the nearest ridge. It had been rising straight up, but then started drifting first to the left and then to the right, as though trying to decide which way to go before its last traces begin to disappear into a robin-egg sky. It is probably coming from one of the peasant huts we pass along the logging roads.

We stand in silence for maybe a minute, maybe more. Gentry has discovered at some point how speaking can distract and scatter, how silence allows us to collect our thoughts like raindrops in a hand, how it can strengthen our spirits. It can also allow us to know the soul of a place, but only when there is no exterior noise and only when you can match that by getting yourself into a state of inner calmness. Then you can listen to the silence. Finally she moves.

"What are you looking at?"

"Nothing in particular. It's just a beautiful country, isn't it?"

"I think that every time we come up here."

"It'll be even prettier when all the trees come back," she says.

"Yep."

"I suppose it's stupid, but I have to wonder why people fight wars at all, when the best thing to do with pretty country is to look at it and live on it."

"Too bad it can't be that simple."

"It should be."

"Gandhi said the earth has enough for everyone's need but not enough for everyone's greed. I guess some people get carried away."

"Yeah." She bends down and plucks a small purple wildflower, looks at it for a moment and then sticks it in her scarf. Again we stand together in silence, as though we want the scene to press itself one more time, like a lithograph, onto our memories. We may also be a little embarrassed: we know without saying so that some of the conversation has been sententious, even righteous. That is a human failure born of idealism, which can be weakened by a temporary tiredness of soul more than body. Finally Gentry speaks. "Let's go, huh?"

We wind down the last part of the path, climb back through the fence, and come to where the others are already gathered. Pablo has returned with the truck while we've been planting. It's turned around and facing down the old logging road, sitting in a circle of muddy tracks. We can see that it's empty.

"Looks like no more trees today," Gentry says.

"That's okay with me."

"I'm gonna let the others load up."

"Me too."

"Are you tired?" Gentry asks, turning to look at me. Her own face looks drawn now, in the different light.

"Yeah, but mostly I'm hungry. I'm starving, in fact."

"You're always hungry."

That is true enough. Right now a lot of us are looking forward to getting back into town. Pablo will drop us off at the restaurant, where we'll wash a little if the water is working in the restrooms. Then we will have a plate of food brought to us, more rice and beans and some of that salad that's probably helping to make us sick.

It is a nice restaurant, full of large plants in a central section that is open to the sky. We'll talk a long time over our late lunch and some cold drinks.

Then we will drift slowly off toward our wooden dormitory at the forestry compound, walking the mile and a half route along the warm and dusty streets of Ocatal, waving and shouting "hola" to the children playing in their shabby dooryards. The skinny old man I call Sandino -- because somebody told me he fought with Sandino many years ago -- will be sitting in his wooden folding chair as we walk past his house, wearing his faded army uniform.

His old dog with the swayback will be standing on the concrete porch or lying beside him in the dirt. The two of them are always there, in the morning when we leave and in the warm afternoons and evenings when we come home.

Soldiers will pass us in trucks and jeeps. Women will be carrying bags of rice and beans home from the market, the bags balanced on their heads. Children will fill buckets with potable water from the city truck. Maybe we'll try to give a few cookies to the children, but they often run away. We'll pass the building where the marines were garrisoned, and we'll go around the town square and past the closed-up church with the clock stopped at 11:30 and the note nailed to the door. The note wants the bishop to return a local priest who was sent away for preaching liberation theology to the people of the parish. Apparently the church establishment didn't like the idea that Christianity might have something to do with people being free and having a life.

Some of us may stop at the *Mercado Municipal* to buy some mangoes or oranges. Maybe Jack and I will go by way of the north end of town so we can pick up a bottle of rum from the man who told us, in perfect English, that he comes from Bluefields, on the coast. If he has any cokes to sell we will have to pour them into our canteens, because he doesn't want us to take the bottles. By the time we get back to the compound the coke will be hot and flat. But we will drink it later anyway, with the rum and maybe some lemons.

First we will take turns washing our work clothes in the tubs under the dormitory, trying to get the worst of the mud out of them. We will probably have to run out to the clothesline that is stretched between the eucalyptus trees with their pendants of pink and red and white to bring the clothes in when one of those violent rainstorms crashes on them in the late afternoon. The shower that we single men use is usually a trickle, so Bob and Brian and I will take turns standing on a chair and dumping buckets of water on each other while we soap ourselves.

Late afternoons and evenings are peaceful times for us, spent mostly on the porch. We will take turns lying in the hammock, and we will sit at the old wooden table to write in our journals, or in the chairs along the railing to read.

We have put all our books into a little community library, a proud collection, and by now we've each read all the popular ones. Somebody always buys a newspaper. Those who can read Spanish will translate the important stories for those of us who can't.

The stories that interest us the most are the ones that deal with recent Contra attacks and with the political situation between the United States and Nicaragua. Naturally we will talk about politics then.

Some of us may walk back to the restaurant in the evening for dinner, but often we're just too tired to walk that far for another plate of rice and beans. Instead we will eat some mangos and go to bed faintly hungry. At least one of us will try to use the old black phone in the forestry office to get through to a friend or relative in the states.

Tonight I want to finish carving two wooden plugs I've been working on for the washtubs. All we have now to hold the water in is an old rag, and it leaks. Gentry says she is going to give me some leather shoe laces she doesn't need; then we can tie the plugs to the water spout so they won't get lost.

Maybe I'll borrow Sharon's guitar and play a few songs, too. Sybil always likes to sing. Jack wants me to learn to accompany "*De Coloris*," which I gather is an important song in this culture, even if I don't know quite why. He wants us to sing it at the party we're going to give for the Nicaraguans at the end of our time here. But I would prefer to hear our night sentry play instead, that Latin-jazz music he did the night he came up on the porch to join us. He was good, strumming and picking with stubby fingers, his automatic rifle under the table.

It is a peaceful time, the evening. People will start drifting off to their rooms eventually, but not before we've filled all of the next day's canteens with water that we pump through a filter to purify. I am usually the last to turn in, staying up late to write in this journal. Brian is already asleep, so I leave the light off while I arrange my sheet on the thin pad stretched over the board I sleep on.

I put my boots up on the window ledge so I won't find any of those gigantic black roaches in them in the morning, the ones that sometimes run across the porch floor in the evening. Then I arrange my sweatshirt into a pillow, though it never seems to come out right in the dark, and I go to sleep to the sounds of crickets and frogs and the occasional gunshots.

Gentry has stopped just on the edge of the flat open area where the truck turns around. She's looking down at her feet. One of the trees we planted in this area has been squashed flat by a wide turn of the truck. Its tiny needles are stuck in the mud, which is molded into the pattern of the knobby truck tires.

"Poor little baby," she says. She is on her knees, pulling at it with thumb and forefinger. It is not going to stand again.

"One down, but a few thousand still up," I say, trying to cheer her. "There's lots more that will be okay."

"Do you really think most of them will live?"

"In this great climate? They'll be fine. About the only danger for them is getting trampled in a fire-fight. Yeah, they'll be okay. Maybe we'll never know anyway. Are you going to come back here someday to find out?"

"Yeah, maybe in about twenty years. I wonder what this country will be like then."

Around the truck are the large wooden crates used to bring the trees from the nursery. Jack is on the truck bed, taking the crates from others below and pushing them toward the cab, where one of the Nicaraguan workers is stacking them. We have to put them all in, then load the picks and shovels, and then squeeze ourselves on as best we can. Sometimes as many as twenty of us sit and stand on top of all that stuff and on top of each other, pushing the truck's wooden railings out to the breaking point. I am afraid that one of these days those railings are going to break right off, sending a few of us tumbling down into the red-dirt gulley.

Nobody is in a hurry, because we're all tired and also hungry. Some people are sitting down, drinking from their canteens, others are lying flat out in the warming sun. Bob has brought his Frisbee again and is tossing it around with two of the Nicaraguan boys. As I watch, it sails over the head of one of them. With a whoop, the boy runs after it as it bounces twice on its side and hops down into some ferns.

Two other young Nicaraguans come over to where we are standing and ask something that I think has to do with taking pictures. They talk with Gentry in Spanish, and when they are finished I ask her what that was all about.

"They want to know if we'd like them to take pictures of the trees in a few years and send them to us."

"What'd you tell them?"

"I said sure. But then they said they'd need a camera."

Gentry goes over to one of the few large, old pine trees and sits with her back against it, knees up in the air. She takes a small book out of her backpack and holds it against her knees. A couple of the Nicaraguan girls come over to where she's sitting and then they wave to a couple of others lying nearby to get them to join the group. Now there are five of them in a semicircle around Gentry, three sitting, one flat on his back, another stretched out on her stomach with a blade of grass in her mouth.

She starts talking to them, and I can hear some of them laugh as she reads something from her book. She reads it again and they laugh some more. I think it's her Spanish-English dictionary, and she is probably trying to get some pronunciation straight with their help. One of them repeats something. Gentry is nodding her head, almost bumping one of the packs hanging on the tree above her.

While Gentry is talking with the children and some of the others are loading the truck, I am sitting with my back against a bank of dirt and thinking about the pine trees. In an infinitely slow process that I am speeding up with mental time-lapse photography, those tiny roots that we liberated today from their plastic bags are feeling their way in the loose soil. A new feeling for them, looser and maybe wet and airy too. The roots are beginning to expand and spread, like fingers from a clenched hand, moving away from each other, finding little spaces in the loose dirt, probing those spaces, making contact with the water and the nutrients in the soil, sucking them in and sending them up into the stem.

Slowly the skinny trunks, many of them bent over from living too long in those plastic bags, are straightening themselves above the ground. They are firming up, adding fractions of an inch, pulling in the clean mountain air and the sunlight, sending out branches.

In my time-lapse images, the pine needles are taking on a deeper green, extending themselves, popping out of those sappy limbs. Some of the lower needles are falling to the ground, where they are slowly decomposing, in the act of fertilizing the tree they fell from, making the soil rich. Growing.

All those twenty years until you come back, Gentry, that is what will be happening. Maybe you will never get those pictures and they will never get that camera, but that is what will be happening. The question is, who will those trees belong to by then? Should they really belong to anyone?

Although I can't hear clearly from where I am sitting, I think she must have turned the teaching process around while I've been thinking about the trees, because she seems to be saying English words. She is repeating them and getting the young Nicaraguans to say them too. She shakes her head and then they try again, sometimes one at a time and then altogether. I can see some of their young faces frowning in youthful concentration as Gentry raises her hand and makes letters in the air with her fingers, trying to get them to see how some word is spelled.

Whenever she smiles they start to smile too, not those shy smiles but big grins that illumine the distance between us. Now someone must have made some kind of joke, because they are all laughing again, rolling around in the grass and the ferns.

Chapter Two

"You're a thrill seeker!"

That is what Ken said would say, more than once, during those times when we would trade stories of our favorite adventures, those risk-takings that are at least as much fun in the re-telling as in the times themselves. And often as not just a little embellished.

There were three possible responses to that. One was to point out that any activity done on behalf of justice, in a world where real justice is often not in the interests of everyone, normally requires some element of personal risk. That would not have been original. Worse, it would have sounded way too stuffy, a better fit for a lecture to a philosophy class or the Unitarians. No, it does not even belong in those places. Anyway, it would have given too much credit to a lot of what we talked about. Not all of our respective thrill-seeking had to do with idealism or high-minded activism.

So I might have told him instead that setting off into the unknown, my preferred way of putting it, can be addictive. But he already knew that, along with a good deal more about addiction than most of us.

The third response was the simplest and best. "Thrill seeker? You ought to know."

We were both right, in our own ways. We were not the first to discover that boredom can be one of the great trials of the modern human condition. It ranks right along with loneliness as one of the downsides of affluence: having too many choices makes each possibility for doing something different seem trivial, or roughly equal to the others, or not worth the effort. Boredom is one of the easiest mental states to develop, since nothing is required to practice it.

Fortunately there are still many people with a low tolerance for boredom and a high need for action. Ken was one of them. That is why he knew the lure of thrill-seeking on a level not usually felt by the average person.

If there had been an element of thrill-seeking during that time in Nicaragua, it got pretty old at the end. We finished our reforestation work fully tired -- tired of the threats of war and the realities of illness, frazzled by the sounds of gunfire in the night, and worn down by those ankle-twisting climbs on wet mountainsides. No one said it directly, maybe out of concern for group morale or maybe from a more personal need to keep up the appearance of revolutionary commitment, but at the end we all wanted only one thing: we wanted to go home.

As it turned out, the return from Central America would be one of those times when getting home proved to be almost as difficult as parts of the trip. That was my own fault.

Here's why. Going to Nicaragua in support of the Sandinista revolution was not illegal, but it certainly qualified as a gesture of political defiance. It was a deliberate in-your-face to the foreign policy of a conservative administration in Washington. That was the point, of course, and it was a point that was not being ignored. Quite a few Americans had worked for the revolution before we got there, and others would follow. But at that particular time, possibly owing to political fallout from the Iran-Contra scandal, those who had actively supported the leftist government in Nicaragua sometimes paid a price at home.

The price we might have to pay was an occasional topic of conversation during those evenings on the porch, and it became a more frequent one as the time for our return came nearer. Several of my companeros had been in Nicaragua before, and it seemed almost as though they enjoyed frightening us novices with stories of political persecution at home. Some of those stories seemed like hearsay or fabrication; others were real enough. A favorite among the real ones had to do with the problems of re-entry into the United States: brief detention, unfriendly interrogation, even confiscation of personal articles by unsympathetic immigration officers.

Maybe because he was a lawyer, Jack liked taking the role of my personal coach.

"You're going to Rochester, right?"

"Right."

"Where do you actually enter the United States?"

"Chicago."

"No way! You couldn't pick a worse place. They'll be all over you."

"I didn't exactly *pick* it. It's just where my flight goes."

"Yeah, okay. But I heard about a guy -- "

"Maybe I don't want to hear about this guy. Anyway, what am I supposed to do?"

"First of all, you can remember that you're a US citizen. You have the right to go wherever you want."

"No," Gentry butted in. "We can't go to Cuba. Or North Korea."

"Never mind that. We aren't talking about Cuba."

"Maybe we should be."

Jack turned back to me. "You don't have to take any crap for coming to Nicaragua. Get a lawyer if you have to."

"A lawyer? My flight gets in at 7:30 on a Sunday morning. Where do you get a lawyer on a Sunday morning?"

"Are you a member of the ACLU?"

"I was, but... hmmm... I guess I haven't paid my dues for a while."

"Doesn't matter, call them anyway. Just don't let anybody hassle you, even for a minute."

My own re-entry would, as it happened, feature some additional complications. Because of the US embargo against Nicaragua, our flight from Managua -- in a jet so old that its overhead lighting consisted of rounded domes attached to the ceiling like large contact lenses -- took us to Mexico City. From there, after promises to keep in touch on behalf of the revolution, each of us would travel to our own parts of the United States. Since some of us had a long afternoon layover, we decided to go into the city. It would be a chance to get those foods we had been dreaming of and maybe do some shopping.

In a quiet mid-town shoe store, I carelessly left my small backpack on the floor while I checked out some boots across the room. It was gone in an instant. With it, I had lost my plane tickets, money, and passport. All the necessary scurrying around needed to get me on the late night flight to Chicago was bad enough, but what really bothered me was the loss of what we considered at the time to be a hard-earned status symbol: a Nicaragua stamp in the passport.

At some point during the long and sleepless flight through the night, it came to me that the loss of my passport could be the perfect answer to any worries about re-entry. My flight, after all, was arriving from Mexico City, not from Nicaragua. My new tickets would show only that I had flown to Mexico City a little more than one month before. Having no passport meant having no incriminating Nicaragua stamp. Here's the cover story: I've just spent a month shopping and drinking margaritas in Mexico City.

Very clever, except for one hitch. On one of the several days we spent back in Managua after the tree-planting, we joined a demonstration against the Contra war, held weekly outside the American embassy. In front of high concrete walls and a heavy metal door that rolled open to admit dark limousines, we circled around with the usual demonstrators' repertoire of signs and guitars, speeches and songs. And we waved now and then at the camera that was filming the demonstration from the top of the embassy wall.

It was that camera that was in a position to ruin my cover story. Could it? How likely was it that an immigration officer in Chicago would have my picture, taken in Managua only a few days before? How organized is the government in its efforts to hassle people who support the Sandinista revolution? Not that organized, surely. Well, maybe. Paranoia, which is often a child of stress and exhaustion, has never been known for logic or probability.

The immigration officer in Chicago -- middle aged, slightly pudgy -- looked harmless enough. No lid-eyed agents in grey raincoats waited in the shadows. It wasn't even raining. I stepped to the desk and explained about the stolen passport.

"All I have is a photocopy of my passport," I told him, "and this note that some friends wrote down there to get me on the plane."

He read the note with no evident interest.

"Why did they write it?"

"Because they can write Spanish and I can't."

He skimmed the note again without interest, or maybe without Spanish. It was about to become the moment of truth. Or the moment of untruth, since I still had not decided.

"Where have you been?"

"Uh, I was..."

He looked up from the paper. "*Don't take crap from those guys. You have the right to go...*"

"I was in Nicaragua," I said as evenly as I could.

There was a slight elevation of the eyebrows, unless I imagined that.

"What were you doing there?"

"I was planting trees."

"What?"

"I said I was *planting trees*."

There was some forced bravado there, but if he heard it he chose not to react. If anything, he was almost too benign.

"What do you do for a living?"

How did that matter? Is this some kind of trap?

"I teach philosophy at a college, in New York."

From his look, I had the impression that he had heard all this, or something like it, before. Or maybe he thought it was too early in the morning to deal with another liberal who had to go plant trees in some place most people could not find on a map. He paused, looked at my papers again, and seemed almost to sigh.

"Okay." He nodded his head toward the exit. "Go ahead."

So much for political persecution. I stepped into the United States. And felt almost cheated. Couldn't somebody at least search me? Take some fingerprints? Give me something to work with when I talk about this at home?

Worrying about immigration hassles was not the only way I spent that long night of flying, staring out over a layer of clouds and feeling that touch of cold air coming off the oval of the cabin window. There was plenty of time to reflect on an experience that even then I began to feel would be life-changing. We had done something -- whatever others might think of it -- that most people do not do. Better still, we did it some years before it became commonplace to talk about making a difference or leaving the world a better place or giving something back.

Those expressions are all sincere enough, even useful to motivate and inspire. But it was interesting that none of us had even once talked in those terms, as though we tacitly agreed that people who do talk about leading the oppressed out of their misery or saving the world for future generations are sometimes the same people who just talk.

Rather, the impression was that there really was not anything particularly unusual about the whole business, even if privately we knew better. It went without saying that if you have certain convictions, you act on them.

It came to me as well how much more advanced some members of the group had been about those convictions. Compared to my own basic understandings, they seemed nearly encyclopedic in their knowledge of Central American history, their grasp of third-world problems, their analysis of the political realities at home. They seemed, to paraphrase an old line, to be people who were against the Contra war well before there was a Contra war. By contrast, I had gone to Nicaragua partly for the sheer novelty and adventure of it all, with only a very general sense of the connection between our reforestation work and support of their revolution.

But even with the breadth of their knowledge, I felt at the same time a welcome simplicity. It was the simplicity that comes from doing what you know is the right thing. Whatever the differences in our backgrounds or political sophistication, we were clearly united in the idea that the Nicaraguan revolution needed both moral support and material assistance. If we had any thoughts about each other, those were only in respect to how much effort each of us was able to put into our work in the mountains. Our one month of bonding measured very little against that, say, of soldiers who share the dangers and sacrifices of a long military campaign. But the kind of community that results from shared convictions does not take long to develop. For me and maybe for some of the others, it was the first taste of that.

As brief as it was for us, that feeling of moral certainty must have been common to others -- and there have been many throughout history -- who were also convinced that they were doing the correct thing. I thought of the young freedom riders in the segregated south of the fifties and early sixties, of abolitionists before the Civil War, of those who dared to oppose Nazism in Germany. Then I was embarrassed to compare our fleeting efforts to the great sacrifices and struggles of people like that.

My thoughts went back to the Sandinistas' anniversary parade a few weeks earlier. Some of the male soldiers looked apathetic or maybe just tired, with rifles held carelessly and shoulders sagging to the left or the right. Their heads turned to watch the crowd, their lines were uneven. One of them carried a guitar and leaned on it, when the parade halted, as if it were a cane.

It was different with the women. We quickly picked out Isabel and Eva, two of the trained foresters who coordinated our work in the mountains. In their dark green fatigues, they looked in that new context more serious and determined, proving that uniforms can transform women as well as men. Like the other women, their shoulders were back, jaws tilted upward in defiance. The women carried no weapons, but they marched in better formation, eyes forward. They listened to the speeches with knit brows and thin lips. Now and then one would raise her hand, work-hardened fingers clenched and forward in a gesture that combined self-awareness with solidarity.

Altogether it was a scene with an unmistakable intensity, one in which even geography had a role to play. Because we were so far north of Managua, tucked into folds of the northern mountains, there was almost no news coverage, a change as refreshing as it was nearly unnoticed. The result was to endow the celebration with its own integrity. There was a complete lack of posing: no jostling for the best position in front of a camera, no shouting into microphones, no mindless and wasteful shooting into the air. This was not an event choreographed for the media, or worse, by the media. What we witnessed was a running up of resolve, not of flags. Their parade was an expression of revolutionary obstinacy all the more genuine because it was orderly and almost eerily quiet. Because the marchers were not so much blindly patriotic as they were committed to their cause, there was no place for demagoguery. In such an atmosphere, it was impossible to be indifferent.

The isolation was not only nurtured by the terrain; it was abetted by an outside world that cared not at all about a parade of small-town revolutionaries. Because it did not care, it could not intervene. In that was an advantage probably unrecognized by the marchers or the speakers.

One part of the advantage was that the people of Ocatal were not fragmented by a greater world that offers dizzied choices among religious and political movements, ephemeral trends, or pseudo-scientific theories. Their choices had been narrowed by their history: either live and die as poor and landless peasants or break with the past and unite against the forces that would keep them that way forever. The defeat of a thousand humiliations was turning steadily into a dream of victory, a kind of hope that was greater even than imagination.

Another advantage of their isolation was the way it created a moral cohesion to accompany their resolve. In the evolution of morality, real progress comes neither from the work of one individual, however exemplary and influential, nor from mass movements. Progress occurs when the moral intuitions of a group are linked with action and the consequences of that action. The intuitions are more likely to develop when the group can make moral choices not only together but also with the least interference from distracting moral alternatives. If they had any sense of a world beyond their own boundaries, it was that of a world defined almost exclusively by the counter-revolutionary forces of the Contras. They may have been equipped and directed by a government in the south, but the message of their celebration was that they had come together in deciding right from wrong. Action and moral values reinforce each other. That was a lesson our own group had learned and one that I did not want to lose.

Thinking of their resolve and morale was another reminder that our one month of living in a war zone does not hold up well compared to fighting that war and creating a revolution. But the *feelings* must be the same, along with the immediacy of it all. The point is to have the feeling at the right time. It is easy, much later, to see that the best-known activists were right, that they had cut through the complexities and ambiguities that had troubled other people, even thoughtful people of good will. Later, those thoughtful people look back and say "of course" and "we should all have realized that at the time." By then, it is almost always too late.

It was not likely that history would have to eventually validate either our own thinking or our actions, any more than that anyone would even remember the whole matter. That would have been to give it way too much importance. For people in the frame of mind that we were in, it does not matter what history validates or forgets. That is the best thing about moral certainty: it spends very little time on analysis or on looking forward or back. And rather than trying very hard to pull others into the orbit, it almost delights in a sense of separation from those who don't share it. At its best, it just causes people to act.

Obviously there are dangers in moral certainty, things like fanaticism, needless self-sacrifice or even self-destruction, the alienation of more moderate people, action that is out of all proportion to its ends. There is also the question of whether moral certainty is ever even possible, along with dozens of complex philosophical responses to the question of what, exactly, is the right thing to do. But to start in on that question was exactly to miss again the point about simplicity. When you are sure about something, you are sure. We were sure that what we were doing was the correct response, however small, to exploitation and poverty and mismanagement of resources in that part of the world. And so we planted trees.

If moral certainty leads in many cases to political activism, the difference between the two is still enormous. The history of modern political activism is one of gradual compromise, of ego trips and infighting, confusion and arguments over goals, factions splintering off and power struggles that drain the movement of its original force. In other words, it is a history of change, because people and events keep changing, sometimes for the better and sometimes not. If they did not, there would be no need for activism in the first place.

Still, the intersection of moral choice and revolution – that extreme of political activism – is made up of many roads, and the more I thought about it the more I realized that I was not cut out to be a revolutionary, never mind much of a political activist. That was not for lack of courage or the ability to suffer hardships, I tried to assure myself. Rather, I was beginning to wonder if any meaningful long-term change, of the kind promised by revolution, is possible.

In a revolution, money and power and privilege flow quickly, often with a minimum of control or accountability. Can moral considerations be expected to keep up with the pace? Along with other questions, it would take more experience and more thought to become clear about that. At the time, the moral certainty and resolve that we both witnessed in others and felt in ourselves was enough.

Memory needs always to be tempered by truth, and the truth was that I had found myself occasionally bored with the evening's political discussions, annoyed by some of the rhetoric, even suspicious of motives. Gentry sensed that, I think, and I thought back to one of our many private conversations. We were sitting on the low wooden steps of the forestry building, watching the evening shadows stretch themselves over the yard. At the gate, the guard sat straight-backed in his wooden chair, assault rifle leaning against one leg.

Gentry understood the difference between idealism and dilettantism.

"So," she asked in her challenging way, "what are you going to do with all this when you get home? Write a book?"

"I haven't thought much about it yet. Tell my friends and my kids. Maybe I'll get a chance to talk to some groups about it, the way they want us to, that sort of thing."

"How about your classes?"

"Yeah, that too. But I'm sort of... reluctant, I guess, to do too much of that, always have been."

"Why?"

"Because I figure that *my* students have signed up to study philosophy, not necessarily my philosophy. There's a line there."

"But people need to learn, to know, right?"

"Sure they need to know. I'm not sure how much of that is my responsibility."

"What course is better than philosophy to get them thinking? You're not just going to do nothing, not after all this?"

"No, it's not that. It's just that I think... what? I think there are other people who are better with the activist stuff, the movements. More..."

"Brave?"

"No, not that either. Talking about revolution in philosophy class doesn't take much bravery. I do it every term, with people like Locke and Marx."

"I meant other kinds of activism, not just teaching."

"Activism needs extroverts. Some of us just aren't that way. So, if we want to do something, we have to think of alternatives."

"Like?"

"Like there's something I've been thinking lately. I mean about after I'm home, that maybe I'd like to find just one person, somebody I could help, you know, on a one-to-one basis. That's probably better for me."

"Like what kind of help? And who?"

"I don't know who, and what, yet. I'll think of something. And I know a few places to look."

TUESDAY'S JAIL

On a Monday I was arrested,
And on a Tuesday I got locked up in jail,
On a Wednesday my trial was attested
And on a Thursday nobody would go my bail.
Yes I'm gone, I'm almost gone...
And I ain't gonna be seein' them
Pretty women no more.

-- Leadbelly

Give us, in mercy, better homes when we're a-lying in our cradles; give us better food when we're a-working for our lives; give us kinder laws to bring us back when we're a–going wrong; and don't set Jail, Jail, Jail afore us, everywhere we turn.

-- Charles Dickens

The waiting room is empty, mostly because the family visits are over for the evening. I step up to the large glass at the far end and slip my ID card under a small opening, like the one in the ticket window of a theatre.

No hand appears to take the card. It is wait time. Standing in front of the glass is sometimes disorienting, because the glass is tinted a greenish-black, making it almost impossible to see through. When the light is right, I can get faint impressions of Main Control behind the glass: a deputy or two, some tables and chairs, and a wall of monitors showing various places in the jail. I try now to look in without appearing to, and then I am startled to realize that the dim outline of a pair of shoulders has appeared right in front of me. At the same moment, my card disappears with a jerk.

"Can I help you?" The voice is low and expressionless, the way people in law enforcement usually talk.

"Yes. I want to see an inmate, please."

I can hear the scratching of a pen. Then my card reappears, followed by the pass, a plastic clip-on saying "Visitor 106."

"Need a locker?"

"Yes, deputy, please." I am being super polite, because I want no problems getting inside. Like many jails, this one is much over-crowded, a situation that can create short tempers and curt behavior.

Now a small locker key with a plastic end appears in the opening.

"Use number 40."

"Okay. Thanks, deputy."

Coat and hat deposited in the locker, I return the key and open a heavy metal door to the left of the tinted glass. In a short hallway, I pass through a metal detector, and then another door. Beyond that is a large set of yellow bars. It will slide open electronically when the deputy sees me standing in front of it. In the few seconds I have to wait, I look up on the wall where a sign used to say "This jail has a no hostage policy." That warning, I assume, explained what should not be expected if an inmate had a knife at someone's throat. This is a maximum security jail, from which it is claimed that no one has escaped. I am not sure why the sign is no longer there. Maybe it was someone's idea of being user-friendly.

Now the bars slide open, rumbling on rollers, and I can step forward. A second set of yellow bars will not open until the one behind has shut. During that time, the feeling is that of a bird in a large square cage. Then the second set of bars clangs once and rumbles open. I turn into another hallway and wait again in front of yet another set of bars. It also opens with a clang. With five doors now behind me, I am fully inside: Inner Control.

To the left is a long wall of bars, with more sliding doors giving access to the elevators. To the right is the control booth, from which a deputy operates all the doors. The booth is glassed on three sides, so that the deputy can see the hall, the bars and the elevators.

As I approach the booth, a tall black inmate passes me and heads down the hallway I have just used. It is a pretend escape.

"Get back here," the deputy yells.

He stops in mid-step and grins at her. Then, walking backward in a comic slow-motion pantomime, he rejoins a group of inmates waiting for the elevator.

Seeing my pass, the deputy rolls up a sheet of paper so that it will fit through a small hole in the glass between us. Having no writing table, I use a concrete pillar to fill out the sheet: my name and pass number, my affiliation, and the name of the inmate to be visited. With this information, the deputy leafs through an inmate list and then picks up the phone. As she makes her call upstairs, she yawns and points with her pencil toward one of the empty visiting booths. For maybe the hundredth time, I think what a lot of trouble all this is for a visit that will probably last less than an hour.

Now it is a matter of waiting until Donald is brought down from his cellblock. Time has a different value in jail, if it has any value at all, so it can be a long wait.

The view is limited, but I can see a cleaning woman as she passes in front of the door.

"Where's Tom?" she yells to someone.

"Here," someone says.

It turns out that Tom is down the hall, delivering some paper cups.

"Tell him to get his buns over here," the woman says.

This booth is one of four, two on either side of Inner Control. The window and door of each booth allow for viewing by the deputy on duty, over a distance of maybe ten feet. Made of concrete block painted beige, the booths are about seven by five feet. There is just enough space for a small Formica table and two plastic chairs.

By chance it is the same booth where I first met Earl, one of my more unusual assignments. We did not meet here often, though. Before long, Earl was put upstairs in the "box," solitary confinement. For fighting, or something. Earl got to like being in the box, he told me. It was more private and less noisy. He would manage to get himself into just enough trouble to get another few weeks of privacy.

The Inner Control deputies would let me see him up there, though reluctantly, and I sometimes had to remind them that I had the right to go upstairs. Since he could not come out, I would sit down in the hallway outside the metal door of the box, and he would do the same on his side. That way we could talk through the small slit that is used to push through plates of food.

The box was near the end of a hallway and also near a locked door that apparently separated that area from the women's part of the jail. Some of the women must have been able to hear us talking, because they called through the door a few times and asked me to send and receive notes under it. I obliged. The process would not have made the deputies happy.

Once, for whatever reason, the door of the box stood wide open. I went inside and sat on Earl's cot to talk. Along with the cot, the furnishings were a toilet and a men's magazine.

Earl's case was interesting for the legal novice. He had done time before. When we first met, he was in jail awaiting trial, unlike other inmates who are here to serve their short sentences. The charges arose, according to his version, from an unusual incident.

"I was on probation," Earl said at that first meeting, "and I was staying at one of those half-way houses."

"Before you go on," I said while pretending to plug my ears, "I have to tell you that I'm not supposed to hear anything about any charges, since you're pre-trial. If you tell me anything, and the DA somehow found that out, I could end up on the stand, against you. That's definitely not the point of these visits."

"It's okay, man," Earl waved away the warning. "I'm gonna beat this one."

"Just so you know."

"Anyway," he continued, "here's what happened. I was out that night, and I was walking home. But the house had a curfew rule, and I knew I was gonna be late. So I was taking a shortcut along this railroad track, going as fast as I could. And it was snowin', too. Cold out there, man. Mostly I was worried about bein' late, 'cause of the probation. Next thing, I seen this loading ramp, out the back of a store. You know the tracks I mean, sort of behind Glendale?"

"No."

"Well, I seen this loading ramp, and there was this big metal door, you know, like a big garage door, and it was open up a few feet. There was light comin' out from beneath it."

"So you were cold -- "

"Not 'cause I was cold. I wanted to call the house I was stayin' in, tell them I'd be a little late. So I sort of got down and crawled under this door. The funny thing was, I didn't see nobody in there. So I says 'hello', called out real loud, so they'd know I was in there. But there wasn't nobody. I went into some other rooms, lookin' around for somebody, you know, to see if I could use the phone. Just nobody there. So then I seen this cash drawer, just sittin' there."

He stopped: the memory of it brought a small smile to his lips.

"How much was in it?"

"About a hundred, maybe a little more. Oh, there was this nice box, too, with nice little speakers."

"So you took the money and the box?"

"Yeah." He smiled wanly, with a twist of his mouth. "And as I was goin' out, the cops were comin' in."

"How'd they know? To come, I mean."

"I must have tripped some alarm or somethin'."

"But how are you going to beat that?"

"'Cause, man, I really didn't go in there to steal nothin'. All I was doin' was lookin' for a phone, like I told you. The thing is, they got to prove I had the intention to rob the place. But that door was open, man. Even the pictures show that. They just don't want to admit it was open, 'cause that means somebody was careless about lockin' up that night. My lawyer's good, man, and he's workin' on it."

Memories of talking with Earl are interrupted by the rumble of metal doors as the deputy throws switches. At a different level is the steady swishing of a broom. Disembodied voices come and go outside the booth, giving me something to listen to and a feeling of dislocation.

We move through many different worlds in one lifetime. Besides the normal and constant ones of home and work and neighborhood, we have our temporary mini-worlds: a favorite vacation place, the gym, a sport to follow or play, a church.

Of these and others, the world of a jail is one of the least well-known or experienced. It is also one of the most likely to inspire fear and revulsion.

The voices that drift into the booth as I wait are those of a world simultaneously similar and different from our normal ones. The differences hardly need elaboration. But the instinct to survive, the need for companionship, the desire for some minimal enjoyment in life are common to every world, including that of a jail. People simply do the things they have to do in any situation; even here, those things are not that uncommon.

"...You know, he wants to talk to you."

"He's over in city, right?"

"He's in reception."

"Right."

A deputy carries two cups of coffee into Inner Control and looks into my booth as he passes. I say hello. No response. Now I hear voices from farther down the hall, harder to distinguish.

"You want it put here?"

"That's okay, right there."

"Sonofabitch is heavy."

They must be bringing in some heavy machine, maybe to polish the floor. Someone laughs loudly over the rumble of the doors.

"... 'Course the guy was stupid anyway."

"He shoulda got a medal for that."

"Got no sense."

Other voices are closer, jumbled together in what must be a small crowd.

"You mean I can't have it till next week, Sarge?"

"You check with me tomorrow. No, make it Thursday."

"...Well, I don't think he was..."

"Hey, you got something you're not supposed to have?"

"No, man, I know the rules."

The voices fade. Each time the doors rumble, I look out to see if Donald has come off the elevator. Finally he appears. Most inmates shuffle, but Donald bounces up to the deputy and sticks his pass into the hole in the glass like someone with a winning lottery ticket. Grinning, he then says something to the deputy. She looks at him blankly and points with her pencil toward my booth. We meet at the door.

"Hey, man."

"Hello, Donald."

We shake hands palm to palm and then loop our fingertips lightly together before pulling our hands back. Donald bounces some more on his toes.

"What's up?" he asks. Not 'sup. Donald enunciates when he feels like it.

"Not much. What's been going on with you?

"It's okay. You know, nothin' happenin'."

Sitting now, Donald waves his hand toward the door of our booth, still open behind me.

"Let's get off the beach, huh?"

"What's that?"

"I say, let's get off the beach. You know, close the door."

I reach behind me and close the door.

"What's that got to do with closing the door?"

"Down in Florida, that's where they say that. You know, if you're on a beach and it's too noisy or windy or somethin', you get in the car and close the door. That's gettin' off the beach. This place is too noisy."

Donald arranges himself as best he can in our small cell. He is not tall, but he makes up for that with a powerful chest and large, hard arms that swell from his wrists and again from his elbows, the biceps almost tearing the loose short sleeves of his jail pajamas. His tight curls run down along his face into a trimmed beard, which he tells me he grows to cover a skin problem.

"So, did you get outside this week?"

"Yeah, I got outside. We went to the park yesterday."

Until just recently, Donald has been working in the jail's kitchen, but now he is on a work crew in the county parks.

"Nice day, huh?"

"Yeah. I was lookin' at the ladies and rakin' leaves and havin' fun with the guys. It's a good thing we went outside and got some air and stuff. Played a little football for about an hour, and we filled about 200 bags of leaves, about nine guys. We was out there from about 9:30 to about 1:30."

"Somebody had a football?"

"Yeah, they bring a football too. Today we got cancelled. One thing about the parks, they always cancellin' us. I like gettin' out, 'cause I don't like layin' around here. I like bein' busy. Around here I don't get enough air, I get lazy and grouchy and all that, you know? The deputy, he always comin' around yellin', 'Get up, get up!'."

"Why does he want you up?"

"I don't know. He doesn't like you to get lazy, I guess. 'Cause he was in the service, and he thinks, 'Okay, I know how to treat these inmates, keep them on their toes all the time'."

"Just like a drill sergeant."

"Yeah, he just like a drill sergeant, whistlin' and stuff, wakin' us up. You know how they wake inmates up? They use a horn." Cheeks puffed out, Donald makes a loud, low noise as his version of a rusty horn.

"That's what he do."

His imitation is almost good enough for radio. "With a bugle?"

"That's what he do, but he do it with a blow horn."

"What do you wear when you work in the parks?"

"Same thing, green." He touches his pajamas lightly at the waist.

"Do people look at you funny or anything?"

"Yeah, they wave and stuff."

"Yeah? That's good."

"We was rakin' leaves, and this lady ran up, says, 'Oh, did you see any glasses?' We was nervous, you know, because this deputy across the street has to watch us, and he was lookin' over at us, probably thinkin' one of us said something smart to her or somethin'. But she just lost her glasses in the leaves, I guess."

"Did you find them?"

"Naw. Then another guy, he was runnin'. You know how these guys jog on their lunch time? He didn't see the sheriff's van over there. So this guy ran up and says, 'Hey, any you guys got a joint?' We started laughin'. We pointed over to the van and we said, 'You see that guy right there? Go aks him. 'He sees the van and he says, 'Oh no, I can't do that!' and starts runnin' away. You know, I was amazed. Guy with a good job like that, a job worth gettin' and takin' care of, and he runnin' around lookin' for drugs. So I aksed another friend of mine, a guy used to have a good job, a BMW, and everything, but he got messed up in drugs, 'Don't they give you tests, like every, uh, six months or so, just for a precaution?' He's like, 'Naw, unless they think that you've got a problem by the way you're actin' on the job. 'I said, 'They should, man, it's an opportunity to be workin' a good job like that, a benefit job with a big salary, you know?'"

Donald is shaking his head at the memory of having discovered some new proof of human frailty.

"From what I've heard," I say, "that guy would have a better chance of getting his drugs right in here."

"Yeah. Some guys got wasted last night." Donald grins, somewhere between disapproval and tolerance. "Wine and reefer together."

"Where'd they get the wine? Nobody can smuggle that in."

"Naw, they make it upstairs."

"You mean in the sink or something?"

"Usually like in a jar, from the kitchen."

"Where do they get the supplies?"

"Well, they take sugar from dinner and get the yeast from the storeroom. Then they use grapes or orange juice from breakfast. You can put a potato in a sock, a clean sock, and put that in with the yeast and stuff."

I've been given the wine recipe before, and I'm asking only to see if Donald's recipe matches. It does, more or less.

"Don't they ever catch you?"

"Naw."

"What about the smoke from the grass? They must smell that."

"It's okay. They burn incense."

"That's crazy, Donald. Why don't they just put up a sign to say they're gonna smoke some grass? Everybody knows you burn incense to cover that."

"I dunno." Donald smiles. "Maybe they think we be prayin' or somethin'. But you know, some of those dudes don't take baths very often, so the incense helps that way."

"So where do you get the incense from?"

"We don't get it, we make it."

"How?"

"Some guys just burn dry orange peels. Even banana skins. You light the stuff, then blow out the flame and keep blowin' on the part that's glowin'. Really smells up the place. The orange peel smells awful." He makes a face and waves his hand in front of his nose. "You can get better incense if you roll out toilet paper and soak it in cologne or maybe deodorant, then roll it up and burn it."

"So the deputies don't care if you guys are burning up all this stuff?"

"Hey, if they do there's other ways to smoke reefer."

"Like what?"

"Like they put it in the end of cigarettes, you know, the kind you roll yourself." He pretends to roll a cigarette between his fingers. "They smoke the reefer first, 'cause it's at the end of the smoke, and then the regular smoke covers up the reefer smell. Or they just mix the reefer in with the tobacco. There's lots of ways. Hey, it's like Rob'sin Crusoe up there, somebody always thinkin' of something!"

"Isn't there ever a bust?"

"Yeah, there was a while back."

"And?"

"They just took the reefer."

It occurs to me that this sort of conversation is typical of what I have learned over the years about life in jail. It is a world that is at once violent and boring, demeaning and creative, stressful and laid-back. In the years I have been coming here, I have heard stories of attempted jail breaks that, if true, rival the worst movie scenarios of bed-sheet ropes and hacked bars, stories of a violence inside that mirrors the violence inmates have known outside, stories of knives sharpened from plastic dinnerware and hidden in the overhead lights until needed, of wine made and consumed in kitchen storerooms, of drugs smuggled in rectums and hollowed-out shoes. And I have seen confrontations between guards and inmates flare up in a moment and as quickly die down.

For all of that, my sense is that of both guards and inmates just trying to make the best of a hard situation. For those of us who have never lived or worked in a jail, the conditions here would become unbearable real fast.

Inmates who have cried in front of me, or begged me to talk to their public defenders or contact their loved ones or go their bail, or who have covered their pain with bluster or piety, have taught me that. But people can apparently adapt to almost anything. Most of the adapting here is in the form of attempts -- both within jail rules and outside of them -- to find ways of making life here more bearable. Smart guards know when to ignore behaviors that are ways of coping even when they violate jail policy. Seasoned inmates know the limits of what the guards can tolerate. What has always caught my attention the most have been those instances of tomfoolery and joking between guards and inmates. They *are* not the rule but all the more interesting for that reason. They suggest an almost natural camaraderie that seems to say "I don't want to be here anymore than you do, but we both are here and we can't do anything about that. So let's just keep cool and make the best of it, maybe even have a little fun."

Calling it fun is a stretch. I have noticed how often our talk turns to those better parts of Donald's incarceration –- an hour of football along with the leaf-raking, for example-- and I know that is his way of distracting me from what he does not want me to know much about. Anyone listening to this conversation would think that jail time is all fun and recreation and good times. It is not. Still, since I already know that, I go along with the deception.

"Well, it sounds like you guys are having a pretty good time up there," I tell Donald. "Now I know where to come for a good party. But I sure hope this place isn't bugged."

Rolling our eyes in a fake conspiracy, we both look up at the ceiling and the concrete blocks, then start feeling for bugs under the table. It occurs to me that Donald has been careful to say "they" in describing all these activities.

"Anyway, you're keeping yourself out of trouble, aren't you?"

"Yeah." He pauses, looks down at the table and then back up at me. "I was about to, but I ain't gonna lie to you."

"Okay, let's hear it."

"You know, I was playin' Ping-Pong, and this guy started arguin' with me. I just play argue, I don't argue-argue. But he got mad and he shot the Ping-Pong ball at me real hard, and hit me in the eye. I got up and everybody was lookin' at me, so I started runnin' at him. I wasn't gonna do nothin' to him, just wanted to see what he'd do. He say, 'Okay, I'm sorry, I'm sorry. 'Everybody say, 'He sorry, DJ, he didn't mean nothin'."

"Well, you'd both just be in trouble for nothing. And they wouldn't care who started it. You'd just end up doing more time. Sounds like you're growing up."

"Yeah, I had to overlook it, much as I was wantin' to do somethin'."

"Was he a big fellow?"

"Naw, he was little. Well, not really littler than me, but you know. I don't want to be no bully. He got beat up down here, some guy bigger'n me. He was arguin' with the guy, and this other guy, he got problems. Ain't got no family, nobody comin' here to see him, and some of these people don't talk to him, so he got an edge on him. He always tellin' me, 'Man, I want to fight, I want to knock somebody out!' I told him like this, 'You know, it might seem like right now nothin's goin' your way, but once you get work release, things start brightenin' up, money comin' in. You'll get a place to stay, the counselor will help you get a place. 'He thought about it and says, 'You're right, man, you're right. 'So I got him calmed down. See, he's been upstate, and people from upstate, they got this kind of thing where, uh, nothing matters. They don't care, 'cause down here is just like a playpen, it's nothin' compared to upstate. Anyway I got him calmed down. He's a good guy, just needs a close friend, somebody to talk to."

"He's your same age?"

"He's about, uh, twenty-eight, but he acts like he's young, you know? He aksed me one day how old I was. I told him I was nineteen. 'You nineteen? You got a good head on your shoulders, man. It's like you're grown up already. 'I said, 'Well, I hope so. Nobody's grown up fully, you learn somethin' new every day. '."

Donald is a bit of a philosopher, or at least on the way to being one.

"You are very mature for your age,"

"I guess 'cause I came up the hard way. I ain't got no sisters, no brothers. So I make friends quick. I like friends to talk to."

"You told me your parents were dead, right?"

"My mother, she died. Remember, I told you my aunt -- he pronounces it to rhyme with 'want' -- and uncle raised me, so I call them my parents."

"And your father?"

"He alive, upstate. No, he's out now. But I ain't expectin' nothin' from him."

"You don't see him?"

"He don't come down here, no. My other uncle's here."

"Here in the jail?"

"Yeah. I see him now and then. First time I seen him, I didn't want to see him, you know? I was in this line, and I seen him and I turned my head. But he come over and he say, 'DJ, what you doin' here? I don't like seein' you in here. 'Seemed like that was a funny thing for *him* to be sayin'."

"So what's your father doing?"

"Dealin', probably. They both slackin' off, so I know I got to make it happen on my own. I never really did like taking things, don't like nobody saying 'I gave you this, I did this for you'. That's how my father was, always expectin' something from somebody. My aunt, she say, 'You gonna be just like your father', but I ain't. I'm gonna be independent."

He stops for a moment, remembering. We have learned not to be uncomfortable with pauses.

"My father's mean, too. Got a real mean temper. He gets mad just like that. Takes a lot to get me mad. That's the way my grandmother is, takes a lot to get her mad. I mean, you could snatch her purse, push her down to the ground, she'd get up and brush herself off and she'd walk. Guess I'm like that too."

"At least that kept you out of that fight," I say. In spite of not wanting to sound too obvious, I find myself wanting to encourage Donald when he talks like this. Compared to conversations with other inmates, this is promising.

"Everybody knows I don't play around, I don't start no trouble. I don't fight, but they know I'm no sucker or pushover, not that type of guy."

He pauses again, as if not wanting to discuss himself further. Then he continues in a quieter voice, signaling something important.

"You know, there's people down here that's older and bigger'n me, and they like me and they know I'm not a trouble starter. I make friends that are solid, like, friends that come to me and tell me problems. I talk to them and they think I bright. They know I got confused, got in trouble, but they say to me, 'Man, when you get out you can make somethin' of yourself. 'I'm tellin' you, I got guys here that's like uncles to me, they beat up on guys musclin' in. I don't got to lift my hand. Like the other day I was playin' cards with this guy and I lost and he was spittin' in my face when he talked to me. I said, 'Hey, man, don't spit in my face', and he said, 'Whatcha gonna do about it, whatcha gonna do about it?' So I stood up and I guess my friends knew I was about to do somethin', but I was slow about it. I'm glad I was slow because my friend, he walked up to me, put his around me and he whispered, 'Man, you know you got two months. Rough it out the best way you can. I know it's frustratin', but just take it easy."

"What did you do?"

"I shook it off and I said, 'Okay, you're the winner' and I walked away from the game."

"Smart."

"So I don't play cards anymore. All I do is read books, watch television, hang out with a couple guys, sit on my bunk with my Walkman. I'm gonna make it. I cut off all the bad things."

"Yeah, you're gonna make it, all right."

He looks down at the table, maybe embarrassed either by my attempts to encourage him or by too much talking about himself. For a time we sit again without talking.

I am thinking now that Donald's resolve to make it could actually come to something. He is sincere at the moment, because he is talking to me, and he knows what I want for him. There could even be an element of manipulation in our talks except that there is almost nothing in the situation worth manipulating.

These conversations are pretty familiar by now, and I know what usually happens when inmates are out on the streets again. Donald seems different, though, a little more respectful of himself.

Along with that, I have an increasing sense of his integrity. He says certain things, deliberately or not, that make him different from others I have been with here. That causes me to wonder about where those things came from. Being surprised to find integrity in an inmate hints at stereotyping; integrity can be equally hard to find on the outside. The word is associated with wholeness, sometimes with purity. In Donald's case, I would even add the element of soul.

Better, soul-making. That is an idea sometimes used to explain the presence of evil in the world: we need it to forge our souls in its fire, to prepare ourselves for God. Without going that far, it does seem that Donald is making, if not his soul, at least an attempt to create a life that he can himself respect. Does he have enough power of will to move beyond this situation? And if he does, how far can he take the effort?

I should have some hope for him. Hope, even if not expectations. "Deliver me from reformers," someone said. The trick is to encourage but not to interfere, and to remember how expectations can lead to major disappointments. Better just to stick with friendship and hope and let him do his own building. Maybe because I am thinking along these lines, I find myself telling Donald about Earl and his robbery case.

"Man, it sounds like they got that dude cold," Donald says when I've finished. "Why'd he think he could beat that one?"

"He wasn't trying to beat it entirely. He said he just didn't want to stand trial for the actual burglary. He'd admit to criminal trespass, but that was all."

"Lesser charge?"

"Yeah. He had a record, and maybe the burglary conviction would send him upstate. I don't remember exactly. But he kept saying that they'd have to prove he planned to rob the place, and they couldn't do that, not with that open door."

"I don't know, man. Sure seems like he robbed it. What do you think?

"I'm not sure if he was right about that intention stuff. He sounded like he knew something about the law."

"Lots of these guys study the law," Donald says. "I mean, do you think he went in there to rob the place?"

"You know, I don't think that, really. He seemed like he was telling me the truth, about that part anyway."

"Sort of a weird situation. Like, you're trying to do the right thing, the phone call I mean, and then this big temptation is right there."

"Yeah, and that's different from planning to rob somebody. Still, he took the stuff, and I don't know how much your intention has to do with guilt."

"Maybe he was just connin' you. What happened to the dude?"

"I don't know. For some reason, I didn't see him after a while. Probably I went away for the summer or something, and got assigned to somebody else when I got back. Anyway, it's your situation I'm interested in now."

"I'm gettin' better at gettin' older," Donald continues. "Tryin' to do good in my life instead of messin' up all the time. There's gonna be a few mistakes a person makes, but you can cover up your tracks a little, anyway. I wrote my parents the other day, told them to send me some towels. I told them I'd soon be startin' work, I might need a dress shirt, a tie, a pair of slacks. Told them it doesn't have to cost a lot, just something I could present myself nice in an interview, get a job. And I sent a card, a nice little card, said some nice things on it. Just so they thinkin' about me. They probably thinkin' about me, but they out of contact."

That does not seem to be a topic to linger on.

"I hope you get that work release."

"Yeah, that's what I really want now. That's the only thing keeps me goin', next to gettin' out."

"Well, you wanted the parks job, and you got that. So it's paying to behave yourself."

"My counselor, he been actually arguing with me, sayin', 'You should go to school, go to school. 'I say, 'I don't want to do that right now, not just yet. 'I want to get released, work for about a year, year and a half, get my head right. I don't know, it's like he don't want me to get no job."

"So he wants you to go to school. Did he say why?"

"Not really."

"Maybe he figures you'll behave yourself more if you don't get a job, like if you get a job you'll have money to fool around, where if you're a student you'll be too poor."

"Well, I told him I need some money, man."

"Yeah, of course you do. I mean, it's not my business, not being your counselor. But I'd say you ought to have a job for a while, get yourself back together."

"That's what I want."

"Anyway, you could at least find out about college from him, the kinds of programs you might want, that sort of thing. But you maybe should enjoy yourself a little first."

"I'd like to get a nice little apartment, like a studio or somethin'. I know I could stay with my parents, but I don't want to. They kind of old, you know?"

"Didn't you say your girlfriend had a place for you?"

"I don't know if I want to stay with her. You know how girls are. I'd rather just spend the nights once in a while, you know?"

We smile together at that, as though we know something important about how girls are.

"Have you got any leads on a job?" I ask.

"I know I'll be able to get a job, like a dietary one, 'cause I'm pretty good at cookin'. I might be able to get a job at a franchise."

"Because you worked in the kitchen here?"

"Plus I worked at a restaurant and at a nursing home for a year."

"Could you go back there?"

"Yeah, I could. Might go back there. I wanted to get a job at the hospital, 'cause they pay pretty good there."

Trying to get more comfortable in our little booth, we have both turned our chairs sideways to the table and pushed our feet up against the wall, waist high. Donald licks his finger, bends forward, and tries to rub out a spot on his purple and white sneakers. The shoes have no laces.

"A guy told me once they don't allow you to have laces so you don't try to hang yourself with them," I say. "Is that true?"

"Naw, we can have short ones. I just like these better without laces. These shoes cost, man."

If you are even tempted toward philanthropy, Thoreau said, don't let your left hand know what your right hand is doing. "Rescue the drowning," he wrote, "and tie your shoelaces."

At a noise in the hallway, Donald gets up and looks out the window of our booth. Smiling at whatever he sees, he slouches back into his chair, puts one elbow on the table, and plays with the side of his beard. We discuss some football scores, and he tells me that he won two packs of cigarettes betting on last night's game.

"And I don't even smoke, man."

"What are you going to do with them, sell them?"

"Yeah, start a store."

"Two for one, right?" The inmates have a loan system, called a "store," for the candy, cigarettes and toiletries they can buy once a week from the jail's commissary. If an inmate borrows one candy bar or one pack of cigarettes, he has to pay back two.

Donald looks up at me. "How you know about that?"

"I've been coming here for quite a while. The first guy I ever visited had a store, and he told me how it works. Soap, cigarettes, toothpaste, all that stuff two for one."

"Yeah, two for one on anything. I guess that's the only way some people survive. My aunt gave me three dollars one time, but I don't eat that much candy and I don't smoke. I just need soap, Vaseline for my hair. I got all that stuff."

"But if you used the money from your aunt, how can you get more stuff for your store?"

"For one," he says, "I sold this guy a Walkman, not the headphones, just the package. That's worth three packs. Then I got a good friend upstairs and I told him I was doing bad down here and I need to start a store. He said, 'I'll tell you what I'll do. Tomorrow you come up and I'll give you a carton', and he just give me a whole carton and sixteen candy bars to start my store. I'll just give it back once I build it up."

"What happens if somebody owes a bunch of cigarettes or whatever and he gets out? He doesn't pay them?"

"If he gets out, he's lucky. If he come back in, whaooo, he's dead then."

"He'd better have the stuff, huh?"

"He'd better have *something*. Even if he just got a sweat suit or somethin'. These guys here don't play around. They don't care if he go up to another floor, they get him somehow. You can't get away with it. It's called the system, and you can't beat the inmate system. I don't care if he's the biggest guy in the jail, he'll get beat up over maybe two or three candy bars. That's what they call money here. They say, 'Gimme my money, man'."

"Isn't there a lot of competition with all these stores?"

"When I start my store, I don't have to worry about nothin'. I be smart. See, I know about the competition, but I'm thinking about a strategy. Here's what I plan on doin', okay? When you buy two packs from me you supposed to give me back two packs. But maybe I just take one pack and three candy bars. So they gainin'. See, a pack costs a dollar and fifty, and those three candy bars is a dollar and five. They gettin' a break."

"Won't that make other guys mad?"

"They can't do nothin' about that. Besides, they ain't feedin' us too good around here these days, so they'll want those candy bars."

Donald the entrepreneur. Sometimes the philosopher. And sometimes even the latent activist with the occasional talk of helping others. I like that last role best. It is something to work on, if I can find more proof of his sincerity. For now, he knows that he will need to get his own act together first.

"You just have a bigger appetite now because you're out in the fresh air throwing footballs around. On taxpayers' money, too. I think I'd better talk to the county executive about this place."

He shrugs and smiles.

"Anyway, what did you have for Thanksgiving dinner?"

"Turkey. Real turkey."

"Yeah?"

"And we had the news cameras watchin' us."

"What were they doing, just some sort of holiday story?"

"Yeah, just to see how happy inmates be here and everything. 'See the inmates on Thanksgiving Day!' "His voice rises in mockery and we both laugh at the idea of the happy inmates." Everybody smilin' and waving,' Hi, ma! There's a lot of crazy people here. I don't understand it. I just kept outta sight, 'cause I don't want my friends seeing me in here."

"People will do anything to get on TV, I guess."

"Yeah. Man, there was this newscaster, this lady, and I seen her. She had this blonde hair, and, whew! She was standin' in front of the camera and everybody's starin' at her and sayin' stuff."

"I can imagine."

"She says, 'I can't do this with you guys starin' at me!' So the sergeant says, 'All right, you guys go back to eatin'. And then he's starin' at her. Oh, man!"

Donald's excitement gets us both laughing, and I can almost feel the deputy staring disapproval into our booth from hers.

"Donald, I've got to tell you, you're a fun one to talk to. Sometimes I get these guys that don't make good conversation. I had this one guy who just didn't have anything to say. I'd say, 'How's your family?' and he'd say 'Fine'. Then I'd say, 'Well, how are you doing upstairs?' and he'd say, "Okay. '"

Donald shakes his head.

"A long hour! I'd sit there trying to think of something else to ask the guy, and it got so bad -- finally he mentioned that he was taking the Bible course."

"What's that?"

"You know, the Bible studies that those guys run here, where you get those certificates. I'm not into that myself, but that's fine if that's what he wanted to do. So I finally got so desperate for something to talk to him about that I said, 'Why don't you bring your Bible down with you?' So every time he'd come down I'd say, 'What'd you read today?' and he'd say, maybe, 'Timothy, Chapter Four. ''Well, read me some of it. 'And then he'd read for a while. Then I'd say, 'That's great. What do you think of that?' And he'd tell me, you know, give me a long sermon. At least it got him talking."

"But not about him in general."

"No. It's more fun to hear about what you're doing here. It's not too often I have those kind, but they make it more fun to talk to guys like you."

"You gotta have a couple laughs," Donald says, "or you just be grouchy all the time."

"Yeah. The guy was way too serious, and I had him for six months."

"You had him six months?"

"He was going upstate. It took him awhile to get there."

"That's one thing I'm glad about, not goin' upstate. I don't want to go up there. I think if I was to go up there, I think maybe deep inside, I don't care how good I would do afterwards, I'd always know I'm a bad person. Down here it's just like, 'Hey, be good, that's all.' And then --." He makes a sweeping motion.

"Then you're out."

"Yeah. But goin' upstate, it's like, 'Hey, you blew it, guy. See you later. 'Here it's nothin'. We just got the wino biz."

"The what?" Jail is a good place to enlarge your vocabulary.

"The wino biz. We call all the winos that. They just in here and back out again, and they tease us and stuff about stayin' so long. One guy got down here tonight. He just got out three weeks ago and he's back. Somebody said he stole some money from an apartment or somethin'. I can't picture myself comin' back here, you know. It's like a nightmare, like the grim reaper with one of those sickles, sayin', 'You're back!'"

Donald stops to fool with his sneakers. It is a sign that he needs a break, and so do I.

It occurs to me that after three months of visits like this one, with lots of talk about crimes and sentences, I do not know what Donald is in jail for. When we are assigned a new inmate, we are given basic information which includes some legalese about the charge, but it is nothing more specific than "Assault II" or maybe "Possession." From other inmates I have heard fairly detailed descriptions of the crime they usually want me to know they did not commit. My attempts to tell them that I should not be hearing about their crime eventually fail, and there are probably a few prosecuting attorneys who would like to have known what I knew.

Others, like Donald, have plea-bargained and have been sentenced to do their time right here. I just assume that their crime could not have been too serious, since no one stays in the county jail for more than a year. After that, it is upstate, the prison system. As a rule, most of the inmates I have known are not inclined to tell me about their charges, almost as if they want to protect me from their world or more likely, keep me from thinking badly of them. They are also reluctant to tell me about the crimes committed by others in the jail. When I ask, they usually say they don't know, and I know that is a lie.

One exception to that occurred when an inmate I was visiting waved to a friend passing by our booth.

"You know him?" I asked.

"Yeah, he's on my floor. And we grew up together, you know, outside."

"What's he in for?"

"Murder." The inmate's expression was deadpan, and he said it with the same interest he might show in a shoplifter. At the time this was all new to me, and the word seemed to hang suspended in the air between us. I thought to myself that I had never seen a murderer before, except on television news.

"You know the one," that inmate added. "That restaurant across the river. He wasted a couple people."

"Did he really do it?"

"Sure, he done it."

"How do you know that?"

He did not hesitate." 'Cause he told me, man."

"He told you? So why is he here, then? I mean, shouldn't he be upstate?"

"He ain't had his trial yet, so he still here."

"But you said he admits doing it."

"To *me*, man. He'll plead innocent. He's talkin' to his attorney right now."

"You think he'll beat it?"

"He might. That lawyer's got a few guys off."

Earlier this evening I had the thought that some aspects of life in a jail are not that different from those outside. That does not apply to the discourse. Things said in these booths -- "sure he killed him, he told me," and "they burn incense to cover the smell of the reefer" -- are not familiar expressions of the everyday. They have in any case a refreshing honesty about them, and they even lend a weird sense of humor to the whole situation.

About then I decided I had learned more than I really wanted to know, and the inmate was looking a little uncomfortable, too. Later, during that time when I was going upstairs to visit Earl, I used to meet up with our city's most celebrated serial killer.

Over a two-year period and while on parole after serving time for killing two children, he had strangled 11 women, most of them prostitutes. The most lurid tabloid could hardly improve on some of the testimony at his trial, which included details of mutilation, cannibalism and maybe best of all for tabloid readers, demon possession.

At the times we talked, he was waiting for his transfer to begin serving a 250-year sentence upstate. I would find him sweeping the hallway that led to Earl's box. We would exchange hellos and a few words about the weather outside or whatever came to mind. Once he brought me a glass of water, and I learned then that serial killers can be at least superficially sociable. If I had not known some of the gruesome details of his killings, I would have judged him to be a really nice guy, the kind who waves to little kids when he is out cutting his lawn. Maybe he did that.

A trustee moves past our window, pushing a broom. When Donald sees him, he jumps out the door and begins a conversation too low for me to hear. Without Donald to entertain me, I study the patterns of the cement blocks. Everything is well build around here -- sturdy, straight, utilitarian.

Whatever else the human race has learned, we do know how to put up buildings. But this qualifies as an odd use for the building instinct. It is not a building to live in, or to look at, or to bring people together for fun or sport or health or learning or worship. It has been built to punish. It is a negative building.

And because it is negative, it does not do what it was meant to do. And it never will. People think we need more jails and prisons, and we're building them faster than almost anything else these days. We now imprison more people than any other country, between five and eight times as many as are imprisoned in European countries. It is not making any difference in the crime rate, but it sure is costing lots of money and creating a growing industry. In New York State the operating budgets of public universities are falling while allocations for prisons are climbing dramatically. In the new priorities, jails and prisons replace classrooms and labs.

Some people think we should make jails less pleasant, but that just shows they have never spent any time in a jail. Even if jails were less pleasant, the people who have to come here would just find whatever ways they could to deal with the situation. They would adapt, but that does not mean they would change for the better.

Other people say that certain people really do not mind being in jail, and some even like it. If that were true, it would be saying something really interesting about the quality of life they have on the outside. But it is not true. I have not yet met an inmate who wants to be in here. They may not care enough when they are outside, but they sure don't like it when they are inside.

We have heard the arguments over and over, the lines are drawn. That they are drawn is the reason why we need some fresh thinking. It is not enough to say either that young black men are somehow genetically or sociologically crime-prone, on the one hand, or that they are universally victimized by a racist and unequal society on the other. Either-or thinking hardly ever advances problem-solving.

Not that we should not do something about people who have offended society, or protect ourselves from those who are dangerous. But those are two different categories, and there are ways to get justice from the first group without always mindlessly throwing them in jail. If we ever get serious about discussing those ways, we would get our justice in a lot of cases without all this bother and expense of so many jails and so many people in them.

People who think along these lines now are sometimes accused of being soft-hearted, naive, even dangerous. The truth is that it is the other way around. The urge to punish other people is what is dangerous, because a lot of that urge is related to fear, which is its own kind of prison. It is also related to righteousness and maybe even to guilt about mistakes of our own that we have managed to get away with. Those are negative conditions, hardly a good basis on which to construct a system. People who want to address crime through education, jobs, better opportunities, community service and restitution for non-violent offenders and other positive measures are the ones who are tough-minded. I call them "pragmatic idealists," a near oxymoron that may be my single contribution to the overwrought vocabulary of philosophy. Such people can be found working here in the jail and outside as well.

In either place, they are enlarging the idea of altruism, which basically means care for others, by including some of society's least regarded members in their notion of others.

The things they do are hard, time-consuming, and uneven in their results. Compared to putting people in jail, their actions seem both unnecessary and unmerited. But they are the only measures that will work, if we really want to deal with most offenders of the kind I find in here. If we do not, that is another matter. We should at least know by now that quick fixes hardly ever work. One of the most disturbing features of the human condition is that it takes a long time to get something right -- whether it is a building or a person -- but it can be destroyed in a matter of seconds.

Donald comes back in, smiling.

"What was that about?"

"A bet. Him and me are always bettin'. Hey, check this out, check this out."

He puts his shoe up on the table and turns up the tongue. Then he slides his finger into a tiny slit in the tongue and extracts some money. It's folded over and over, so I ask him to unfold it so that I can see how much. A five-dollar bill.

"Another violation of the rules," I wag my finger at him. "You know inmates can't have money. Do I have to tell the corporal about this, too?"

He ignores the teasing, except for a sly smile.

"Man, this leg still hurts."

"Did they ever give you anything for it?"

"Naw."

"Not even aspirin?"

"Nothin', man. The doctor, he just looked at it, said it wasn't nothin'. But it's swollen, see?" It is swollen.

"Well, take it easy. You can rake those leaves more slowly and don't run the deep pass patterns."

"Anyway, I'm still workin' out. Check this, huh?"

He flexes his biceps and turns his arms around so that I can see the bulges in his forearms. Donald is in a contest to see who can produce the biggest arm muscles.

"Where are you now?" I ask.

"Second place. I'm workin' out two hours a day, three days a week."

"Well, I'm impressed. Your girlfriend will be, too."

"I can't wait, man. I want to get my clothes back, and see some ladies. I like to dress up for the ladies."

"You'll be wearing all the clothes you want before long. Just keep out of trouble upstairs, huh?"

"Don't worry."

"Well, I do worry." I give him a stern look, which he probably sees right through.

"I'm doin' okay, man, I really am."

For a moment, his own glance reflects mine: serious, or as much so as we can make it. Our conversations are often trivial, like most of tonight's, but he knows I want him to get his life straightened out. I wonder if he really knows what the odds against that are. Life on the streets he will soon return to offers more temptations than viable opportunities. He may not know the exact statistics on crimes committed by young black men, or just how low their life expectancy has become, or how slight are their chances for decent jobs or college educations or high incomes or any other indicators of success.

But he does know how many of his friends and relatives have spent time in here and how often they have returned, some of them on their way upstate. And I know that an hour or so of joking and trivial talk is hardly enough to profoundly change the course of his life. Every inmate I have visited has wanted to stay in touch with me after he is released, but only one ever did, for about two months. What does that say? Still, it's better to think that Donald is working on his self-esteem, something in short supply around here, and even reaching out to others.

"I'm doing okay," he repeats.

"Yeah, you're doing really well. As far as those ladies are concerned, you better be careful or I'll tell your girlfriend. Then you'll wish you were back in here."

Now he is smiling again, less at my threat than at the idea of being out on the street with the ladies. I am just happy to be ending our visit on a good note. The deputy looked into our booth a few minutes ago, maybe indicating that somebody else wants in here.

"Time for me to go."

"Yeah?"

There is a hint of disappointment in his voice.

"Next Tuesday, huh?" I reassure him. "Is Tuesday still okay for me to come?"

"Yeah, it's okay. Unless I get that work release. Then I don't know."

"We'll find another day if we have to. I'll just come as usual next week and see what's happening."

We stand up and shake hands again, then step out into the foyer in front of the glass booth and the deputy. A small crowd of inmates is standing by the sliding doors, waiting for the elevator. One of them recognizes Donald and comes over to us.

"Hey, man," the inmate says.

"'Sup, man?" Donald says as they shake hands.

"Two weeks," the inmate says, "I'm outta here."

"Where you gonna stay?"

"With my lady. She was here tonight, visitin', and she says she be waiting for me. She ain't give up on me yet."

They smile at that, mutually impressed with the constancy of girlfriends. Then the inmate looks at me.

"You his lawyer?"

"No, I'm a friend of his. I just come down here to get him on the straight and narrow, keep him away from you bad asses."

The inmate's grin shows a missing front tooth.

"But he's corrupting me," I go on. "A bad influence."

"Me?" Donald turns to the inmate. "Man, this guy's corruptin' *me*. You oughta hear the stuff he's tellin' me. Next thing, I be comin' to visit him."

The inmate looks at us as though all this is not making much sense, and then shakes his head when he realizes that it is not meant to make any sense. While we have been talking, the others have passed through the open bars and entered the elevator, and behind me I hear the deputy yell something through the round hole in the glass.

"You guys are gonna miss your ride," I tell them.

The two of them get into the elevator, where the other inmates are poking each other and a deputy is looking at them impassively.

"Beam us up, Scottie," one of them yells to the deputy in the glass booth.

The last one in, Donald turns and looks back at me through the bars, which have rolled closed. He mouths something through the bars and the noise, and it seems like he's saying "next week."

Chapter Three

If the world really did run according to logic and the operations of cause and effect, Ken and I would have met in the county jail. We did not, but it is possible that we came close at one time or another, with him in one of those groups of inmates that would occasionally pass by the visiting booths, bumping and jiving, or even on one of the elevators.

A few years later we would compare notes on that, intrigued by the possibility. We enjoyed trading our impressions of the nastier deputies or the memorable inmates. Sometimes we would even hit on a mutual acquaintance.

"How about No Neck?" I asked once.

"You know *him*?"

"Sure. A real short guy with a head that sort of popped right out of his shoulders. I had him for a while."

"Yeah? We called him Pit Bull, too. A crazy son of a bitch."

"He was pretty funny. I remember that his favorite word was 'motherfucker. 'It was amazing to see how he could use it in every possible way in a sentence. To amuse myself I used to watch him move it around grammatically. First it's a noun, then an adjective, and so on. Or he could even make a whole sentence out of it, like 'That motherfucker almost killed the motherfucking motherfucker'."

Ken shook his head, vaguely disapproving. It was not clear whether he was disapproving of the language or of the company I kept.

"Dude liked to fight too," he said, probably as a way to change the subject.

"We got along okay."

"Man, it would've been something if you'd been assigned to me."

"Well, I am, now, and I like it better on the outside."

"You wouldn't have liked me then. You know that, don't you?"

He might have been right about that. I had related well enough to my jail assignments on a personal and individual level, but those personal relationships that cross racial or ethnic or class lines have to be arranged with some care. Without that arrangement they fail, and we find ourselves retreating to the comfort zone of our own kind. So while I had enjoyed the one-on-one meetings, I felt no connection to the groups of inmates I would sometimes encounter.

On a simple level, the scenes they created suggested a paradox of happy anarchy in a highly regimented environment. Palms slapping. Hips or shoulders hanging. Their voices were often raised a near octave, and it was not always clear if a sentence was declarative or not: "You here?"

But their bluster had a flat quality, and it fooled no one if it was meant to hide the realization of where they were. It was not meant to do that, nor was it an expression of hopelessness or anger or the forced rituals of bonding. It was necessary only as a commonality: they were together in a jail. What they did not seem to realize was that being in jail was only the immediate and material aspect of their imprisonment, and thus a temporary architecture of their worldview.

It is unlikely that most of them understood the existential dimension of their incarceration: they lacked freedom in a far more important sense. Freedom is the ability to imagine other worlds; it is the consciousness of what is possible. Neither on the outside nor in the jail had they been made to understand the possibility of their own freedom or the responsibility that comes with that freedom. As a result there was little likelihood that they could turn against their pasts to create the first stirrings of autonomy. Or that those stirrings could be forged into actions that would negate a condition that was one of near non-being. They were, in that regard, a microcosm of the larger community of young black men in our time.

"You wouldn't have liked me then."

Or could it be that he was wrong? That would have depended on how far he had moved from the forced conformity of jail life, how much progress he might have made in creating his own values in an environment where the development of any values was hardly a priority.

If he was beginning to do that before we came into each other's orbit, it might have been because his early years were not passed in the dull air of a northern inner city. He was born in the south and lived there long enough to have memories that were different. Even if his first years were spent in a low-income housing project, like all children he was able to find innocent fun. There were good times with aunts and uncles and cousins in the country, meals of collard greens and smoked ham and baked macaroni. In the humidity of southern summers, sitting on the banks of slow-moving streams, he fished for carp and yellow-bellied bullhead. Afterwards the same water became a cooling balm for a tentative swimmer.

Early life was not entirely idyllic; this was still the south of segregation and injustice and a growing backlash. At a Black Panther rally he learned for the first time about strange concepts of injustice and inequality. Wide eyed, holding close to his father, he saw black men with guns. He heard angry speeches in words and phrases barely understood, and his eyes smarted from the tear gas as local police moved on the crowds with clubs.

Such events are usually described as the end of childhood. For Ken that end came at age six from another direction, when his parents separated after years of marital struggle. It took some prompting to get the full story from him.

"On a mid-summer afternoon my mother told me to take all four of my little brothers and sisters upstairs. We could see some bags in a closet with an open door. She said we should go into one of the bedrooms and not look out the windows. A horn honked, so of course we did look out. We saw her in the front yard with the bags as a black car pulled in. It was our aunt. They embraced and moved around the car silently, like conspirators. We called down but she didn't look up, and I barely kept one of my sisters from falling out the window. I never felt so abandoned in my life, and I didn't know if I was the cause of it or not. My mother had mental problems because she had seen the murder-suicide of her own parents. Dad got custody of all of us."

The family was split up, with the five children sent to three different foster homes. Eventually Ken's father brought them together again under the care of an old lady. Not long after that the family became part what is known as the Second Great Migration, identified as the largest voluntary movement of black people ever seen in this country. At the beginning of the twentieth century, nine out of ten blacks lived below the Mason-Dixon Line. Between 1940 and 1980 nearly five million of them left the south for a better life in the industrial cities of the north or west. It was an escape from Ku Klux Klan violence and Jim Crow indignities as much as from share-cropping and disappearing agricultural work. It was a search not just for jobs and better educations for their children, but for hope. For Ken's father the destination was Rochester.

He arrived in a city with an impressive history. Rochester's early economic success began with the completion of the Erie Canal in 1825. The city quickly became a supplier of flour to an expanding nation, at one point said to be the largest supplier of flour in the world. It was also a leading builder of canal boats and, during the Civil War, more money was made from the demand for clothes and boots.

Rochester was progressive as more than just an upstate economic power. Frederick Douglass arrived in 1849 and used his influential newspaper and his oratorical powers to make the city into a locus for the abolitionist cause. It was also one of the last stops on the Underground Railroad. A few decades later, Susan B. Anthony broke the law by registering to vote. Shortly after, she actually voted. She was famously arrested and fined, and the modern women's movement had one of its first heroines. Both are buried in the city's loveliest cemetery.

That was then. The progressive political mentality would gradually fall victim to the force that is always most likely to stifle change: money. Rochester's wealth grew steadily through the efforts of its third most famous citizen, George Eastman. The founder of Eastman Kodak was an inventor, businessman and later philanthropist; above all he made the city wealthy.

The considerable fortunes of leading Rochester families were most often based on ownership of Kodak stock, which by the middle of the twentieth century was valued at 80 times its original price. And the rich were learning an old lesson: that a good way to stay rich is to hold on to your money. Along with that tendency toward preservation, they were also developing a complacency and a lack of social sensitivity that are common features of inherited wealth.

It was fitting, then, that a partly tongue-in-cheek history of Rochester at mid-century was entitled *Smugtown*. Rochester had become, in the author's words, "safely republican" and "entirely unprogressive," a city with a "beguiling lack of political and civic consciousness." Decisions were customarily made in clubs that were private and exclusive, clubs that, in the original sense of the word, excluded all but the rich and privileged. Change was not a favored word in those environments, and, probably for lack of use, it lost favor among Rochesterians as a whole.

Still, the city enjoyed a lingering reputation for benevolence, even if it was the last city in New York State to institute a public housing program. It was also well known for its manufacturing jobs, even if many of the arriving blacks got only the lowest paying jobs. The black population grew 300% between 1960 and 1970. What became known as "white flight" to the suburbs became common, with predictable effects on the schools. As "inner city" came to mean black neighborhoods, downtown would gradually become a place to be avoided. Concern for the welfare of the black community did not grow with the increase in the black population.

So it should not have been a surprise that an arrest of a young black man for public intoxication at a street dance was the catalyst for the riots of July, 1964. The black community's frustration simply came to a head. Bricks and bottles and Molotov cocktails flew, the police chief's car was overturned, a helicopter crashed. Over three days, the riot spread through several of the city's black wards, leaving four dead, 350 injured, almost 1000 arrested, over 200 stores damaged or looted. The numbers were small in comparison to the riots that soon followed in places like Philadelphia, Watts, Newark, Detroit and dozens of smaller cities, but Rochester had the distinction of being the first northern city to require the services of the National Guard.

It was shortly after the riots that Ken's father migrated to Rochester. He came alone, but within a year he returned to the south for his children. At age seven Ken was on a Greyhound bus heading north, looking at snow for the first time, happy with the idea of being with his father again.

At first the six of them stayed in a one-bedroom apartment, sleeping in one bed. Before they could find a better place, the children were again split up among other families. Eventually they found a suitable apartment, and for Ken the best thing was that they were together again. But his father's gambling habit combined with a nervous breakdown and a suicide attempt to make their lives anything but calm. A sister was eventually diagnosed and institutionalized as schizophrenic.

Mostly Ken missed his mother. In primary school he was teased about his southern accent and for saying words like skreet instead of street. Efforts at special education did little good. He became defiant, skipping school as often as he attended. At age ten he was sent to a home for troubled youth. It was becoming the textbook case of a black youth going in one direction only.

In a newspaper interview I would much later dig out of my files, Ken returned again and again to the themes of hatred and anger. "For years and years," he told the interviewer, "I hated my parents, I hated society and I absolutely despised anything to do with the law. So I broke every rule in the book. I pushed my parents away from me. And I found out that the root was that I simply hated who I was every day."

Elsewhere in that same interview were some lines that were possibly more important than all the others, prophetic lines that explained some things about our later relationship: "Never in my life did I allow myself a chance. And those who tried to be a friend I shoved away, because I didn't want them to see the true me."

Life at the Hillside Children's Center was an overdue improvement. Counselors provided positive role models and took an interest in him. He liked being taken to amusement parks and to the lake for water skiing. In a wonderful incongruity, he even became a boy scout. But only briefly: he continued to break the rules, and he ran away frequently. Eventually his mother re-entered the picture as a last resort, and he was sent to live with her again in North Carolina.

Not a good idea. They quarreled constantly. He was thrown out of the house more than once. What he wanted the most was to return to Rochester, and the opportunity for that presented itself in the form of a new friend. This was one of the first crime stories Ken would tell me, and like many of the others, it had a quality of incompetence that made it almost as droll as it was reprehensible.

"I'll never forget this guy. He was a light-complexioned black kid with freckles, the first black kid I'd ever seen with freckles. He knew I wanted to run away to Rochester and said he could find a way to help. What did I know? I followed him to a house he said was his cousin's house. He went around to the back and minutes later he re-appeared at the front. Later I found out he broke into the place."

"When I got in he told me to go in the bedroom and search the drawers. I opened up a drawer and found this blue bag. I'll never forget it because it was loaded with coins. Then I looked in another drawer and there was a .380 automatic pistol. I put it in my pocket."

"That day we broke into three houses. The following morning I went back to my mom's house and there was a knock. These two white guys were asking my mother if I was there. I could hear them because my bedroom was in the basement. My heart was pounding and I heard my mother yelling for me: 'What'd ya do now? Come upstairs. 'I came running up the stairs and the guys handcuffed me. They sent me to a detention center while I waited for court. Then I was sentenced: six months in a place for juveniles."

There he cut trees all day, taunted by redneck guards. The first time he tried to escape, he hitched a ride with an old farmer who drove him quietly back to the gate. It had not been hard to identify a thin black youth in institutional clothing and chain-gang boots. The second time was not much better. He escaped in the company of another inmate and with $20 his father had sent for better purposes. They had been told that putting black pepper on their boots would throw off the hounds. It did not. Face and hands torn, he was pulled from a briar patch and put into solitary.

"That was a horrific time for me. My mother would never visit, the whole time. But my father drove from Rochester to see me. I can recall him crying one time because he saw how hardened my face had become from months spent in that place. I was never going to be the same after that experience."

Eventually he was back in Rochester. His father was working as a cook, and he managed to get Ken a job washing dishes. It was not the right job for a teenager.

"I went to work in a head shop. I was a counter person, selling records and drug paraphernalia – bongs, hashish pipes, stems, and paper. The guys who owned it were a bunch of whites from the suburbs. They liked me, and Dad was glad that I was working behind a counter."

"These guys were big druggies, left over hippies. They always had pot and speed and amphetamines. You could pick up a quarter pound of weed in those days for $95. That's when I started smoking pot – Mexican Weed, Acapulco Gold, Panama Red. I also started hustling weed. I got a quarter pound of Colorado Gold and started selling nickel bags with quarter ounces and half ounces. I was good at it."

He left there eventually for a job managing a submarine shop for two Italian brothers. Just turning 18, he was proud of the way he was allowed to open and close, even to hire another person. It may have been fitting that his employers were themselves operating somewhere outside of the normal business world.

"These guys were mysterious because a lot of their friends were associated with the mafia. They were having the drug wars back then. I was somewhat scared about being in there because they were having shootouts and bombings. I always thought somebody would come by the shop and toss in a Molotov cocktail. Still, I worked for those guys probably a year or a year and a half, an under-the-table job. About the same time my mother came up. She would help in the shop and my baby brother would come down and I put most of my family to work behind the counter. So that was pretty cool."

Cool it may have been, but things were about to get hotter.

"The first time I ever got arrested as an adult was when I just turned 18. I was old enough to buy a shotgun and I had an obsession with guns since the day I started a mock SWAT team at the children's center. I had also purchased a pellet pistol for my younger brother – he was 14 then – because he wanted one so bad. The air gun was a replica of a .357 Magnum and looked very real. I gave it to him and told him he could practice up on the flat roof."

What happened next could easily have been predicted: a neighbor saw the boy playing with the gun and called the police.

"The next thing I knew cop cars came speeding around the corner. One even had a blowout from hitting the curb."

If I had not heard this story directly from Ken, with no good reason to doubt it, I would not have accepted that detail about the blowout. It is exactly the kind of cheap comic relief that does not belong in a serious story of early crime, the sort of detail that one does not make up, and I laugh every time I think of it.

"I saw them hopping out of the car and they got their guns drawn and they're telling him 'Freeze, freeze, put your hands up in the air. ' They didn't know it was an air gun. So I panicked and I rushed down there. I had my hands waving and I'm saying 'Don't shoot, don't shoot, it's just an air gun!' But my brother kept the gun and when they pulled their hammers back I just... you know. I remember that before I could reach him the cops intercepted and threw me against a wall. I said 'Don't move man, stay still' and then the cops grabbed the gun and saw it was just a pellet pistol."

"They ended up arresting me for endangering a minor, and when the cop checked me he asked if I had any illegal drugs. I said no, but in the panic I forgot all about the weed and lo and behold when he checked me he found two nickel bags and a couple of joints. They took me down to the county jail and put me in a cell. The toilet was loaded and it wouldn't flush, disgusting. I remember a guy with no teeth was sitting across the cell and he was laughing at me. That was my first real run in with the law, and the judge put me on probation."

A forgiving judge. What makes the whole story special in retrospect is that the judge would later sit with others of us on a board Ken would create. The arresting officer would become a friend.

He was not to be so lucky the next time. With a friend who would later be killed, Ken started a gate house, selling five-dollar bags in small manila envelopes. They were being careful.

"We had a mirror in a corner to see customers as they came in the hallway, and a thick oak door with heavy steel bolts and a small hole in the center. We installed a buzzer to tell us when somebody was coming and we didn't shovel the snow so the cops would be slowed down! But the customers started to complain about all the snow and ice. We gradually came under steady surveillance, cruisers slowly going past or even just parking across the street. That didn't slow the customers at all. We started every day with 200 five-dollar bags and we were sold out by early afternoon."

They had to open the door when the police finally arrived with a warrant. There were ten of them, equipped with surveillance photos to make sure they got the right people.

"Before they got to me I threw a sack with 40 nickel bags out the window and onto a roof. The problem was that one of them heard the sound of the window and looked up to see me doing it. Next thing, I was lying on the floor and one detective kept dropping a sledgehammer inches from my head and asking me where the stash was. The other wanted to know which one had a white shirt on -- he had seen my arm out the window. A fire truck with an arm retrieved the sack while up and down the street more police were raiding three other houses. My father appeared just as they were taking all of us away."

Here is a complaint, one that is likely common among non-fiction writers. Non-fiction story-telling suffers from a huge disadvantage when compared to the writing of fiction. Fiction writers can create literally anything they want to, the only restraint being the extent to which their readers might expect the story to bear some semblance of reality. If the bar of realism is low enough, the fiction can include the most unlikely characters, the most improbable events, the most exotic locales, and all of this with plots that twist and turn upon themselves and end in skin-tingling, heart-thumping, throat-lumping climaxes. They can even allow for supernatural intervention when all else dulls.

By contrast, a non-fiction story, if it is to be honest, has to tell what actually happened. The sad fact is that events that actually happen are rarely as exciting as the creations of even the least imaginative writer of fiction. Yes, real life narratives can be embellished and told, we hope, in some compelling way, but non-fiction cannot escape the confines of its own truth. Here we have the reverse of an old dictum: too true to be good.

This book, for example, used its most dramatic moments in the first pages: a murder (even if it happened before the story began), a break-in, blood, a drive-by threat. Of course all of that was meant to get the reader's attention, but it used up some of the best material without even the promise of some further drama to come. That is why I am grateful to Ken for telling me so openly and specifically about his youthful exploits: they provide the reader some excitement while allowing this narrative to remain, yes, real.

There is another problem, and that is that some of this is getting too far ahead. I was still looking.

THE CAVE

And you will not go wrong if you connect the ascent into the upper world and the objects there with the upward progress of the mind into the intelligible realm -- that is my guess, which is what you are anxious to hear. The truth of the matter is, after all, known only to God. But in my opinion, for what it is worth, the final thing to be perceived in the intelligible realm, and perceived only with difficulty, is the absolute form of Good.

-- Plato

If any truth has come to assume greater importance to me during these peaceful days, it is the insignificance of all our cares, even those we take to be the most serious, once we shut our eyes to all but the inner, divine element in them.

-- Teilhard de Chardin

The lazy creaking of a door cuts gradually through the layers of sleep. Like an experienced baby-sitter, I have learned to doze with ears tuned for the important sounds. That creaking door is the one to the women's enclosure.

Raising my head only slightly from the sofa, I can watch as Marilou emerges, dressed in pants and a loose-fitting black halter. She moves soundlessly past the tables and down between the long row of beds. She is a cat that never trips, and then in my imagination she is a dark-hour wraith that glides past the last beds as though she needs no feet. I watch her until she disappears into the women's bathroom at the far end of the basement.

Ron, another of the homeless who stay here regularly, warned me once that she is not to be trusted, saying that there have been a number of "accidents" in the shelter. My first thoughts were of knives stuck into sleeping chests, but he probably meant stealing. It is hard to know what to believe around here, but in this case I have decided that Marilou is a bit unbalanced. The one morning I tried to talk to her, the response was a fearful, black-eyed stare, directed somewhere over my left shoulder.

My watch says it is 5:45 in the morning, which means that I have slept almost two hours. That is longer that I meant to. Colleen, the other volunteer for this late-night shift, said she didn't mind if I slept. She's not at the desk, so she must have decided to stay out in the kitchen, where it is warmer. I need now to shake off the grogginess and get some life back into the limbs. A second creaking of the door signals that Marilou is back in her bed and that it's time to get up. The lights will come on at 6:00 a.m. sharp.

I fold my blanket and put it back into the storeroom, then go over to the desk, still trying to wake up. The desk sits near the hallway to the kitchen, in a circle of light from a large desk lamp. This main room is a fairly typical old church basement -- a high ceiling supported by large pillars, with steam pipes running to various corners. Although that was not their original purpose, those pipes are providing the heat which makes this basement into a reasonably warm winter shelter for some of the city's homeless.

Most of the basement is in deep shadow, broken only by the lighted bathrooms in the far corners and the red exit signs. A dim light filters through the casement windows from the parking lots outside. There is just enough light to see the seventeen beds, each with a sleeping man in it. Beside each bed is a chair serving as a nightstand. Clothes and boxes and bags lie around most of them. Two years ago a business donated some of those half-wall enclosures used in offices, and now each guest is able to sleep in partial privacy. Inside a higher, four-sided enclosure are four women's beds.

A sound comes from about halfway down the first row. In the shadows, a figure is sitting on the edge of bed number eight. He pulls a top over his head, stands up, moves slowly toward the bathroom. When he comes out, I can see that it's Ron. He stops by the last bed and stands there looking down, or maybe he's holding onto a chair. Along with all the shadows, a concrete pillar makes it hard to see. Then one of his racking coughs comes rattling down the wide aisle, a serious event of the thoracic cavity.

That causes more stirring in the shadows. What appears to be someone else sitting up turns out to be only a pair of knees bent upward, or maybe a shirt across a chair. Shadows within shadows, frustrating focus. This place can sometimes be on the edge of frightening, as with a scare story told to me by another volunteer.

A woman was brought to the door by the police. Late in the night. Found lying in the street, she was apparently not drunk enough to book. She was also near the end of a pregnancy, and claimed she was trying to get to Canada. Since all the beds were taken, she was given one of the couches. Shortly after settling in, she claimed she was having contractions. With two volunteers on duty, it was possible for one of them to drive her to the hospital. Once there, she was found not to be having contractions. She then proceeded, so it was told, to nearly destroy the emergency room. Eventually sedated, she was taken back to the psychiatric center from which she had escaped.

It is a story not inclined to foster peace of mind. There is some comfort in the knowledge that most troubles occur on the early shift, after the guests have been admitted and before they are tucked away for the night. The notes in the log book, most of them by early shift volunteers, make interesting reading.

"Angelo started fighting at the table again. L. wanted him out. Gave me a hard time about leaving, started swearing."

"Willi M. left medication in the men's room Sunday night. No sign of it. His name is on the bottle. Says he has no more."

It looks like some of the women can be trouble too.

"Hazel left, angry again with Scott. She says he speaks to her rudely. He also said something to (?). Led to verbal confrontation with Hazel."

“At 1:15 Marilou presented herself at the door. She thot it was 10:00 p. m. Since we had a spare bed in the women’s dorm, we accommodated her. She wanted to know if today was Saturday. She probably was out drinking for the night -- such was the scent on her breath.”

There’s a diplomatic way to put it. The next one is more detailed, with a sense of style.

“Ronnie and Fred had a ‘simmering spat’, i.e. exchange of words, threats, minor physical combat. Police were called immediately, but situation was in control soon after it began. Police came, some words continued through 11:30. No action recommended at this time unless situation escalates.”

Next, and less interesting, are notices on the wall above the desk. One sign gives the names and addresses of all the shelters in this city. Three are in Catholic churches, one is a Bible mission, and the last is non-sectarian. Another sign, which I will someday be sorry for ignoring, details first-aid procedures. Next to that are the rules for the guests: no stealing, no fighting, no weapons, no TV after 11:30, make your bed in the morning.

Here is an announcement for the City Hall “Atrium Series,” various free afternoon concerts. Maybe it is put here as a suggestion for a place to get out of bad weather, since this shelter is closed in the daytime hours. There’s a nice surprise for government workers and business people: they sit down for a free concert and find themselves next to a homeless person, with bags. Along with the music, an unwelcome reminder of life in the modern American city. Another poster concerns stress management, and under that are hand-written messages and phone numbers taped to the wall.

Twenty or more sleeping people can make considerable noise. Someone whimpers in his sleep and murmurs something, unintelligible. A drawn-out sigh, the dream of a lover lost, comes from somewhere closer. Snores are in various tempos and cadences, as though answering one another. It becomes a challenge to distinguish among them. A nasal snore ends in a whine, another rumbles in a chest, and a third gurgles. An old man’s voice trembles, maybe the vocal part of a nightmare. There is Ron’s racking cough again, deep down, followed by another cough that is cut short. Somewhere a throat is cleared, inadequately, and I wait for the job to be completed, swallowing myself.

There is a rise and fall to the competition among the sounds. When it is the quietest, other sounds emerge: the trickling of water from a leaking toilet, the squeak of a bed and rustle of covers as someone turns over, a hum whose source remains a mystery. Above all the noises are the occasional cracks and bangs of the steam pipes when the heating system kicks in, a violent crashing that only the soundest sleeper can ignore. Like a summer thunderstorm whose sounds move back and forth in the night sky, it travels with the push of steam from one part of the long room to another.

It is just a few minutes now until the lights come on. I am thinking back a few years to my first night of volunteering. A friend who also works here said they always need more people. I chose the second shift, from 2:00 to 7:00 a. m. because he said it was harder to get help during those hours.

A little before 2:00, I knocked on the door that leads to the basement. Hurry up someone, it's freezing out here. A married couple appeared and led me downstairs. They conducted a brief orientation, in tired whispers, as they put on their hats and coats.

And then we waited, and waited, for the other volunteer. He or she would appear. No one should ever work here alone, they said. It is against the rules, too many potential problems. We waited again, and they looked more tired as the minutes passed. When it was finally clear that no one was coming, I sent them away. It won't be a problem.

But it was. The door had hardly shut behind them when the panic hit. I am alone here with over twenty homeless people, some of them drunk, some disturbed, maybe some sociopaths and psychopaths for good measure. Every noise raised my pulse, every shadow threatened. I paced, sat, paced some more, tried to read, listened, jumped. Finally, unable to take it anymore, I lay on the sofa and dozed, if it is possible to doze in a state of low-level dread. Somehow the five hours passed.

So it is sometimes with fear: if it is suffered through sufficiently the first time, it does not come back. There have been a few other nights when no second person has come, and that is no longer a problem. Still, it is better to have a partner. If nothing else, it is a way to lighten the hours.

Finally awake now, I suddenly remember something. A note in the logbook said to wake Vic, bed seven, at 5:30. Just as I start toward his bed, he gets himself up and begins pulling on his pants. Even in the dim light it would be hard to miss a large blotch under his left eye, either a particularly nasty birthmark or an unsuccessful fight.

"You must be Vic. I guess you got yourself up on time. I was just coming to get you."

"Yeah. That's okay." Vic is pleasant, forgiving.

"You want some cereal or something?"

"No cereal. Maybe I'll just have a few pieces of toast. If that's okay."

"Take whatever you want."

"Thanks."

In a few minutes Vic appears at the desk, fully dressed, asking for something. His voice is so soft it's hard to know what he wants. Maybe he's asking if it is all right to leave when he's ready, so I nod a sort of generalized permission, one that is meant to cover all requests.

"Do you want to sign in for tomorrow, Vic?"

"Tonight, you mean?"

"I forgot. It already *is* tomorrow. Yeah, I mean tonight."

"Can I?"

"Sure. Actually, you have to if you want a bed again."

We turn the pages of the log book until we find the sign-up sheet for this evening. Vic signs under bed seven.

"Where you off to so early?"

"Have to go to the labor pool."

"You must be the first one there. Are you getting any work?"

"They been sending me out to this lumber yard. But I didn't work yesterday. Had to have stitches removed."

It is best to leave that information alone. Vic puts on his outer clothes as we're talking, and then together we walk toward the kitchen.

"Well, I hope you get some work. Anyway, it looks like a nice morning out there." There is no basis for that claim, as we might say in class, since I have no idea what it's like outside.

As Vic passes on into the kitchen, Betty returns from the bathroom. She walks with the tiny steps of a geisha, moving her feet as though she is pushing sand ahead of her.

"You're on your way too," I say to her.

"I have to work up on North Clinton. I can leave at 6:30 and make it fine."

"You're going to walk?"

"It's not far."

It is a fair distance, but that's not the issue. No more than five feet tall, Betty would not have the strength to fight a small dog, much less the kind of people she might meet on North Clinton. Maybe she should at least fortify herself, in the literal meaning of that phrase.

"Have some toast or cereal before you go."

"Just coffee. That's all I want."

Long lines run down an impassive face that might, in better times, have been expressive. Her short brown hair barely protrudes from under a grey stocking cap. She is frowning at the coffee urn as she watches clear hot water pour into her cup.

"Where's the coffee?"

"The first shift didn't have any real stuff last night. Or else they drank it all. You'll have to use hot water and instant."

Another lesson in the clash between large expectations and smaller pleasures. In an effort to come to terms with that, Betty stifles a sigh and spoons some instant coffee into the cup.

"Say," she turns to me, "do you think there's any extra socks I can have?"

"Socks? Maybe in the storeroom. Let's look."

There are no socks in the storeroom. This is not Betty's morning. She returns to the women's enclosure, and then emerges carrying her large plastic shopping bag.

"Good-bye, Betty."

She takes a last look around, like an organized mother who needs to be sure that nothing is forgotten

"Bye."

Now it is time for the real awakening, and Lincoln is up, right on schedule. Lincoln used to occupy bed number one, but not in the usual role of a homeless person; he was responsible for the janitorial chores. Over the years he has become more in charge than those of us who volunteer, and he now sleeps in his own private enclosure, over near the clothes cupboard. Although he is not young, he has a vitality and an air of authority that gets respect from both the guests and the volunteers. It also goes a long way toward keeping the peace around here. He says he has his own apartment somewhere in town.

He nods as he goes out to the kitchen. The snap of circuit-breakers as he flips them is simultaneous with the yellow glare that bursts from the long ceiling lights overhead. Lincoln is all business in the morning, and he seems to be enjoying himself as he walks down the rows of beds.

"Hey guys, it's time. Let's go fellows, let's go."

He leans over one sleeper. "Let's go, buddy." From there he walks over to the women's enclosure, knocks, and talks through the door with his mouth inches away. "Okay, ladies, let's get going." He waits a minute.

"Yvonne!" There's no response. Again, "Yvonne, time to get up."

Still there is no reply, but he must be satisfied that she is awake, because from there he goes to the kitchen. In no time he and Colleen are carrying bowls and boxes of cereal to the tables over by the wall. By now a few of the men are out of bed, while some are slower to wake. The white-haired regular whose name we don't know is up on one elbow, squinting the length of the room. Another man, wearing long johns, sits on the edge of his bed, head hanging low so that his back arches in a half circle above it. A thin man wearing only shorts and a towel over his shoulder heads for the shower in the back.

"Hey," Lincoln shouts at him. "You don't go 'round here dressed like that."

The man turns slowly and looks at him. "I'm taking a shower."

"Okay, but put on some more clothes. This ain't no honky-tonk."

That makes me laugh, for the first time today. Whatever this place may be, it sure ain't no honky-tonk.

As though in slow motion, the basement is coming to life. Movement is silent. Some of the men raise their heads and blink into the new light above them, others stare with the melancholy eyes of Tennyson's lotus eaters, dark faces pale.

There is a noticeable dignity in the simple acts that prepare them for the day: the shower, the drawing on of socks, the choice of cereal. It may be that the care they imbed into morning rituals is in reverse proportion to the anticipated insults of the day. If the coming hours promise that activities without meaning or value are to be done in public places, so much greater is the demand that attention be given to these private preparations for them. Even if those preparations are trivial, only the withered roots of dignity, they sustain.

So it is on a larger scale for the man who sits by himself at the end of the table. In a refusal of refuge, he has not favored us with his name. He has dressed carefully in a dark suit that fits well, completed with a white shirt and tie and a leather briefcase that sits under his chair. Last week he identified himself as a banker, "temporarily unemployed." He will look to improve his prospects again today.

Someone has put on the television, and the voice of an early-morning evangelist leads his audience in prayers. A man named Iggy motions me over and asks, hand over his mouth like a conspirator, if we could change the channel to the news. I oblige. We are just in time to watch the business report, including the Dow trend for the week and the possibility of a shortfall in a pension fund. A few of the men stare at the screen as though this is a matter of some importance to them.

By now other guests have made their breakfast choices; they are sitting at the tables or on the sofas, watching local news. The weather report always draws the most attention and a few comments. Today, we are told, is going to be a fine spring morning. It is already 38 degrees.

Ron is drinking a glass of powdered milk.

"Good morning," I say to him. "I heard you were in the hospital." Actually, that information came from the log book. "Are you okay?"

"I've got hepatitis. Liver's all fucked up."

He smiles, wanting the world to know that a fucked-up liver is not a big deal.

"So what are they doing for you?"

"I don't know yet. But I got a good doctor. Got two good doctors. I could have wept for joy."

"They're not just laying on the hands, huh?"

"No, Jesus, none of that." He laughs forcefully, just short of what would bring on one of his coughing fits. Then he winks.

"Tell you something. I'm thinking of getting married."

"Really?"

"God's truth. Maybe that little woman over there." He nods his head to the left, where Marilou is sitting at one of the tables by herself, eating a piece of toast.

"She's my kind of woman, don't you think?" Ron is grinning and talking very loudly. I have a vision of Marilou coming over and throwing a cup of coffee in his face, but she pays him no attention.

"You know," he continues, still hoping for a reaction, "a woman who is gentle and loving. Could do a lot for a young guy like me."

"I don't know. She might be a bit more than you can handle."

Ron starts telling stories of his years in the army, in Alaska. While he talks, a man comes over to our table and starts picking cigarette butts out of the ashtray. The longest butts are less than half an inch. He tears off the filters while we watch and sticks the remaining tobacco in the breast pocket of his shirt.

"Getting my day's tobacco," he says to us. "Can't stand to see it wasted."

"You got any cigarette paper?" Thankfully Ron has shifted his attention from Marilou.

"Oh, yeah. As long as I got paper, I'm all set."

He sits down across from us in his search for tobacco and company.

"This place closing soon?" This is somewhere between a question and an answer.

"Right. In the middle of April. I don't know the date."

"And opens again in October?"

"Sometime in early November, I think."

"Depending on the weather," Ron advises us. "They wait for it to get around 32 or 33. Don't want nobody freezing."

"I suppose not."

"I got me a warm rock, down by the river. Gonna stay there when this place closes," he says. "The water goes around both sides of it."

How this keeps the rock warm is unclear, unless I have missed something. Thinking it is better not to pursue the matter, I try to picture him sleeping on top of a rock, with the river flowing around it.

A man with several days of snow-white growth on his face comes to our table and asks if he can have a razor. In the storeroom we find a box full of disposables. We inspect one and decide that it looks dull, so I tear open a package of unused ones. He doesn't ask for shaving cream, which is good because there isn't any.

"That'll do fine," he says, running his thumb along the new edge.

As we come out of the storeroom I see that Sean is up and sitting at his usual spot, a large overstuffed chair beside one of the pillars. He's watching the news with a bowl of cereal on his knees. It's time for our regular visit, which offers some relief for both of us from the commonplaces around us.

"Morning, Professor."

"How's it going, Sean?"

"Oh, okay. About the same."

"How's the math coming?"

Sean is studying math, he has told me. He's trying to pass the math sections of the Graduate Records Exam. When he first told me that he was taking those exams, I put it down to some fantasy on his part. He claims that he had spent a few years studying at a college somewhere in the south but hadn't finished his degree, which was to have been in industrial arts. Studying for the entrance exams to graduate school made no sense in that circumstance, I thought. Now he tells me that he can receive his undergraduate degree if he can demonstrate competency through the GRE in subjects he didn't complete during his college years. Sean is more competent and better informed than he appears.

He is very thin, dressed always in an over-sized brown sweater with a stretched neck. Right now one point of his shirt collar is outside the neck of the sweater, the other safely inside. His dark hair hangs loosely to the sides of a sallow face, and his hand shakes a little as he lifts his spoon from the bowl. There is an air about him that suggests he is familiar with public hostility, has become reconciled to it and has decided to bear it with patience, maybe even with agreement.

"Well," he says slowly, "I'm studying every day, but some of it doesn't make much sense to me."

"What kind of math is it?"

"Geometry mostly, some trigonometry. I've got these books that are supposed to help you prepare for the exam, but I can't make sense out of them sometimes.

"You're not the first person who couldn't make sense out of math," I say in an attempt to encourage him. "That's why a lot of people work in areas that don't have a lot to do with math. But I actually liked geometry when I took it in high school, maybe because it had more concepts and fewer numbers to worry about. A guy who teaches math told me once that people who are good at geometry are not good with the other kinds of math, or else it's the other way around."

"Yeah?"

"Uh huh. And I'll tell you something else. Plato said that doing geometry well is one of the highest kinds of intelligence."

"Yeah?"

"Yeah. So stick with it. Maybe it will start to make sense. Next thing, you'll be coming up with some great new theory in geometry, proving that the earth is really rectangular or something."

Sean smiles faintly at that, either at the teasing or at the idea of achieving fame and fortune in geometry. Then he looks quickly down at his bowl of cereal as though the new theory is about to emerge from the flakes. He tips the bowl so that the remaining milk can run onto his spoon.

"Have you got any plans for when this places closes?" I ask him.

"I might go back to Washington. I like it down there."

"You've been there before?"

"I used to work there. For *The Washington Post*." He emphasizes the name of the paper, proud of the association. "Sort of casual work, you know. Actually pretty ideal for my purposes. You can work two days, three days maybe, even all week if you want."

"Where do you stay when you're there?"

"At one of their shelters. I've got a friend down there, he stays in the same shelter. Sometime maybe he'll visit up here."

It could be that this is the way homeless persons entertain out-of-town guests: a couple of nights in their personal shelter. Watch some television in the evening, have a choice of cereals in the morning. Then it is off to the local public library for part of the day. And later, with any luck, a free concert at City Hall.

"So why did you come back here?"

"For a funeral."

"Who died?" Sean usually has to be prompted. But he wants to talk, so there is value in the prompting.

"My father."

"I'm sorry to hear that. How old was he?"

"Sixty-four."

"So your mother lives alone now?

"She died a long time ago."

"How did you find out that your father died?"

"My grandmother told me." Sean must think he knows the next question because he adds, "She's eighty-seven."

The idea that Sean has some inheritance he doesn't know about pops to the surface of a flat conversation. It is a plot straight from a nineteenth-century novel: homeless but diligent young man trying to finish his education against all odds discovers that he is actually the legitimate son of a filthy-rich local industrialist.

"Did your father have a house, that sort of thing?"

"Naw."

So much for nineteenth-century novels.

"He had a lot of paintings, though," Sean says. "We went down to get some of them after he died."

"Where was that?"

"Washington."

Now I am confused. "Didn't he die up here?"

"He got sick down there. Cancer. Then he came up to the hospital here."

"Okay, I got it. So what about the paintings?"

The plot revives: art treasures hidden behind old paneling, needing only minor restoration.

"There weren't any left. You know, people were supporting him. They took the paintings."

"So there wasn't much left. Much for you, I mean."

"Yeah." He looks regretfully into his cereal bowl, also with not much left.

"I just remembered. You're an artist too, aren't you?"

"Well, I have been. Can't make any money that way, though. I got an artist's certificate once from an art school. Had to send some money to get it. 'Course that doesn't mean you're an artist, just having a certificate. You also got to do something. What I need is the right friends."

"What do you mean?"

"Like rich friends, you know," he says with a shrug that is meant to dismiss friends of that kind. "My dad, he had the right friends, the ones I ought to have. But then those are the friends you don't really want, if you know what I mean."

"Yeah, I know what you mean."

"But I think I need to get into computer graphics. I was just reading about that, in a magazine."

"Can you do that sort of thing?"

"Naw. I don't know enough about the new programs. And I don't have enough money to go back to school right now. Almost had it, but then they raised the tuition. Anyway, I didn't like some of the professors. They didn't know what they were talking about."

"I've heard that somewhere before."

There were some hopeful signs the last time we talked, but now it is becoming less likely that Sean will fit my loose profile or plans. It is not just the negativity, which is understandable in these circumstances, or the evident pain, or even what seems like a long history of self-abasement. It is as though he practices being submissive and finds an odd kind of personal nobility in lacking autonomy and hope. How long would it take to break through the tyranny of his alienation? How much patience would be needed to turn indifference into energy, never mind into a passion for living?

Sean is wiping at some milk that he has spilled on his pants, and that reminds me of the clothes that are probably still in the dryer. On a rotating basis of about three bed numbers each night, the guests can have their laundry done. Earlier, Colleen and I did the night's laundry, but it might not all have been dried and folded.

"I've got some stuff to do, Sean. We can talk again."

"Sure."

In the kitchen, Colleen is sitting at the other desk, the one near the long stairs that lead up to the parking lot. She puts down the book she is reading and points a finger at me, like a teacher at a child caught whispering across the aisle.

"Good morning, sleepy-head."

"Oh, I didn't sleep. Constantly on the watch, taking care of you through the long night."

"You must be good at pretend sleeping, then."

"Well, maybe a little. Did you sleep at all?"

"No. I'm reading a really good book." She holds it up to me: *God in the Evening*.

Colleen and I have worked together before. She is quiet but far from shy, and the impression given almost from the start is that of a person deeply committed to her faith. She calls herself a re-committed Anglican. That is in reference to a past not entirely in accord with the more conservative side of that religion: she lived with a man for several years without the sanctity of marriage. They did eventually marry, but the relationship went downhill and ended in divorce. She tells me she has a new life now, new beginnings. She is back in school, studying science education.

From the Gaelic, the name Colleen means young woman. Although likely around 40, this colleen carries a lingering youthfulness in more than just her name; it's a loose garment she barely recognizes. Her height and form are not sprite-like, but there is something ethereal about her, as though the words sprite and spirit have become mixed in a near-anagram. It is something more playful than it is serious, brought from a far-away and fantasy-laden place. More, the spiritual legacy is matched with its genetic counterpart: blue eyes and a tremendous head of auburn hair that threatens an Irish temper.

There is no more time for imagining. "Did you get that last load out of the dryer?"

"Oops, I forgot. Is somebody asking for it?"

"Not yet."

With the plastic clothes basket on the floor between us, we start folding pants and shirts and underwear.

"And did you read that book I told you about last time?" She narrows her blue eyes, trying to look serious without succeeding.

I don't even recall that she recommended a book, but this is not the time to admit it.

"No. I forgot the title."

"I'll write it down for you. It'll be good for your religious development." Emphasis on the last word puts a light irony into her tone.

"I've had plenty of that. Maybe I'll just start calling you Sister Colleen."

"Where do you go to church?"

"Sometimes right here, when I feel like it. But I go to Quaker meetings sometimes instead, or to the Unitarian service."

That earns me a disapproving look over the shirt that she has tucked under her chin to fold the arms. I remember now that we had a similar conversation last time. Normally I would cut off this sort of hectoring, but Colleen gets away with it by managing to keep her tone playful.

"Well, I like Quaker meetings. Nice and simple, you know? Just people sitting around and talking when they feel like it. No big organization, no ego-tripping or authoritarian stuff, no complicated liturgies."

"You're running from the church."

"Hey, I'm *in* church."

"You're in the *basement* of a church. And you know what I mean, so don't play around. I mean the Eucharist."

"What about it?"

"You're forgetting, or else you're dodging. Because you're running. I mean the Incarnation. That's what. What do you think the Eucharist means?"

"I really don't think about it much at all. It's about the same as meditation to a Zen Buddhist, isn't it? Let's be a little more broad-minded."

She gives me another of her squints and shakes her head, flinging the temperamental hair left and right. Behind her, hanging from a steam pipe, is a banner. It is decorated with bright flowers, probably left over from a mass or celebration upstairs. It says, "May the Christ that is resurrected in you beckon forth to the Christ that is not yet resurrected in me."

"I hardly think it's narrow-minded to accept Christ into your life," Colleen says, now with a little pout.

"I didn't say that. I just thought Christianity had stopped seeing religion only in its own terms. Why can't spirituality take other forms than the Eucharist? Didn't you read any John Dewey in one of those education classes of yours?"

Bringing an atheist into the discussion could be asking for trouble. After a pause, time taken to think of a response, she hands me one end of a sheet and backs away with her end.

"What about your John Dewey?"

"I'm thinking about a distinction he made between 'religion' and 'religious'. Religion means what you're talking about. Religious means any activity that you do on behalf of an ideal end. Like teaching or medical work. In other words, anything altruistic is what he means. Like what you're doing right now for the people in the other room. God isn't just upstairs in this place, and you know it. What's wrong with developing your spirituality this way?"

"That's not enough, if there's no faith to relate it to. 'Faith and Works' together, remember?"

"Uh huh. And that is exactly the kind of thinking that puts social responsibility in the hands of the church, like right now. We shouldn't have to have shelters in church basements so people can do faith and works. All we're doing is letting the government off the hook. A government that can't even take care of its own needy people, it's happy to have you running around talking about faith and works."

"You're just being naughty. Maybe you should have slept some more. Read the book I told you about."

That is a dodge, as she must know. We are not close enough, in these brief times together, to push our differences into a full collision of principles. Is she a case of doing charitable work -- the heart of Christianity -- to assuage an errant past, or is it a substitute for self-questioning? Is she looking, in the dark hours of a homeless shelter, for an alternative definition of holiness, finding divinity in the ordinary needs of those in the other room?

Works of charity are challenged to be disinterested, actions done without regard for failure or success, undertaken for their own sake. Colleen does not generally interact with the homeless, surely not because of any antipathy, but because she agrees with the mystic Meister Eckhart that temporal things and temporal affections are a hindrance to knowing God. Detachment is key. She can accept the human situation in all its pain and frailty and disappointment because it is a relative one. The only absolute is her faith; it is the path to God. Acts of charity are, by comparison, her compromise with the world as it is. By preserving that compromise she sustains her personal integrity, even if that means being unable to fully extend it to others. It is as though she knows something, or feels something, that is in another dimension.

Now we seem to be in agreement that it's time to change the subject. One way to do that is with reference to the past. The last time we worked together, Colleen was excited about a production she was involved in with some other graduate students. It was a modern dramatization of Plato's touchstone "Allegory of the Cave."

One of the most famous passages in western philosophy, the allegory is part of Plato's attempt to explain his theory of the "forms." It is a theory that has been central to western philosophy for 24 centuries. Plato's argument is that real truth and ultimately goodness can be known only if one moves away from our world of immediate, particular, changing reality and toward the greater, changeless reality of ideas, or what he calls forms. The forms are universals, and as such they create the world we inhabit, as the idea of, say, "bicycle" creates all the bicycles in all their variety throughout the world.

The theory is a valuable early contribution to discussions of knowledge: what it is, where it comes from, what we can hope to do with it. But a point sometimes missed is that Plato also argues for an ultimate form, that of Goodness. The form of Goodness, he says, causes all that we know of as good and right. Without having a vision of this Form no one can act with wisdom, either in his own life or in matters of state.

In the allegory, prisoners in Plato's cave are chained in such a way that they are able to see only shadows projected on the far wall of a cave. Shadows are thus the only reality they can ever know. One of the prisoners is able to get free and make his way painfully up and out of the cave. At first, the light outside is too much for him. But once he becomes accustomed to that light, he's amazed to find a world of substance, not of shadows, a world of greater and literally higher reality. A considerate fellow, he returns to tell his fellow prisoners about that world above, to free them from their ignorance. They naturally are not inclined to believe him. Anyone who keeps trying to convince people in the cave that there is a reality beyond the one we're accustomed to is going to be thought insane, Plato says. And if that person tries too hard to move people toward this higher reality, this truth, he is likely to get himself killed.

It is unclear now exactly how Colleen and her friends made all of this into a contemporary playlet, but getting her to talk about it is at least a way to get her away from the Eucharist. We discuss her play while we finish folding the clothes, and then we carry the basket to the main room and put it on the floor where it can be seen by whoever owns the clothes.

Now our conversation has me thinking how odd it is to be discussing Plato and John Dewey within the same five minutes. Plato, the first and greatest of the idealists, consistently seeking the transcendental "good," contemptuous of the distracting trivia of everyday life. The eternal ideas are the only reality worth knowing, he argues. Even though we are presently burdened with bodies, our minds should be constantly in motion, working toward the eternal. Rather than giving in to the transient and temporal, we can use philosophy as the means to the world of truth and wisdom. From there it is only a step to enlightenment. At that point, most important of all, we would know how to act correctly.

Then there is Dewey, the foremost American pragmatist. He is contemptuous of vague, unattainable ideals and wants instead to address real, everyday problems. As a philosopher, ideas are important to Dewey, but it is right here, the now, that we need to fix. Morality has to do with the actual events of everyday existence. It depends on actual connections between human beings, not with ideals and philosophical debates about distant transcendentals and spiritual aspirations.

Both of them are immensely valuable, for exactly opposite reasons. But which one of them would best understand what is going on in this place, this morning?

Most of the guests have eaten by now, and a few have come through the kitchen and gone up the stairs while Colleen and I were talking. They are careful about the 7:00 a. m. departure time, maybe out of fear that they won't be allowed to return when the shelter opens again at 9:30 in the evening.

In the main room some of them are bending over their beds to straighten covers. Others are pulling on outer clothes, and a few are finishing their coffee as they spend the final minutes watching the morning show. Lincoln has begun pushing a mop around the chairs and tables, his hat tilted back on his head. A man comes over to me.

"Do you think I could get a couple aspirin?" he asks furtively.

"Sure, if we have any."

In the storeroom we find a bottle in one of the cartons of toiletries. As we are opening it, two other men appear, palms out.

"Lincoln said there wasn't any," one of them says.

"Well, I found some." I don't want to contradict Lincoln but also wonder what little policy we might be violating. Still mopping around the chairs, Lincoln doesn't notice. The first man thanks me as he places aspirin on his tongue.

A large young man is on his knees over in the open area near the tables. He is bowing, over and over, hands folded in prayer, then spinning on his knees and bowing in the opposite direction. Now he gets up and paces rapidly back and forth.

He turns to those of us who are watching him, and in a deep voice begins to shout something at us about the next presidential elections, the ones in '64 and '68. That is only off by about 25 years. One of the men near me says something about too many drugs, and another looks at me and explains that he just wants some attention.

Another man is shadow-boxing in front of the television, which is now turned off. Probably he just saw the sports news. Someone starts imitating a sports announcer: "Live from the homeless arena..."

The regular guests, knowers of the rules, are careful to sign the book as they leave as a way to secure their bed for the coming night. We try to watch for newcomers, to remind them to sign in if they want to return. Two of these are a young man and woman who are just now putting on their heavy clothes. He is helping her to get into a long black coat with a fur collar. It is a prize possession judging from the way she strokes it as he stands back to admire her. As they turn to leave, I go over to them.

"Do you want to come back here tonight?"

"Well, maybe," the women say. "We aren't sure yet." Of the two of them, she is obviously in charge.

"Why don't you sign the book anyway, so you'll have a bed in case you do come back?"

We go to the desk and I show her where to sign. She writes "Venus" under one of the women's bed numbers.

"Which bed did you have?" I ask the man. He looks at me as if we were speaking different languages.

"He didn't have no bed." This comes from Lincoln, who has apparently been listening. "He was on a sofa."

"All right, put your name down anyway, and then write 'sofa' after it.

He hesitates, looks at the woman. Then he looks over to Lincoln, and back at her.

"You write it," he says to her. To no one in particular he adds, "I can't."

She writes for a second time, and then they pick up their bags like tourists about to board a bus and they leave. An older woman, with make-up carefully applied, comes out of the women's area to sign in next. Her coat matches her bobby-socks, which are rolled above her ankles.

"Thank you," she says to Lincoln, who is now wiping the tables and picking up dishes. He says something in return, but it is muffled in his quiet southern accent.

"The jam was especially good this morning, Lincoln," she adds.

It is the same jam every morning, just like everything else. Her mother must have told her, in better days, to find something specific to compliment her hosts on. Lincoln, wiping tables with his back to us, makes no reply, so in the silence that sits heavily among us I tell her that we're glad she enjoyed the jam. Satisfied now that good manners have in this way been preserved, she pulls on her mittens, adjusts her hat, and goes out through the kitchen.

Except for two young men who are drinking the last of their coffee as the clock moves to seven, and Lincoln wiping the tables, the main room is empty. I go to the logbook and make the standard entry: nothing happened.

"See you next week," I call over to Lincoln. "Think you can manage without us till then?"

"Guess I'll get by. I can't wait till this place closes for the year."

"Are you kidding? You love it here. Where else can you have so much fun every night?"

"Think I'll go to Memphis this summer," he says. Got a brother there, he's dyin'. Maybe I'll just stay there. Nice down there."

"You'll come back."

In the kitchen Colleen is putting on her coat and tucking her unruly hair under the collar and shoving books into a canvas bag. One of the men stops in front of her.

"Hey, I didn't see you last night," he says to her. "My name's Lonnie."

He puts his hand out, then abruptly pulls it back as though aware of an impropriety.

"I'm glad to meet you Lonnie," she says. "My name is Colleen."

"Are you a single girl, Colleen?"

"No, I'm not," she lies with a disarming smile.

"Oh," Lonnie says, "That's too bad. I thought maybe you were a single girl."

The other man is struggling to pick up three large garbage bags that Lincoln has tied and left at the bottom of the stairs. They are meant for the dumpster, which sits just outside the door. One bag has a hole in the bottom, and drops of cold coffee are leaving a brown puddle on the concrete floor as he picks it up.

"You guys can each take one," I tell him. "I'll get the other."

"How about that one?" He points to another bag, filled with dozens of stale bagels and shoved partly under a table. Through the semi-clear plastic we can see mold growing on some of the bread.

"I don't know what Lincoln wants to do with that. Let's just leave it for now."

"Maybe we can sell them on the street," Lonnie jokes. "The homeless capitalists."

With that they pick up the garbage bags and head up the stairs. On the fourth step Lonnie turns and asks if either of us can give him some change for bus fare. I give him a dollar and receive as security the promise that he will pay me back "the next time."

"Looks like you've got a new boyfriend," I say under my breath to Colleen as they go up and out the door. "Maybe you'd better come back tonight."

"Just stop it, right now," she hisses.

Now it is our turn to go up the long stairs, being careful not to bump our heads on a steam pipe that hangs low near the top. We push open the heavy metal door and breathe in the sweet spring air. It is a welcome surprise after the smells of smoke and sweat that have accumulated below over the long winter months.

"The air feels wonderful," Colleen says. "All I want to do now is take a long shower." She breathes deeply and shakes her hair from under the collar of her coat. Then she stretches her arms in the air, like a child playing with balance, and turns a full circle.

After most of the night in semi-darkness, the morning light is also a fine surprise. The sun is up. Its rays slant across the parking lot and reflect in the windows of our cars and of the school building. For a moment we have to squint and look away from the windows.

Lonnie and his friend have paused in the alley between the church and the school, lighting cigarettes and looking back at Colleen. They say something to each other, then turn and walk in the direction of downtown. Far across the parking lot, one of the guests is picking through a wire-basket refuse container. Some of the garbage has fallen around the sides of it as she roots deeper into the basket.

The last three, going wherever they are going for the day and maybe coming back tonight, maybe not. Three out of more than three million homeless, the losers in the national lottery, the dark side of the American dream. Today people will likely turn to look into shop windows as they pass by with their bags and their mismatched clothes, or cut wide swaths around anyone sitting or lying on the sidewalk, or quietly hustle them from fast-food restaurants, with feelings that will range from embarrassment to disgust, from pity to fear.

The government estimates that more than a third of a million people sleep on the streets of America every night. The number is increasing. The lone hobo, in earlier decades seen near the train yard, has turned into hundreds of people sleeping in alleys or subway tunnels or on the doorsteps and sidewalks of any average-sized American city. The classic skid row panhandler is no longer older and alcoholic. The problem of homelessness had broadened to include more women and more destitute families. Worst hit now are the young, Afro-Americans and Hispanics.

Part of the reason is the recent closing of government-sponsored facilities for the mentally-disturbed as part of cost-cutting. Some of the anti-poverty programs of the 60s have also been undone. Another reason, of longer duration now, is the shrinking demand for unskilled labor as a result of a declining industrial base in the economy. Many other reasons – such as lack of education or adequate family support, abuse in childhood or in a marriage – make the problem more complex than it was thought to be in earlier times.

The good news is that help is taking shape in the form of shelters like this one. There is also an increase in private distribution of food to the poor along with legal assistance by advocacy groups and projects to provide better short-term housing. It remains to be seen if these efforts can keep pace.

They are the welcome results of activism on the ground rather than in the mind. But it is there that the most important change has yet to happen. The American philosophy of individualism has a long history and much to be said in its favor. It is not helpful when it allows us to ignore the problem of being down and out by recourse to the familiar "well, I made it on my own." The truth is that our governments and our communities have helped each of us to make it, when we have done so. A better society would add to its individualist philosophy a healthy measure of communitarianism.

"Well, it was another quiet night," Colleen says, "but I'm always glad when it's over. Are you going to work now?"

"I've got two classes this morning, but then I can go home and get some sleep. How about you?"

"Uh huh. But I'm not going in till about ten. My boss doesn't mind if I'm late."

"Remember the last time we came out of here together? We had to knock snow off our cars."

"I was afraid mine wouldn't start that morning." She looks down at her car keys. "Where do you think they'll all go when this place closes?"

"Some of them stay with relatives or friends, I think. The others, I don't know. Are you coming back here yourself next year?"

"Maybe. We'll see."

We walk over to her car, which she's parked alongside the school and under a light to keep it safe during the night. A bottle of wine with an inch of liquid in it is sitting by her front wheel. I pick it up for the dumpster. Colleen fishes around in her purse for something, and then unlocks the driver's door. As she gets in, she hands me a piece of paper, torn from a small notebook by the looks of it.

"I wrote down the name of that book I want you to read. No excuses this time."

"Okay." Her earnestness deserves a reply. "Next time I'll be prepared for arguing with you."

"Do you know where we all are, Derek?"

The question seems to come from nowhere, and before I can think of an answer she pulls shut her door and starts the car's engine. As she drives off I go to the dumpster and toss in the garbage bag and the wine bottle.

On the piece of paper, in large block writing that looks like a child's, she has written the name of the book she wants me to read.

Below that she has written, "Answer: In the Cave."

Chapter Four

So, after those years in which Ken and I probably circled one another in the jail, or even elsewhere in the city's less savory locations, it would be in a shelter, a different one, where we would finally meet. This one was an all-male facility, situated in a newly-renovated building in a rough part of town. It was designed for long-term rather than overnight care, with programs for counseling, job placement, drug rehabilitation -- a transition from broken lives and troubled pasts to the possibility of something like mainstream existence. This was a time when cities everywhere were waking up to the dimensions and complexities of the problem of homelessness.

I had been helping out there mostly in a security role when the new director asked me if I would be interested in a mentoring program.

"This is all pretty new and we're still developing the guidelines."

That was meant as code language to say that I could do about whatever I wanted as a mentor. Once those guidelines got written, probably nobody with any imagination would want any part of the program. So it was a good way to get me interested, and he knew it.

"The main thing is to be a friend and sort of an advisor to one of our residents. Spend some time one-on-one and help him whatever way you can. Does that sound like something you could do?"

"It sounds like something I would *like* to do."

"The guy we have in mind for you just got out of prison. Nine years. He's new here, so like a lot of the residents he's sort of an unknown. Can you handle that?"

"Yeah, I've had some experience."

As though the weather knew to cooperate with this kind of story, it was a nasty winter night, one of those nights when a light Northeastern snow comes down not in soft flakes but in tiny sand-like grains that fly horizontally in front of the headlights and snake across the road before piling up on curbs or in corners out of the wind, or sticking briefly to headlights and windshields.

It was also not an auspicious night in the fresh history of the facility, and I was partly to blame. The week before, one of the older residents had asked me to bring him some pipe tobacco. I did. He stepped outside for a smoke on the sidewalk and came face-to-face with a mugger, knife in hand. The mugger at least had no interest in pipe tobacco, and the hapless resident had no money, so the incident ended there. The smoker came back inside looking a little pale and maybe even temporarily cured of his habit. As for the mugger, we all agreed that he would do better in the suburbs.

There was little sympathy being shown, maybe because the homeless are used to doing without much sympathy themselves. The discussion turned quickly into a symposium of war stories.

"Man, it's just good he didn't stick you," said one resident. "Look here." He turned half away from us, pulling his collar as far as he could toward his left shoulder and exposing the side of his neck. A long white scar began at his hairline and disappeared into his shirt. "Knife fight," he said with the laconic pride of the survivor.

"Yeah?" from another resident, pulling up his sweater. "How about *this*?" Another scar, this one uglier and wider, ran around his side just below the rib cage and ended above the hip in a pucker. "Got that one in prison. 'Nother one too, but I ain't gonna show you that."

Just as well, since there was barely time. More clothes were being pulled and tugged by the warriors, while those of us with nothing to show for ourselves looked on with something like mild envy. Eventually the interest died, and one of them remembered that I had come to meet the guy I was supposed to mentor. Somebody called upstairs for him.

In a minute, a young black man came bounding down the back stairs and, without even a glance around the room, came toward me with his hand far out in front of him, as if wanting to reach across the gap between us. Because he wore a sleeveless sweatshirt, my attention was drawn first to long, thin arms on which hard muscles twisted upward on themselves and ended in very straight shoulders. A tattoo of a scarecrow ran down along one forearm. The rest of the body seemed equally thin, tensed in a way that took him to above average height, as if he were in the habit of walking on his toes.

"You work out a lot," I said as we shook hands. A whitey shake.

"Yeah, lots of time for that where I've been." His mouth turned up to a one-sided grin, and I liked it that he was laughing at himself in front of a stranger. Still, he was quick to change the direction of the conversation, even if not the subject.

"This place needs some weights and stuff. There's a perfect place downstairs to work out, and I'm gonna get us some equipment, somewhere."

His narrow face was made even thinner by ears that seemed nearly flattened against his head. As he spoke, his eyebrows rose dramatically and creased the skin of his forehead in two equal waves, at the same time causing his eyes to bulge slightly. It was an animated face.

But it was the voice that got my attention, all the more so because it came from such a thin neck. It was the low, powerful voice of the rural preacher, the kind of voice that carries across the largest room, causing heads to turn and drowning out other sounds, maybe rattling loose glass. Along with the strength of it, there was also a tone of self-assurance and conviction, as though discussing weights and workouts was, for that moment at least, the only important matter in the world.

"Let's go talk in my room," he said, dismissing everybody but the two of us with a sideways shake of his head. He took the stairs ahead of me, two at a time.

At that first meeting, he was nothing like the many inmates I had known. They had been at times reticent, awkward, some nearly inarticulate, often simply unable to cross the racial and social barriers that had defined most of their lives and separated them from me. About Ken there was neither diffidence nor hesitation, above all when it came to his criminal past and multiple prison experiences.

He handed me a worn paper folder, the record. Like an employer with a resume, I thumbed through it while he went to get the coffee. A quick look, since I was not sure how much time there was. I skimmed through robbery, weapons possession, drug dealing and endangering the welfare of a minor, among other charges. His age was given as 29. By the standards I was used to, the prison record was not all that extraordinary. What I found heartening was what the pages did not include: for whatever violence he had undergone, he had done no serious violence to others.

"You name it," he said as he returned with the coffee, "and I got it." He was holding a tray with cups and little packets of sugar and artificial cream, but when he looked at the record in my hand I knew he wasn't referring to the coffee tray.

Then he laughed for the first time, a laugh that was as loud and distinctive as the voice. It came out literally as a "ha-ha-ha," which seen here in print may seem artificial, a caricature of laughing. At the time, I heard in it a defensiveness and maybe the insecurity that could be expected at a first meeting. In fact, as I heard it more often, I realized that it was entirely sincere and joyful and even communal, as if he not only found something to be funny but also wanted to be sure everyone was in on the joke. Still, forming on the spot a habit I never was able to break, I immediately imagined it as the ha-ha-ha enclosed in cartoon bubbles, drawn over the heads of cartoon figures.

The record told me that he was obviously a saver, a keeper of materials most other people would want to hide or destroy, and I had the impression that he wanted this white guy to know things that, in other times, he had been telling only to fellow inmates. It was almost as though he had been saving up for a different, or a better, audience.

The hint was clear in any case, so I turned to the second page and pointed randomly to one of charges.

"That one?" He took a little breath, in the manner of one about to start a long story, not for the air but for the attention.

It was an early crime, and it confirmed the argument that bad management gets what it deserves, almost every time. It is frightening, I would rediscover after many earlier conversations in the county jail, to think of the consequences if more criminals actually planned their operations.

"The guy who was with me didn't even know I was robbing the place. In a sense I wanted to get caught because I had a Jamaican posse after me for robbing drug houses."

"Why were you robbing drug houses," I asked, and immediately remembered Willy Sutton's answer to an equally silly question. But his own answer was different.

"I owed money for my addiction and I was on the lam. I was going crazy then, kicking down doors, breaking in places. So a lot of people were looking for me and I was scared shitless. That's why I wanted to get caught. I had already robbed an OTB and didn't get caught that time, got away with five thousand dollars. Cash."

It seemed to me that saying "cash" wasn't necessary, since they would not likely have written him a check. I let that go.

"So I went back and this time it was stupid because I tried to rob the place in broad daylight. I had a fake gun in a leather jacket and I walked in the place, right across from the Federal Building and around the corner from City Hall. Police on every corner."

"The guy with me drove up in front and parked – a canary-yellow Cadillac Eldorado. How stupid could you be to have that for a getaway car? And he had just got the car out of a repair shop but it couldn't go over 40 without stalling."

Those last details were too inane to be true, I thought then. It was another of those times when I wondered about the line between truth and invention in his stories, but again I decided that it was precisely those seemingly inappropriate details that made the stories credible.

"I didn't realize that until I went in there and showed them a note that said this is a robbery. The woman handed me 4000 dollars and I walked out. We were like a block away from home when out of nowhere a cop car flew in front of us at the intersection. There were also some guys on mounted patrol, horseback, and back then they had those police jeeps. About 15 cops came out of nowhere and surrounded us. One of them put a .45 Magnum over the hood and the guy that was driving, the guy who didn't know I was robbing the place, said "Hey, what the hell you did?"

"They took me downtown and interrogated me and I said 'you know, the guy that was in the car didn't know anything about it. ' After a while they released him. That was good. I remember seeing him after I got out, and I thought he was going to hit me. But he was like, 'man I got to shake your hand. Most people would never have done that. 'He was grateful that I didn't implicate him."

And I was grateful to discover that, folk wisdom to the contrary, there *is* honor among thieves.

"They gave me a year and a half to four and a half for that robbery. That was the first time I ever went to prison. Before that I was just in juvenile detention centers and in and out of jail a lot."

We had not talked long, but it was becoming obvious that there would be no difficulty with bonding, even if the bonding was to be based on things other than personal histories. So I felt free to press a little.

"You said you were on the lam. What was that all about?"

"I had got hooked up with those Jamaicans and some people from St. Kitts Island and St. Croix. One time I had this house on Avenue C with a guy named Bill, a Jamaican immigrant. A couple of hundred dollars came up missing. I had fallen asleep and when they came back they thought I had stolen it. They wouldn't let me leave, held me at gunpoint. Then they started beating me with sticks until I would tell them where the money was. They had one stick with nails in it that they broke over my leg and I still have a scar from where the nail stuck in me."

He could have joined the scar competition from earlier in the evening. But there was more.

"I got hit on the head with a skillet. That knocked me unconscious. I remember waking up and my shirt was all wet because they threw a pot of water on me. They kept questioning me. One guy took a wooden chair and broke it over my head. Another kicked me in the ribs and broke some of them. I had internal bleeding from where something got punctured. I don't know what."

"This went on for a couple of days. I asked to go to the bathroom at one point and they let me. So I jumped out of a two-story window and landed in some hedges. Ran and tripped over part of a sidewalk and fell almost in front of a car. The guy stopped. I begged for help, and he put me in his car and drove me to a hospital. Of course the cops had to come and make a report. I told them I was jumped."

He talked, I listened, and the coffee gradually ran out. His openness was natural, not calculated, and I suppose it helped that I made no judgments. The listening had been practiced over many years, although I was careful not to tell him I had heard some of the same before, even if more haltingly and with less flair. By contrast, his stories came at me directly, glossed by a touch of bravado and a feel for the dramatic. I found that directness disarming, as would many others. Neither of us knew the extent to which he was practicing on me. And only he knew if the stories were as true as he made them sound.

I knew one thing: this was the one I wanted. After that first meeting things moved fast.

By the time we met again, he had the weights for the basement, a first exercise in working people for donations to a worthy cause. The shelter could not hold him long once he discovered the power of his personality. Soon he had his first apartment; a few of us threw in some used furniture and some decorations to get him started.

The apartment, on the second floor of a flat-topped brick building that hung over a busy north-side avenue, offered new challenges. Twice, when I went there for early visits, I was greeted with questioning looks from young men talking just inside the door. Words broke off nearly in mid-sentence. Their eyes followed as I passed, and I felt them fixed on my back as I went down the wide, bare hallway with its stale smells of last week's cooking. Making some little business deals here, fellows? Sorry if I came at a bad time. It was a relief to turn the corner and mount the stairway to Ken's unit, wondering if it was hard for him, in that environment, not to fall back into old habits and familiar friendships.

No, he was headed in a very different direction. Or better said, several directions at once. Over dinners of okra and pork that he took evident pride in cooking, he would replay his latest conversations with people he was meeting. If I was his official mentor, there were plenty of others who were willing to share the work. Soon enough there were benefactors, too. An ex-inmate making good gets the music going for many people, hitting the high notes of hope in a world looking for something positive to hear.

Into his net fell activists and journalists and politicians, even, incongruously, policemen who had arrested him over the years and, as noted earlier, the judge who had sentenced him. We both loved to laugh at that. The net widened quickly, and the plans widened with it. My own work would become little more than that of encouragement, easy enough to do. Why give advice when advice is not needed?

Gradually the role of mentor turned into that of a friend among many friends, and I was content simply to share in his accomplishments, however modest at first. He began with small talks at schools and parties and recreational centers, finding the power of his voice and his message. The message was that too many of our "children," as he called the teenagers he talked to, were living with anger, hatred, resentments and feelings of abandonment and despair. And when they can't hold it in any longer, they end up exploding in violence and abuse.

"My dad always said I wouldn't amount to anything." It was a dinnertime theme. "So I never had the idea that I deserved a chance. That's why I feel close to the children and why I praise them for the smallest accomplishment. But we have to go through the fire to really understand."

Mostly he talked about his own life. He told them about how he dropped out of school and grew dreadlocks. How he began to sell drugs, over time becoming his own best customer. How he used drugs even in prison. He asked them how many of them had used drugs and alcohol and watched as most of the hands were raised. He showed them his arrest record.

He talked about wearing chain gang clothes and being forced to strip and pour de-licing powder on himself. About the sounds of screaming and sobbing carrying down prison corridors, about blood pouring out of chests and heads, about guys who thought they were tough until they hit the big house where they "melted like ice cubes in the summer sun."

He knew the power of story over lecture. He was also aware of the value of connecting the story teller to the story rather than setting up an artificial distance. With that audience it would not have worked any other way. For him there must have been something purgative about the process: the telling was a way to turn humiliations into victories and disorder into salvation.

The students would not have understood that, but they could appreciate his feeling for them, something akin to love. They probably also shared the fascination for temptation and trouble.

As he talked, he saw the hurt on their faces and sensed their despair. In turn, they told him that they knew exactly how he had felt in his own childhood: lonely and afraid. "I'm opening doors," he would tell me and others, "helping these children to identify their emotions and deal with their problems. God has kept me around for some purpose, and that is to try to reach some of these children. I just want them to believe in themselves."

At a children's center, he asked his listeners to identify three positive traits about themselves. They rarely could. When he asked them to identify negative traits, the number rose quickly to ten. "They've never been told they're special, loved, cared for."

They did not need to be told that they were poor. Ken began his work with youth at around the time when the United States was becoming, among advanced nations, the country with the greatest inequalities of wealth and income. The figures had become so skewed that they defied belief and frustrated understanding. One family, for example, was then on the way to accumulating more wealth than 40 per cent of the entire population. Our two richest individuals were not far behind. In New York State, one per cent of the population held 35 per cent of the wealth. It is hard to imagine that even the worst medieval monarchies could have been more successful in capturing the riches of a country.

Meanwhile, real annual income for average American families had been steadily falling. The reason had nothing new to recommend it: it was old-fashioned greed. Like war, natural disasters and epidemics, greed has a long history, but at that time it was steadily becoming institutionalized as an integral part of the corporate structure and the financial system. All of that is obvious now. What was not so obvious then was the connections that were just beginning to be made between such inequalities of wealth and various social ills.

Those connections were turning the world's richest nation into a leader in drug and alcohol addiction, rates of violence and crime and imprisonment, poor educational performance, mental illness, shorter life expectancy and higher infant mortality, less social mobility, more anger and cynicism.

A list of societal dysfunctions of that sort was unimaginable to earlier generations, and it was not a subject that many wanted to talk about. Worse, it was even less popular to point out that problems usually associated with the lower social classes were magnified in countries with greater economic inequality.

If inequality was creeping its way steadily into the national economic picture, in Rochester it moved at more of a saunter. The city was on its way to being ranked as the ninth poorest city in the country for children and the worst in that regard among the cities of New York. The statistics relevant to every aspect of the well-being of young people –- child abuse, teen pregnancy, mental health, detention, among others –- were alarming to anyone who took the trouble to consider them.

Ken knew the situation more from experience and intuition than from sociology or economics. So did his listeners. If some of what he had to tell them had been said before, he was saying it differently. Or maybe it was that *he* was different, a relief from all the sociologists and psychologists and politicians: he had been there. His audience of young people could feel the energy, hear the passion in that voice. Caring, he knew, is not an intellectual exercise; it comes from a heart that has been wounded and chooses to respond with love rather than hate. Most of all, he was one of them. His knowledge of their stunted and dangerous lives was personal and unmediated. His story was their story, except that his was much longer and had seen consequences that he was determined they should never see.

He wrote articles for the local opinion page, graduating from his street talk to a sophisticated prose. "Lack of education and opportunity, the disintegration of strong families, racism and the feeling of exclusion from mainstream society have resulted in the frustration, despair and hopelessness of today's black youth."

"Although these social illnesses are concentrated in our inner city, as well as cities across America, we cannot forget that the cities are in integral part of our macrocosmic society: a malady in the former affects the health of the latter. The blight of crime and violence in our community is like a gangrenous limb of the body politic, which we cannot simply amputate to prevent its spreading infection."

"Who will arise and say to our youth: stop selling drugs, stop killing each other? Who will tell these young people to go to school, get a job, and live a productive life? Who will be the strong advocates who will get involved, stop a fight in progress, stand by a young person's side, or go to his home to speak to the parents? Who will arise and assist a youth whom no one wants to help -- those youth considered too far gone, those youth whom community agencies, the court system, and even their own families have given up on?"

"No wonder this generation has given up on themselves, when we as adults turn them away and offer them the bleak future of the deadly streets."

It was not all immediate success. His first attempt at serious organization was a disaster.

What he had in mind was a rally and a march through downtown streets to City Hall. A rap group was booked, speakers invited. He prepared and distributed fliers, devised forms on which kids were to write out their concerns about drugs, disease, violence and education. He estimated a crowd of between 500 and 700, and he naturally alerted the media.

About 40 young people showed up, easily outnumbered by the few of us who had come to give our support, some camera crews and reporters, and a few cops who looked like they would have been more interested escorting a funeral procession. Ken spoke and the rap group performed just the same. The little group of demonstrators marched as planned to city hall. Within minutes city officials came outside and asked them to tone it down. The officials were holding a meeting to consider ways to deal with violence in the streets.

A large headline the next day announced: "Youth Event Flops."

The story included a picture of Ken consoling two discouraged young women, their heads bowed and his arms around their shoulders. Of course he was disappointed, he told the media. "I don't want to find fault. They're not here. It's that simple." Someone asked where they were. "I'll tell you," he said. "They're out on some street corner, in some drug-infested neighborhood, because for years this is what they've adapted to."

I called him that evening, a call I didn't want to make.

"What am I supposed to say?" I asked when he picked up the phone.

Expecting anger or depression, I got the opposite. The voice was as strong as ever.

"It's okay," he told me. "Just a bad start, and I need to figure out what went wrong. One thing is, I relied on the schools to get out the word. Next time I'll do it myself."

"Anyone would be discouraged. Do you want me to come over?"

"No, there's need for that. I'm not giving up just 'cause of this. No way."

He may not have needed encouragement, but he did need some recreation. His schedule was exhausting even him. Could I take him fishing, out of town? "I haven't been out of this town in years," he said, "except for trips to places I didn't want to go."

Fishing bores me, I told him, but I can always read. He borrowed some gear, I collected a few books, and we spent three days camping in the Adirondacks and driving from lake to lake looking for fish. He waded happily into shallow waters at the edges of those mountain lakes while I sat on the shore reading, and on warm, clear evenings we talked over campfires while the fresh air revived him.

The connection between fishing and philosophy has a long history, reaching back to Izaak Walton and probably further. It could be that certain insights come more easily in the quiet and solace that are major elements of that sport. Something must happen when you stand stolidly in the presence of water, waiting, waiting. If virtues like patience and acceptance are thus fostered, Ken must have made some progress on those fronts, since he caught nothing. Looking back, I think of the fishing trip as one of the better things I did as his mentor.

I discovered something interesting: Ken was afraid of my disapproval. He called after an appearance on a local radio station, one of those programs on an early Sunday morning when there is airtime to be filled.

"How did I sound?"

"Yeah, well, you said all the right things... "

"But?"

"It was like you were trying too hard to be profound. Like an old man. You aren't one. Or maybe like the whole thing is getting to you."

"This is serious stuff, Uncle Derek." There was clear hurt in the voice.

"I know it's serious. But it puts people off when somebody sounds stuffy. Or pretentious. Just relax more, be yourself."

The last bit of advice was not necessary, the one before it was at that time impossible. For my part, it was a lesson in using criticism sparingly, which may later have been a mistake.

That and a few similar incidents caused me to wonder about the dynamics of our relationship. We were an odd couple at the very least: a two-time felon turned inner-city activist paired with a bookish, semi-reclusive suburban academic, not to mention the 20-year age difference. My college students had the same youthful energy, so I could relate to that, but they did not have his enthusiasm or his concern for social justice. While my tendency was to think and raise questions about what constitutes right action, he had no doubts on such matters. Where I was inclined to hesitate, he pushed.

We raised eyebrows in restaurants when Ken would come on to the waitress while I studied the menu and told him to keep his voice down. ("What's *wrong*, Uncle Derek? Chill, okay?") He found to his amusement that he could sometimes embarrass me by direct talk about things I thought to be private and personal. It could have been that he was simply doing and saying things that I would not or could not myself. But what was I to him? Did I offer, by virtue of some professional success and middle-age stability, the contrast of genteel respectability? One thing was certain: both of us had been many places the other had not been.

Early on I asked him why he agreed to have me as his mentor. He had several reasons, as though he had been waiting for the question.

"You reminded me a lot of people who came into my life when I was younger, and I always thought of you as, I don't know, an uncle that I always wanted because my father has only one brother and they were never close. After I got out of prison they told me they could get me a mentor and it could be this guy who comes in and works at night, and I said sure. And I remember coming up to you, and you told me you were a professor in philosophy and I said, wow, maybe this guy can help me with my writing skills and stuff. And, I don't know, I became interested because I always liked smart people, aha, ha, ha, ha, because I always wanted to be smart, that's why. And you were a nice and caring guy and I think we have the same perspective on life too, that of caring for other people and trying to help be, you know, somewhat of a humanitarian, seeing some of the issues and burdens that society has put upon us."

He spoke sometimes about wanting to make his father proud. Was I serving as some sort of alter-father? He had a father, a quiet man whom I met now and then, and who did seem proud. So I became "uncle" Derek, one of the more reputable members of a family that otherwise included brothers in and out of jail, an addicted sister, and another who was mentally ill.

Gradually I met the people who were closest to him, knowing that it was important to him that I do so. But I could never get past the sense that I was moving around no more than the edges of his inner-city world, a place of relationships and values and even language so long established that it was nearly impossible for a suburban white to gain entry. None of that feeling came from Ken. It did come from a few of his friends, young black men with serious faces. They were not particularly imposing, but they seemed so because they were broad-chested and muscular, and I noticed that the power of their bodies made most adornments of jewelry or tattoos unnecessary. As a rule they did not smile when we were introduced, and their quick handshakes suggested some unspoken impropriety in the matter, as if to say that while *he* might think we should get to know each other, *we* are not so sure.

We met in various contexts, and for all of Ken's attempts to bring me into that orbit of his life, they remained just courteous enough to satisfy Ken's need to prove his legitimacy in the world I represented. If I was welcome, it was only within narrowly-defined limits and only because Ken had signaled his approval. In other circumstances their distance and even mistrust might have been intimidating, but after a time I understood that I had nothing to fear from them. A line from a Dickens' character sometimes came to mind: "You'll find us rough, sir, but you'll find us ready." I came to think of them as the "guards" at the point when I realized that they were protecting Ken from *me*.

For his part, Ken had no time to waste on negotiating awkward relationships. There was much to be done. Soon kids were approaching him on the streets to tell him that what he was saying mattered, and they were calling him at home with their problems. Then people began coming to me, asking if that guy in the newspaper was the one I was telling them about. Yeah, that's him.

Gradually he became more sophisticated about his contacts and venues. He started getting appointments at our city hall and he began talking to city school administrators about plans for therapeutic sessions in which students could talk out their feelings. "Fillings" he called them, and I, wanting to be the mentor in small matters if not in larger ones, tried to make him be more careful about differences in pronunciation and, more importantly, between words like ideas and ideals. He mostly ignored that sort of help. For him those were purely academic distinctions and therefore they made no real difference. In the larger picture he was right. And it could be that, sensing that I had no necessary role in shaping his work and his future, I could at least shape his image, in the best tradition of *Pygmalion*.

Especially in the beginning, the energy seemed inexhaustible. It did not matter to him that the problem was greater than most of us wanted even to think about, much less act upon. The change in his own life was going to be the agent of change in the lives of the children. They should never have to face what he had faced or do what he had done.

It was all about the children.

REFUGEE LUNCH

The best of hospitality and of generosity
is also not in the will, but in fate. I find
that I am not much to you; you do not need me;
then I am thrust out of doors, though you
proffer me house and lands. No services are
of any value, but only likeness. When I have
attempted to join myself to others by services,
it proved an intellectual trick -- no more.
They eat your services like apples, and leave
you out. But love them, and they feel you and
delight in you all the time.
-- R. W. Emerson
Where can I find a man who has forgotten
words?He is the one I would like to talk to.

-- Chuang Tzu

Rabbit hutches.

I have been trying for weeks to think what the refugees' living quarters remind me of. Just now it came to me. When we were children growing up out west, our parents raised rabbits for a time, in an old hutch built of small wooden boxes, three or four rows high. The front of each hutch was a framed screen, which we would open to feed the rabbits.

Inside what used to the cell-blocks of Hei Ling Chau Detention Centre, the Hong Kong government has built the same arrangement. Metal poles rise like scaffoldings to the ceilings, over twenty feet above. Attached to the poles are sheets of plywood. Each layer creates a living space maybe five feet wide and eight feet deep, but nowhere near high enough to stand up in. Each of these spaces contains one refugee family and all their possessions. It is the equivalent of living day and night under an oversize dining room table.

Nhat and I are on our way now to his hutch. Walking along the wide outside corridor that runs between the cell blocks, six of them on each side, is an experience of waiting and welcoming. The Vietnamese refugees sit in small groups in the shade of the cell blocks' north sides. Women are holding infants in their laps and men are squatting in circles. Defying the heat, children are running around on the concrete. There is not a tree, a flower, or a blade of grass to be seen in any direction. The mid-day sun pounds on the concrete, creating a reflecting heat and a dulling humidity that goes nowhere in the still air. Our eyes narrow against the glare.

Apparently these people don't see an American very often, so I am the center of their attention whenever I appear. This is a classic case of Gulliver among the Lilliputians. They wave and smile and call out greetings as Nhat and I pass. So I smile and wave back, like a politician acknowledging his constituents. The group just outside Nhat's cell block includes some young men I vaguely know, so we stop for a minute to talk. Any normal conversation is impossible, since only a few know a handful of English words, and I in turn have learned only a few Vietnamese expressions.

First there are hellos all around, including the usual struggle with the "l" sound. They know the word, anyway.

"How are you?" one of them asks, carefully separating each word. His friends grin proudly at this mastery of English and look to me for approval.

"I'm fine. *Ka moon zit nee-ow*." That is as close as I can come to saying "thank you very much," and it is not very close. Still, they smile broadly and nod in appreciation.

One of them points to my right ankle, heavily taped above a dirty sneaker, and indicates that he is worried about it. The others nod that they are worried too.

"It's healing," I tell them. I make a motion with my hands as though I am breaking a stick and then give a negative shake of my head to indicate that the ankle is not broken. They bob their heads happily at this news. Then I hop up and down on the good ankle and say "ow, ow, ow" to let them know that it still hurts plenty. That makes them laugh. Their smiles are wide and genuine, blissfully unaware that they would never qualify for a tooth paste commercial.

It is a distressing collection of terrible teeth: many are simply missing, some are yellow stumps, and others stick out at impossible angles. This place would be an orthodontist's paradise, except that no one could pay the bills.

"American, yes?" one of them asks, as though he needs to confirm the fact yet again.

"Yes, from New York."

"Ne-u Wok. Nu Yawk. Nou Jzak." Several of them are now trying to get it right; doing so could create a valued connection.

"New York." I repeat it a few times.

"Noo Wurk," one says, extending his lips and caving his cheeks.

"That's a little better."

At that they laugh and clap their hands, repeating it as we wave our good-byes and pass into Nhat's cell-block. It is even hotter in here, as if the humidity has trailed in behind us and stuck to our clothes and the walls. It is also more crowded. We pick our way around more mothers holding their children and slip down a narrow passage between stacks of hutches. The refugees watch us, their dark eyes reflecting boredom, anxiety, or simple curiosity. Laundered clothes hang everywhere on makeshift lines and their sandals sit in neat rows at the base of the scaffoldings. Red and blue plastic food containers dot the plywood floors of their hutches in those spaces not taken by a person.

We stop for a moment to admire a young baby in the arms of its mother, and she is obviously pleased by the attention. It is feeling even more like I am in training for a career in politics.

Immediately small children gather around us, one of them pulling at my leg. A small hand extends a toy truck to me, so I take it and spin the wheels and bump it into a couple of toes before handing it back. The child and the truck disappear between pairs of legs.

Nhat's wife and baby are inside their hutch. Her name is Hieu, which I have been trying to pronounce correctly. Nhat says I am not getting it right. He speaks to Hieu, probably telling her that he has brought me home for lunch again. Since there is no way the three of them could make room for a fourth person in there as well, she scoops up the baby and vanishes into the crowd.

Their hutch is on the middle level of the scaffolding, which puts their plywood floor just below my shoulder. To get in, we have to jump slightly and at the same duck our heads and turn ourselves, almost like gymnasts. Nhat goes first, and when he is far enough back to make room for me, I follow. The ceiling is so low that even sitting up straight is almost impossible. It is necessary to scrunch down slightly, back against the outside pole and legs stretched out almost to the opposite side. The walls of the hutches are bed sheets, separating the families and giving a bit of privacy.

The first thing I do is take off my shoes, for I am in an oriental home now. Nhat already has his sandals off, and he pushes our two pairs out of the way and begins to rummage in one of the two cardboard boxes behind him. In those boxes are his family's entire possessions.

First, he produces two plastic cups. He inspects mine carefully for cleanliness before he puts it down beside my outstretched leg. Next comes the most curious teapot I have ever seen. It is nothing more than a soda-pop can. Nhat has carefully cut away the top, which now rests loosely on the can. Into the top he has somehow fixed a straw. The top is removable, presumably to allow tea leaves to be put it. I don't see any real need for the straw, but I suspect this whole thing somehow replicates real teapots back home in Viet Nam.

It is also hard to understand how the tea stays hot in this metal arrangement, but it's always plenty warm when Nhat pours it for me. On the other hand, it would be almost impossible for anything not to be hot in the relentless heat of a Hong Kong summer.

This tea ceremony has become a ritual for us by now, a way to pass the time until the food arrives. While we sip our tea and wait, we also try to converse. Conversation between the two of us has become a little easier, since Nhat is quick to pick up English words, and we have become more skilled at a simple sign language and pantomime to get our thoughts across. Nhat is definitely intelligent. That has become clear not only through our makeshift conversations but also from the chess games we play down at the playground. He wins easily almost every time.

The few times I have won, he probably set it up so that I would. Maybe he thinks I need to save face. Sometimes, when I've made a really dopey move, he will indicate on the chessboard what will happen if I don't take the piece back." No," I try to tell him, "I made the move and now I'm stuck with it." "No pwoblem, no pwoblem," he says. Then he moves my piece back to safety and shows me what needs to be done instead, playing both sides of the board with as much respect as it is possible to show under the circumstances.

Right now he is working me again on the matter of the beer.

"Please help me buy box beer," he wrote on a piece of paper the first day I met him. I was puzzled as to what "box" beer might be, but then I realized that he meant a can of beer.

The beer is not for him, he is explaining again.

"Wife... not milk... for childrens. Wife have beer, milk for childrens."

He is making breast-feeding motions and shaking his head negatively, and I am supposed to understand that his wife has been unable to nurse their baby. Apparently someone has told him that beer may start her milk flowing; maybe that is even true. As much as I would love to bring him the can of beer, I simply cannot. The rules for volunteers who are allowed to enter Hei Ling Chau Detention Centre are clear: no alcohol, no weapons, behave yourself.

In fact, it would be easy enough to smuggle in a can of beer. We are never really searched by the Hong Kong Chinese guards who work for CSD, the government's Correctional Services Department. But I have learned that there are no secrets in the cramped quarters of Hei Ling Chau. News travels fast. If I brought Nhat his beer, most of this cell block would know it before Hieu finished her first few sips. Even if I wanted to jeopardize my own chances of entering the camp, I am not willing to compromise the organization we are working for. But how to tell Nhat all that?

"No, Nhat. I'm very sorry. The rules say that no beer is allowed."

It is not easy to pantomime words like "rules" and "allowed." Along with some gestures, I say "If I bring beer in Hei Ling Chau, the CSD will throw me out. No come back." I know that he understands "no come back" and CSD, and with this I dramatically grab myself by my shirt and pantomime being thrown out of the camp. Nhat does not look convinced.

This little problem will not affect our friendship. Nhat can be moody at times, but we have grown close during the weeks of working together at the playground. Hei Ling Chau holds over 3000 Vietnamese refugees, probably half of whom are children. No refugee is allowed to leave the camp, even though it is on a small island that is part of the Hong Kong archipelago. The only exceptions are workers who go out each day to tend a vegetable garden, and groups of children. That is one of the reasons why we are here. The children may leave the camp to play at a small playground down the road, but only if volunteers come from outside to take them.

Each morning, a dozen of us meet at a pier in Hong Kong, from which a small government ferry takes us on an hour's ride to Hei Ling Chau Island. From the dock, we are taken by truck up the hill to the detention centre. Once past the guards inside, we are met by Nhat and a few other refugees, who are paid a tiny salary to organize groups of children and then accompany them and us to the playground.

It is the same routine every day. Many of the children hold large red and white striped umbrellas to ward off the sun as we walk down the dirt road; they call out "otto, otto" and scamper to the side as the occasional car appears around a corner. We take a morning group, return them to the camp by noon, and then take a second group after lunch. The number of children at the camp is so large that each child gets to the playground roughly once every two weeks. Once there, they have two hours of play time.

Nhat and I sip our tea, trying to think of new ways to communicate. Somewhere he has picked up an old Vietnamese-English dictionary, and right now he's looking up a word. He points to the Vietnamese word and I follow his finger over to the English equivalent. The word is "demonstration." I nod my understanding and pronounce it slowly for him several times.

He checks the word again before he speaks. "In Hei Ling Chau, we... we demonstration." He thrusts his fist into the air and then squares his shoulders with determination. "We demonstration," he says. "No come back Viet Nam, no come back Viet Nam."

"I understand, Nhat. You don't want to go back to Viet Nam."

"Yes! No come back!"

Last week's demonstration is by far the hottest topic in the camp right now. It was partly in response to a recent government raid on another, larger camp, a raid that was controversial for its use of armored personnel carriers and a helicopter and also for its attempt to get refugees onto planes headed back to Viet Nam. The camps will have to be emptied sooner or later, but that is not a future that is accepted by the refugees.

To date, over 50,000 Vietnamese boat people, as they like to call themselves, have left Viet Nam. They are fleeing variously from political danger, poverty and unemployment. Packed into small boats, they have crossed the South China Sea and been picked up by the Hong Kong government. Some refugees don't make it, becoming instead the victims of open-sea accidents or even piracy. Some countries have simply not allowed the boat people to land, pushing their boats back to the sea. To its credit, Hong Kong has given them temporary asylum. It has no choice, though, but to put them into a growing number of detention centers until someone can figure out what to do with all of them.

The main responsibility for that falls on the United Nations High Commissioner for Refugees. Formed in 1951 to deal with refugees from the Second World War, the office has seen its mandate grow enormously. That mandate now encompasses internally displaced persons as well as conventional refugees, whose numbers worldwide have grown into the tens of millions. It is considered to be a growth industry; the UNCHR now employs lawyers and interpreters as well as the usual administrators and clerical staff. The original task of protecting refugees has been enlarged to include providing the kind of aid traditionally given by the Red Cross: medical care in its various forms, orphanages, even homes for the elderly.

The biggest challenge is to figure out what, in the end, is to be done with all these refugees. As usually happens, the situation is complicated by political realities and cultural sensitivities. Any solution has to balance the interests of Hong Kong and Viet Nam as well as neighboring countries -- even to a degree those of the United States and other nations which may become destinations for the refugees.

One solution, called mandatory repatriation, is simply to ship them back to Viet Nam. The Hong Kong government has tried that in a few cases, but the process was stopped by an international outcry, part of a humanitarian protest against forcing people back to a totalitarian country where they might be imprisoned or killed. That makes sense for those Vietnamese who are actually in political danger at home. But by now it is clear that not all the boat people are in fact political refugees. Some are, but others are being designated as "economic migrants," that is, simply people looking for a better life than the one they've known in poverty-stricken Viet Nam. No country is morally required to accept economic migrants. The problem is to determine who among these 50,000 refugees are truly political, and that is slow going. If you are claiming to be a refugee rather than a migrant, how do you prove that you are in political danger and thus deserving of asylum? And how does a government prove that you aren't? That is where the lawyers come in.

Nhat claims that he is a political refugee; he insists that the communists would kill him if he is sent back. For the time being, he and the rest of the refugees sit in camps like this one, waiting for someone, somewhere, to determine their fate. Some of them have given up hope and chosen to return home voluntarily. But for those who are still waiting, hoping for repatriation and the chance for a better life, Hong Kong's recent attempts to force them to return were a reminder of a continuing threat. Thus last week's demonstration.

Now Nhat produces a set of photographs from one of his boxes. Since taking pictures inside the camp is forbidden, I'm surprised to see these. I'm even more surprised to see that they are pictures of last week's demonstration.

The first picture shows a group of Vietnamese men marching down the central outside corridor, fists raised. Their large banner says "Down with Mandatory Repatriation" and then its equivalent in Vietnamese. The second picture is of little children, sitting on the concrete and holding dozens of identical small signs with "Freedom for Vietnamese Boat People" written diagonally across a photo of the Statue of Liberty.

Another presents a young Buddhist monk, white robe over dark slacks, walking with a group of teen-agers. They are holding a sign which says, among other things, "We shall overcome someday." This had apparently been a cross-cultural demonstration.

Nhat flips more pictures. A group of girls dances in a circle, arms outstretched and heads tilted left and right. Their bright orange skirts are accented by orange scarves over white blouses. This is a marvel of ingenuity: how do you take forbidden photographs, print posters, and create gorgeous costumes for dancing girls in a refugee camp?

Other pictures show more groups carrying more signs. Someone on a makeshift podium addresses a crowd of refugees, who sit cross-legged in the sun. Their faces are strained, angry, worried. A man climbs a guard tower to hoist the flag of the Vietnamese boat people. Laboriously, Nhat pantomimes how this man was pulled down by the guards, the flag taken away, destroyed. He makes punching and grabbing motions. When we are finished looking, Nhat hands all the pictures to me.

"Souvenir," he says, the word they use for 'gift'.

"No, Nhat, these are yours." I try to hand them back.

"No, souvenir. For you, for America."

He apparently thinks that these pictures will make some difference. They are going to convince the American government to convince the Hong Kong government to take in all the refugees. How could he think otherwise? He is a father and a member of this community. For him that translates into responsibilities.

We wait until Hieu appears with several bowls of food and hands them in to us. From the cardboard boxes, Nhat produces two red plastic spoons and several plastic cups. He hands a cup to me and, sweeping his hand almost grandly across the bowls, indicates that I should serve myself. From one container I spoon rice into my cup, and from another a few pieces of what appears to be over-cooked pork. A third container holds an unidentifiable vegetable, maybe a melon, floating in a dark-green liquid. This is meant to go on top of the rice and the pork. An oatmeal-like food in another bowl is too spicy for western tastes.

Not sure if Hieu will eat our left-overs or if she is eating with another family, I have been taking very small portions. As we eat, Nhat keeps urging me to take more. Over my attempts to pantomime that I am not very hungry in this heat, he spoons more, and then more, from each container into my cup. He is attentive to every move I make, the perfect Oriental host. When two pieces of rice fall from my spoon, he picks them delicately off the plywood and puts them on a paper plate. Then he hands me a napkin.

"This is really very good, Nhat. *Ka moon zit nee-ow*."

He bows slightly and brushes dark bangs back from his forehead, the host satisfied that the guest is comfortable.

"Daren my good friend," Nhat says. He has not yet been able to master my name. "I like... give food my friend."

"You are very kind. I enjoy having lunch with you."

In spite of speaking slowly and trying to use words that I think he may know, I have a feeling that not much of this simple diplomacy gets through. It does not seem to matter.

Nhat produces some oranges and begins to peel them, using a small knife with a blade that hooks at the end. He hands most of the pieces to me, keeping only a few for himself. In silence, we eat the soft pieces of fruit. Then he collects the peels, our utensils, and the left-over food. As he does, a thin man appears and speaks to him over my outstretched legs. He wears a wide-brimmed straw hat with a grey strap holding it under his chin, and his eyes look puffy, as though from a bad sleep. As they talk they both look at me, and I realize that I am being introduced. The man and I nod, smile, and shake hands. His hand is also thin, his face older than that of the average refugee.

"He --. "Nhat stops, searching for a word, and finally turns to his dictionary. The English word beside his finger is "mayor." When I show my understanding, Nhat waves his hand around the cell-block. I assume he is explaining that this man is somehow in charge of this area. At this, I smile again and try to express my appreciation for being visited by a dignitary. Their own nods and smiles assure me that my appreciation is being appreciated. The mayor says a few more words.

"He... happy know you," Nhat translates.

"I am very happy to know him. Please tell him for me, Nhat."

They exchange what is to be assumed are other gracious sentiments to fit the occasion. Then we all three nod and smile some more, and the mayor is gone.

Nhat indicates that he too will be leaving in a couple of minutes and that it is time for me to rest. After he has maneuvered around and over me to leave the hutch, I stretch out full length on the plywood. Nhat has left me with their pillow, which is a 1984 edition of the *Reader's Digest Almanac*. Each time I use this book, I wonder if its editors could ever have imagined that it would someday serve as a pillow in a Vietnamese refugee camp. That would take a lot of imagination.

Sleep is impossible. Above and below, and on both sides, voices and scurryings of neighboring families in their hutches are mixed with the noises of hundreds of other people in this cell-block. Babies cry and children shout, while adult voices are raised above the general din. The food has made me even hotter, so that beads of sweat run off my forehead and fall onto the almanac. The plywood trembles ominously from the movements around me.

Lunch with Nhat has become an every-other-day affair. On the other days I am the guest of Duong and her husband. Duong is another of those who are paid to accompany us to the playground. She is a tiny young refugee woman whose graceful movements and delicate features sometimes make me think I am looking at a Vietnamese doll. Early on, Duong decided that I would replace her father, since her real father is one of those who had given up hope and returned to Viet Nam. Now, when we walk together through the camp, she links her arm in mine and proudly shows me off to groups of refugees, especially other young women. "My fah-zer" -- she enunciates the word carefully amid their giggles, and her black eyes shine. She has taught me to say something in return, which I assume is "my daughter."

Duong picked up on the idea of lunch from Nhat, and now she enjoys her turn at hosting. Since she and Que live on the top level of their scaffolding, they have more headroom. They also have more space, because some other people who had lived there with them decided to return to Viet Nam. Duong and Que will probably lose the extra space soon.

On my first visit to eat with them, we climbed a wooden ladder to get past the first and second levels of hutches. I noticed immediately that the two of them have used their extra space to advantage. Besides the usual cardboard boxes, they had a child-sized stretcher resting on two other boxes and serving as a shelf for clothes and dishes. A clothesline holding underwear ran between the poles of the scaffolding. They had also decorated. A large poster of a beautiful lake and forest covered much of one wall, with "Finland" written at the bottom of it. Pictures, cut from magazines, were taped to other walls. One showed three women dancing, another was a group of Christmas candles. There was a trace of pathos in their hanging of pictures advertising clothing and cosmetics.

Que, wearing white slacks and a yellow tank top, greeted me with a wide smile on a thin face. With gestures, he introduced me to another young woman who I understood to be someone's sister. Duong immediately removed my shoes and left me to talk with Que, which was impossible. Slightly embarrassed, we smiled and nodded to each other several times. Finally, he resorted to the inevitable pictures, which I took to be of family and friends back in Viet Nam. Taking the example, I showed the pictures of my own three children, pulling each slowly from my wallet. Then, using my fingers, I explained all of their ages to him. It was slow going, on both sides, but a good way to fill the time.

Mercifully, Leah appeared. Leah is a Vietnamese-American who coordinates the volunteers, and she is bi-lingual. As Duong and the sister organized lunch, Leah led the conversation.

"Can you tell them that I am happy to be their guest for lunch?" I asked Leah.

She did, and they all smiled and talked to her about that for several minutes.

"They say they are glad that you are here, but they're also worried that you won't be comfortable. They know that they are poor and that you are rich and used to more comforts."

"Tell them I'm very comfortable. I think their home is very nice, and I'm not all that rich anyway. Tell them I've been in worse places than this. No, skip that last part."

Leah translated for me, and we all began to relax. I let Leah talk to them in their own language for a while, but it was obvious from their glances in my direction that the talk was about me. Having the American for lunch was a very big deal.

While we ate, they talked among themselves, and I talked with Leah.

"How many meals do they get every day?" I asked her.

"Three, but it's about the same thing all the time."

"At least these two don't have any kids to worry about."

"They probably will soon. There isn't much else to do around here. That's another problem. The numbers in the camp are growing even while the government's trying to figure what to do with them. Duong's already had one miscarriage."

"I just hate seeing all these people sitting around with nothing to do. All that young energy and all these lives, going to waste."

"In one of the larger camps the government's trying to organize some work for them," Leah said on a note of optimism. "Private industries could use them to do hand work. Maybe just part-time, but it would be something."

"But what they really want is to get out of here, into Hong Kong itself."

"No. Maybe some do, but mostly they want to get to the states or Canada. A few of them actually make it, if they have relatives there. Hong Kong is sort of like a funnel right now, and they're just stuck in it."

"How long before the situation will change?"

"Who knows?" Leah shrugged. "It could be a long time. The screening process is slow."

A shaven head, and then the torso of a young man appeared on the ladder, and in a moment we were joined by the young Buddhist monk of Nhat's pictures. He wore the same white robe, buttoned down the entire front and ending at his white sandals. Deep-set, serious eyes contrasted with another open smile and better teeth as we were introduced. The monk had something for Duong and Que, and as they huddled over it in one corner Leah and I continued our own conversation. The scaffolding shook with the weight of the six of us, and I imagined the whole structure collapsing like a triple-layer sandwich made of air.

"He seems awful young for a monk," I told Leah. "But most of these people seem young."

"I suppose when you get older you don't leave your own country and run the risks these people have. Not worth it. He is young, but there's some people around here who don't want him to get any older."

"What do you mean?"

"There's a contract out on him."

"You mean to kill him?"

"Uh huh."

"Why? He seems harmless enough."

"I really don't know. There's stuff goes on with these people that it's better to stay out of."

"Okay, I will. But monks need a temple, right? Is there a Buddhist temple of some kind around here?"

"Sure. There's always a temple. His is over by the offices, in a sort of trailer."

"Can I go to it?"

"Why not? I'll take you there."

She did, another day, and we sat with the young monk in his temple, in front of a small collection of incense sticks and statues and pots filled with flowers. We ate oranges and cookies as people came and went, and as usual I was treated like royalty. It is hard to accept that there are gangs making trouble in the camp, threats of violence, and actual violence. Behind the kindness and friendliness shown to me on all sides,

there is a tension here that is inevitable when 3000 people are forced to live in close quarters, hot, hungry, bored most of the time, and likely on the edge of despair over their futures.

Since that first lunch, there has almost been a competition between Duong and Nhat to have me as their guest. Diplomacy is difficult without a common language, but we have pretty well worked things out so that I eat with each family every other day.

Although the refugees always seem to have just enough food, some of us have begun bringing cookies and other things from Hong Kong to share with them. Sometimes we have some small purchases made for them during our evenings back in the city. Most of the refugees have very little money, but being locked on an island means they cannot spend even what little they have. So we end up doing little shopping chores for them.

I barely knew Duong when she first mimed shyly that she wanted me to buy her a pair of sandals. She took one off and showed me the size, a six, imprinted on the instep.

"Okay, I'll get them for you tonight," I told her with the usual gestures. But I was a bit surprised, and even slightly annoyed, at being asked for a gift by a near stranger.

The next day I handed Duong her sandals. She clapped her hands with almost childish delight at the ones I had chosen for the bright pink design of flowers woven into the cloth.

"How many?" she asked.

"How many what?"

"How many? How many?" she repeated. Then she pulled the equivalent of four dollars from a pocket of the pajamas she always wears.

"Oh, you mean how *much*."

"Yes, yes, how many?"

"No money, Duong. They're a gift. You know, like a -- souvenir."

She accepted my gift with evident hesitation, turning the money over in her tiny hand and looking around as though we were complicit in some improper transaction. Since then I have noticed how careful they are to give me the money first when they ask me to do some of their shopping.

Now I am lying once again on the plywood floor of Nhat's hutch, musing, as anyone in this situation would do, on the strange meanderings of life. How could a person, growing up in a middle-class suburb of a large American city, predict that he would one day be an honored guest in a refugee camp? I have just finished a simple meal in a hot, noisy, claustrophobic space.

I am sweating and thirsty and my ankle is throbbing. Still, this is the kind of moment and the kind of feeling that cannot be bought. No travel agency could possibly think of arranging this way of spending a summer month, or if it did, it would not be in business long. Experiences like these have to be arranged on one's own; they involve some luck and some connections. Right now the value of what I am starting to think of as alternative vacations is becoming clearer: the value is in the people and the situations you could never know otherwise.

The oddest thing is that we came here to help them in various ways, and I suppose that taking their children out to the playground is a help. Children need a chance to play, whatever the circumstances. But it seems somehow that the attempt to help has gotten turned around, and the kindness is all flowing toward us. For them the simple fact of our being here with them is the most important thing, not whether we do some shopping for them or provide some medical care or take their kids to a playground. We are on the other side of the situation, so it is hard to really understand that the most important thing for people who are poor and desperate is to know that someone they consider rich cares for them and wants to spend some time with them, to visit and become friends and to appreciate their experience, which is what friends do.

During one of our charade-like conversations, Nhat slowly wrote out a sentence on one of the pieces of paper we sometimes pass back and forth.

It said: "Daren does not despise the poor."

"No, Nhat," I said, "of course not," turning to hide the burning I felt suddenly in my eyes. It would be tempting to be suspicious of their acts of kindnesses if those acts were done in the context of wanting something. They rarely ask for anything. They have almost nothing, not even the promise of a better future, but they want to give.

Oriental philosophies make much of paradox and mystery: being arises from non-being, we gain by losing and lose by gaining, the further one travels the less one knows.

I am right now developing the first paradox of benevolence, as follows: desiring the good for other people, and acting on that desire, makes benevolence impossible. That is because the objects of benevolence return it with acts of their own, and after a while there is no malevolence against which good motives and actions can strive. This might be what led the Roman lawgiver Solon to say that no more good should be done than the people can bear. No, probably not.

Only the most wild-eyed idealist would accept that reasoning. Even if every egoist turned into an altruist as a result of benefitting from some kindness, which is itself unlikely, the natural world offers more than enough of tragedies and troubles and even simple inconveniences to keep the benevolent-minded busy. Altruism will survive.

In any case, people who go around *looking* for the chance to exercise their benevolence may be too fond of what is disagreeable. That is a human tendency that should not be nurtured, and people like that deserve whatever ridicule comes their way. The people I am working with here strike me as anything but saintly, for which I should one day light a candle of thanks over at the temple. It is not the case that their work here is tied to some otherworldly excess of good will any more than to some bloodless utilitarian calculation. If they have an ulterior motive, it could be nothing more than to combine some acts of benevolence with the chance for an unusual set of experiences.

A second paradox might be wrung from the refugees' own Buddhist doctrines. The First Noble Truth of Buddhism states that life is suffering. Since altruism aims to alleviate suffering, it follows that altruism is contradictory to life, a doctrine of negation. This begins to sound like Nietzsche, and again it is getting me nowhere. That paradox would be acceptable only if there were no further Noble Truths. But the second of these holds that suffering arises from craving.

It follows that we can damp down suffering to the extent that we can eliminate or reduce our cravings. That would not be good news for people who work in marketing or advertising or even many areas of manufacture. On the other hand, it can be a mantra for anyone who believes that freedom and personal happiness come from substituting being and doing for having.

There is more at stake than freedom and happiness. Altruism is optimistic. If you believe that the world is in a tug-of-war between good and evil and further that evil wins every game, there really is no good reason to act altruistically. The refugees must not believe that. They have gone to considerable trouble to get where they are now and they are accepting a pretty miserable existence because they are optimistic about their future. That explains why they are so eager to return acts of kindness with kindnesses of their own. They know the reciprocal nature of benevolence. In their own way they are teaching that to those of us who have come here to be with them. Because their own generosity is being practiced in difficult times, they deserve more credit for it. It carries an even greater aura of love.

So much for paradoxes.

Nhat's finest moment, certainly the incident that best defines the experience here, was the day my watch was stolen. That was the same day that I sprained my ankle.

We had lunch that day at his hutch, and because sweat was making my watch stick uncomfortably to my wrist, I took it off and set it on the plywood floor, near my leg. When I reached for it after lunch, it was gone.

After I checked and re-checked my pockets, we searched his little living space. Turned over the bowls and shook out clothes. Scoured the hutch below his and the floor of the cell-block on the thought that maybe it had fallen off the ledge when I moved my leg. Looking became a way to avoid the obvious: someone, probably some child among the many who come to see the American, had simply taken it.

The truth was that I did not even care. It was not an expensive watch, and there is probably no better place to have to buy a new watch than Hong Kong, where street vendors offer an endless variety. Before long, the idea of shopping for a new watch became rather appealing.

But it was impossible to mime all that to Nhat, who would not have accepted it in any case. Buying a replacement watch was not the point. I could tell from his face that he was absolutely mortified. A guest in his home had been robbed. By one of his own people. At one point, he tried to force his own cheap watch on me, but I pushed it away.

"I very... sad," he kept repeating. He does not know the words for angry or upset, but that was what he meant. It was made clear from the red that had spread across his face.

"No problem, Nhat, no problem," was the best I could offer.

"Yes! Pwoblem!"

We looked some more. Back through the clothes. In all the corners again, under the lower hutch. I said no problem, Nhat said pwoblem. And for him it was a very big problem. Nhat had lost face.

It was time to join the children for the afternoon trip to the playground, and I indicated that. Nhat gestured angrily for me to go. He was staying behind.

Down at the playground that afternoon, I was trying to organize some of the older children into a soccer game when somehow my foot slipped off the side of the ball and the ankle twisted inward under my full weight as I fell. A sickening pop came before the pain, and then I was rolling in the dirt. Within minutes the ankle was three times its normal size, and all five toes had turned a deep purple. Duong and I poured water on it and watched as the purple spread steadily along the sides and top of my foot.

It would have been better not to have walked the long dirt road back to the prison, but there really wasn't much choice. For part of the way, Duong used her shoulder as a cane for me, and I think she would have carried me if she had been able.

Leah said she would go inside and sign me out for the day. The grass outside the prison would be more comfortable and the truck that would take us down to the ferry would come soon. Sitting against a lone tree and trying to stay calm, I cleaned my fingernails and looked obsessively at the triple-sized ankle.

Before long, a voice rang from behind me. It was Nhat, waving and beckoning from inside the double cyclone fence. I got up carefully and hobbled over to my side of the fence. We were separated by two cyclone fences with ten feet of concrete between them. Nhat mimed a worried face as he pointed to my ankle.

"Yeah," I said, "I hurt it. Playing football."

"Yes. I... hear. Childrens talk me."

"It will be okay. No problem, Nhat."

We wrapped our fingers in our sections of the fence and stared at each other over the concrete no man's land. The low afternoon sun sheared off the guard tower, making it hard to see him clearly.

"Daren no come back Hei Ling Chau?" he called across.

"I don't know, Nhat. Maybe I can come back. Maybe not. My ankle may be broken. Then I will have to go home. I need to have an x-ray before I know."

Not much of that was getting through, I realized. Nhat does not know most of those words. In the silence that stretched between us I heard the rumble of the CSD truck as it pulled into the parking lot.

"You no come back Hei Ling Chau?"

The look was plaintive, oriental stoicism fled. Again we stared in silence.

Then Nhat's face brightened. In his right hand, held high as though by a magician for an audience, my watch appeared.

"Hey, you found my watch! Where was it?"

"Daren go playground, I go childrens. And I go -- "He made punching motions, downward. Then he pantomimed slapping little faces.

"No, no, Nhat!"

"Yes, yes!" He made more punching motions and slapped some more, dancing around almost comically on his side of the fence. "I go --. And childrens go --." He pantomimed a child reaching into a pocket and sheepishly pulling out the stolen watch. Proudly, he held it up for me to see once more.

"Now I go --." His slapping motions became even more violent.

"No, Nhat. Don't hit them anymore. That's enough. We have the watch now."

"Yes! I have Daren watch. I give Leah for... give you."

Then his look was triumphant. Nhat had saved face.

The clacking diesel motor of the truck was loud behind me, and I saw that most of the people heading for the ferry were already inside. Someone called my name. I had to shout to Nhat through the fence.

"I have to go now."

"No come back Hei Ling Chau?"

"Maybe I can. I don't know."

I turned toward the truck, then back to Nhat.

"No, NO! That's not right. I'll come back. One way or another. I'll see you."

The doctor in the Hong Kong hospital said it was a serious sprain, but the ankle was not broken. Probably better if I had broken it, she added not very helpfully. Her orders were to stay in the apartment in Hong Kong for at least three days, keeping the ankle elevated. I took pain-killers and thought about life out at Hei Ling Chau, missing them all and regretting the lost time with them. Leah called to report that practically everyone in the camp was worried. Poor fah-zer, I could hear Duong saying.

On the fourth day I limped back into the detention center and was surrounded by smiling refugees. Duong flung herself into my arms, and little children pulled me down onto the concrete with total disregard for my throbbing ankle. Nhat tried to look nonchalant.

Now time is running out. This is one of the last times I will have lunch with the refugees. They have been asking me about that, making airplane motions with their arms, but I have been deliberately vague about the date of my departure, trying to hide from it myself as much as from them. Leaving is the very last thing I want to think about right now; I am just settling into solidarity.

All there is to do now is lie here until Nhat returns, using the chance to freeze the sounds and other sensations of this place into a solid mass of memory. But how can I possibly explain to people back home what it is like to lie here on this plywood, wrapped in the kind of love and caring these people have been showing? Who could understand?

For that matter, how can I know what it is like to be in their situation, even after all these experiences with them? A month with them, or even a year, cannot get me inside their emotions.

From certain places in the prison, and from the road we use to walk down to the playground, they can see a part of Hong Kong in the distance, a hazy dark outline over the blue water. So close. What must that feel like?

Each evening I ride the little ferry to the place they tried to get to, glad to return to a shower, a cold beer, and a soft bed in an air-conditioned apartment. Ironically, it is a gorgeous apartment, a loan from a generous American friend. It is all marble and brass and luxury bathrooms and doormen and tennis courts and swimming pools and dizzying views.

If I really wanted to come unglued I would think hard on having lunch here in Nhat's hutch and then spending my evening in such luxury. Instead I think of a line from Marcus Aurelius: "Even in a palace, it's possible to live well."

While I sit by the pool and drink that cold beer, they will lie on their plywood and dream of the lives they want to create. Vague dreams. They can have little idea of the commercial bustle and sounds of Hong Kong, the skyscrapers and lights, the smells of expensive restaurants. How can they imagine America?

In a few days, I will board an airplane. Fourteen hours later, I will enter their promised land with little more than a flip of my passport. It will be good to get home to a place most of them will never see.

What can I know of their days at sea in an open boat? Water slaps wood inches below the gunwales, threatening to swamp the small boats. Women hold squirming children and men watch anxiously for land. Storms may be on the horizon, fresh water is running low, pirates are waiting for their next victims. Are these people this century's equivalent of our own Mayflower pilgrims, fleeing over dangerous waters, looking for that elusive better life? History plays tricks. For our pilgrims, the reward was a vast continent of nearly untouched resources. For these people, it is a refugee camp.

Now Nhat re-appears outside the hutch, Hieu and their baby with him. As she scrambles into the hutch, he hands the baby in to me. The child's face is smeared with a white cream for heat rash, but he's chubby and he wiggles a little in my arms.

Hieu is holding up a tiny pair of shoes I bought last week for their baby and making gestures of appreciation. That reminds Nhat of some further shopping he wants me to do. He points to the child's torn shirt and hands me some money.

"Okay, but I'm not good at sizes." I pantomime my concern about getting the right size.

Ever resourceful, Nhat opens his fingers as wide as they will go, places his thumb below the baby's chin, and shows me that his little finger is extended nearly to the child's waist. I do the same, and my larger hand marks out the correct size. He nods encouragingly.

"I got it. I'll look for his shirt this evening."

I force the money back into his hand. The shirt will make a good going-away present. But it is difficult to imagine how we will ever manage to say good-bye. It is not helpful to think about leaving when I am only now arriving.

Chapter Five

We need to go back for a moment, before we can go forward.

It was several years before all this happened when I had said that it might be better to find someone I could work with on a one-to-one basis. At the time, I was not sure what that even meant, since the idea had been little more than a line tossed off to end a conversation. It became one of those ideas, like a promise made long ago or a plan hatched without being fully awake, that only occasionally work their way back to a conscious level. Probably that was just as well. It may be that I was thinking of some young person I could help with his or her education, or maybe even an older one, someone who had for whatever reasons missed the fast train of American life and was still poking along on the local.

Still, I had looked now and then and I probably did some projecting, but it would have taken considerable imagination to create someone like Ken. Though he fit my rough outline, I could hardly have predicted that anyone could move so quickly from being helped to helping so many others. Here it would be easy to fall back on that old cliché, much exaggerated, that the teacher learns more from his student than he teaches. It was not that: we learned different things from each other. For my part, I was re-examining my doubts about the value of direct activism.

It is reasonable now to wonder if he even needed much help at all. He was simply a born activist. Unlike, say, the owner of a new car who gingerly tests the pedals and adjusts the mirrors and twists the steering wheel, Ken just started driving, full throttle. There were absolutely no doubts about what he wanted to accomplish and no change in the direction.

If it was hard to keep a count of Ken's growing number of contacts and supporters, it was even harder to keep track of his activities. No one could have guessed that one person, starting with literally nothing, could do so much for the city's endangered youth in a few years' time. He was becoming, I told him, a one-man challenge to the statistics on recidivism. Or he was just becoming.

Contacts with community leaders and agencies are vital to any attempt at community improvement, as Ken knew, but he also knew that he needed other voices than his own. That is what he was creating through the hundreds of lectures and workshops. Talking and listening, he created his message and then stirred it into a blend of his own experiences and the concerns of his youthful audiences. Young people, when they sense that someone is genuine, will speak with no inhibitions. He and his youth became mirrors for each other.

Some of what they discussed was not new. They talked about schools that would include mechanisms for dealing with anti-social behavior, school patrols for hall monitoring, crowd control and weapons detection. They wanted meaningful jobs and apprenticeships for dropouts, rehabilitation programs for youthful offenders, community policing to create safer neighborhoods, alternatives to incarceration, recreational activities for after-school hours, and anti-drug campaigns that would actually speak to them. Like activists throughout modern history, they found it easy to make wish lists but harder to be heard outside their own little groups.

Altogether, it would come to over 600 presentations in four years, a schedule that can exhaust one even with the thought of it. He was not appearing only before groups of young people. Still the keeper of records, he showed me a file of thank-you letters -- from colleges and universities as well as high schools, from television and radio stations, from community groups and psychiatric facilities and government agencies, from directors of foundations and corporate executives and city council members. Support letters came from congressional representatives, state senators and members of the state assembly, teachers, police officers, academics. I thought back on a very different file he had shown me on the night we first met.

He loaned me a video of his reading of Martin Luther King's "I Have a Dream" speech, which he delivered to a high school audience in a way that linked his personal and local dream to King's larger one. "You must have the confidence to look inside yourself for your dreams and goals," he told the students when he finished the reading. "Never let anyone belittle your dreams. I don't care who it is. For not to have a dream is just to exist."

Over time, Ken discovered that community activism is big business. He became aware of the millions of dollars that had already been committed to youth projects and of how much of that money disappeared into the hands of complacent bureaucracies. Money that actually produced useful programs, he complained to me, was being controlled by politicians and government agencies, not by the youth and the parents who were most affected. It was a quick education in the paradoxical realities of idealism.

Mainly he learned that grants and programs are only marginally effective because they are impersonal. What was needed was someone who could take both the rhetoric and the action and give it personhood. Without bothering to read the right books, he found that leadership is more than organizational skills and political acumen; it is that dedication to a cause that makes one committed individual into the real life, real-time embodiment of what needs to be done, or is being done. Ken became that embodiment, with a connectedness that would have been the envy of a Zen master. What especially interested me was that his ability to remain focused and organized for a good cause was in direct contrast to the bungling of his crimes.

Eventually, as these things go, he saw the need for a recognized structure and community legitimacy. He established his own organization, named himself executive director, and put those of us who were his earliest and strongest supporters on the board of directors. We named it Voice of the Future; its mission would be to develop and implement programs providing constructive activities serving the common welfare of the city's youth.

When our lawyer arranged it so that contributions to the organization were tax-deductible, funding became more reliable -- from corporations, foundations, banks, private donors, government agencies. The amounts were teasingly small, the normal indications of a wait-and-see attitude.

Board meetings were spent mostly on finances and ideas for programs. My notes from one of them are fairly typical.

K: "We're late in the process of developing a proposal for our "Do the Right Thing" programs.

J: "Okay, so let's start it as a pilot project."

K: "I've got a bank interested, maybe two of them. And they like the Moviethon idea, too. Can we purchase a large-screen TV?"

A: "Probably not, Ken."

K: "What about the Drug Free Dance? We just got $3000, maybe we can use part of that for it. I've already got the high school, they're waiting for us to decide."

A: "Okay then."

K: "Oh, almost forgot. I met with those state senators, and they listened, they support what we're doing. They gave me an application for state funding, a, uh, a September 1 deadline."

D. "So, what's our balance now?"

K: "$2,097. 29. Don't forget we've got over $1600 in in-kind donations for Youth Day."

A: "But we've got to get a lot more than that in real dollars, Ken; it's only two months away."

J: "And we've got to get Ken some kind of salary."

K: "Yeah, those bus fares are killing me, and the telephone bills. I've got to get some office equipment."

A: "Look, we can't afford a fax machine, along with the computer. Could we get a refurbished computer somewhere?

J: "Those really aren't all that reliable. Anyway, we'll have to wait on that until all the current bills are paid."

K: "Can I have a board decision by the end of the month?"

J: "Let's get back to talking about a stipend. How much can we give Ken, right now?"

D: "We'll make it $75 a week, okay Ken?"

K: "Yeah, okay. I know you guys think I always want to spend more money than we have, but I'll get the money somewhere. Right now it's more important to keep the momentum, reach more kids."

When it came to the fiscal battles, I generally took his side. Why not, since he always *did* get the money somewhere? The best thing was to watch him doing exactly what he had said he would do, changing his life by changing the lives of others. He was choosing the excitement of activism and politics over the thrill of crime and drugs.

No mentor ever had it so good.

We agreed that saving the world was the best adventure of all.

"But you're just saving this city, and only the kids at that," I told him. "A lot of us think we can save the whole world."

"You're not serious."

"No. That's just a running joke with some of us. But that reminds me -- there's something I want you to think about."

"What?"

"Not to take things too seriously. Yourself included."

"This is serious stuff, I told you before."

"I know. But there's always room for some laughter. Especially at your own expense. It's maybe a good way to... yeah, not just to keep things in perspective, but also to preserve a little bit of dignity when things aren't otherwise too, umm, ennobling, shall we say?"

"I'm not following."

"I'll tell you the story of one time when I ran into a burning building, to save whoever needed saving in there."

"You didn't."

"Yeah, I did. Well, sort of."

"What does that mean?"

"What happened was, I was in my car – this was back when I was in college, and I was in a neighborhood near downtown, mostly old houses – when all of a sudden I saw smoke and flames above the roof of one of the places. So I got out of the car and ran up the hill. Like a lot of them, this house had a wide porch across the front, and I can remember jumping up a couple of steps onto the porch and grabbing the front door handle."

"Were you scared?"

"You know, people usually say that things like that happen so fast that you don't really think about getting scared. And that's the way it was. But I remember, just as I was turning the door knob, I got a picture in my mind of some flaming beam falling on my head as I went in."

"And?"

"A couple of funny things happened. First, it was odd that the door wasn't locked, even though this was maybe 10:00 pm, or later. So I was surprised that it came open. But it did, and I stepped into a little foyer. It took a second to realize that there wasn't any falling beam, and then I realized that there wasn't any smoke, or flames. Instead, just then a family came flying down the stairs – mother, father, and a couple of kids. They were Oriental, I remember, all of them in their pajamas, and they all looked pretty scared."

I paused for effect.

"So what did you do?"

"That was the next funny thing. I just ended up holding the door open as they all tumbled down the last stairs and ran out, without even looking at me. They must at least have wondered why some stranger was standing there holding the door. At that point I was beginning to feel a little stupid, or useless anyway, but then I noticed some pegs on the left wall, with coats hanging on them. So I grabbed every coat, sort of scooped them up in my arms, and took them outside. The family was out on the sidewalk, looking back at the house, so I put the coats on them and then I took off. By that point the fire trucks were coming anyway."

"So was the house on fire?"

"No, that's the joke. It turned out that there was an alley behind those houses, with a row of garages, and that's what was on fire. The flames were high enough to make you think the house was burning."

"But the family must have thought it was. And the fire department too."

"Yeah, that made me feel a little less foolish."

"Still, you *thought* you were saving them. Did they say anything to you?"

"I think I left too fast for that. I probably was seeing a headline: "Stranger saves armload of coats, rides away like the Lone Ranger."

Ken laughed.

"So you get my point, I hope. I've met people and groups in a few countries that take their work way too seriously, like they think they really *are* saving the world. Righteous and self-important. If that's actually how they think, they should save themselves first, and then save other people a lot of trouble, by just staying home instead. Save money too. People who can't laugh some, even at serious stuff, make me nervous."

"Why nervous?"

"Okay, maybe not nervous, but they're just hard to like. Life can be tough, even tragic sometimes. We have to decide if we're going to cry about it or laugh at least some of the time while we're trying to fix the few things we can."

We were walking along the Erie Canal trail on a summer evening, and the topic had actually been women. Trouble with some woman in his life, or was it in mine? Probably both, with neither of us offering useful advice.

Slightly unnerved, joggers and bikers swerved around us as we poked each other in the shoulder or chest and flung our arms in the air to exaggerate our frustrations, shouting and laughing much more at ourselves than at women, repeating the eternal complaints of men.

Eventually we got back to talking about struggles where we had better odds.

"A kid came up to me the other day," he said, "and told me he hardly knew me from the stories I'd been telling them. But he understood. These kids I'm with every day, it's like they sense they don't have a chance, not the same chance anyway. Like there's a conspiracy against them."

"I've never liked conspiracy theories," I said. "Partly because I associate them with people who read tabloids, but also because most of the people we might think are conspiring are too stupid to create a real live conspiracy. Let's leave conspiracies to the political novels. And even if there were a real conspiracy, somebody would shoot off his mouth sooner or later, if nothing else to make some money. So forget about conspiracies. It's more like some people just arrange things the way they want them. And that leaves other people out, and wondering, whether it's actually planned or not."

Ken didn't agree, and I wasn't surprised. "Anyway," he said then, "you can joke about saving the world, but what do you really want?"

"What do I want? That's easy. I remember once getting a letter from a friend of mine. I was going off on some trip or another, I don't remember where, but this was sort of a bon voyage, good luck letter. Then she wrote one thing that really got my attention. She said 'I hope you find what you're looking for. 'That was a better line than she knew, because it got me thinking 'Uh huh, and what exactly is that?' The answer sort of popped out at me."

"What?"

"Justice. And when I say that word, it always has 'social' in front of it, even though there are other kinds of justice. And social mostly means economic for me."

"Yes! That's it exactly. Did you tell her that?"

"No."

"Well, you should have."

"It didn't matter, that I told her or not. Could be I never even saw her after that. But it was one of those -- what can I call it? A great revelation of the obvious. It's not that we don't spend a fair amount of time in philosophy classes talking about justice, since philosophers have been discussing it and trying to define it since Plato. I guess I'm at the point where I'm more interested in seeing it. Like seeing it in people's actions and behaviors toward each other. And you know what? I do find justice, more often than you might think, even if it's only little examples and it doesn't always last."

That must have sounded both self-serving and way too dramatic: Antisthenes the cynic and Plato's *Republic* and John Rawls rolled into one. I don't think Ken noticed.

"I've been on both sides, lots," he said after a minute. "If you've been on both sides you can feel it a lot more. That's why I know how the kids feel."

"A philosopher named Hume said that the demands of justice assert themselves after a little reflection. Sorry to put it so formally. He could have said 'after a little experience.' 'A nine-year old who has been treated unfairly understands easily enough what justice is. You already got the point. The main thing is that you're doing something about it."

"Sometimes I think I'm not doing enough."

"I'm not sure what 'enough' means. Whatever you do is some help obviously, but in the end it's your own sense of working for justice that counts."

"I want to see some results."

"You're seeing results. Anyway, look at yourself for results. Though that makes the whole thing sound a little self-centered. In a paradoxical way."

"What do you mean?"

"I've thought about this a lot, and there's one thing that would really bother me and I think it would bother other people too -- to be lying on your deathbed, with a little time left to think back over your life, and to think that what you mostly did was live for yourself. That seems to be okay for a lot of people, but it's not enough for others. When I said self-centered I just meant that living some of the time for others means also living in the way that is best for you yourself. But that is a personal thing and we definitely shouldn't be telling other people how to live their lives."

"I need it, for sure. Sometimes it's like being driven."

"I don't especially like the idea of being driven, because it sounds like you aren't choosing.

"I *am* choosing."

"That's a bigger problem than you think. Whether a person chooses a certain kind of life or course of action is a major question, one my philosophy students like to argue about. It's usually called the free will problem. Do we make really free choices? Or are the choices more like reactions to the world as it comes to us, reactions that are determined by everything that's happened before, and especially by what's happened in our childhoods?"

"I like the free will side better. Nobody wants to think of being pulled around like -- like a dog on a leash."

"Most of my students take the side of free will too. The problem is that a lot of modern science tends toward the determinist side. But I don't think it has to be totally one or the other. It's more likely that we have fewer choices than we like to think. Our early environments, which we surely don't choose, have a tremendous influence on us. Our physical make-up, our genetic inheritance -- we don't choose those either."

"Physical make-up is different from environment."

"Sure, but it comes to the same point about free will. Would anybody choose an environment that includes family problems, crime, or poverty? Those are a matter of bad luck. The better things about us are a matter of good luck. That's generally true even if we like to *think* we are making the choices that bring us better lives. It's fine to think that's the case, and sometimes I do too. But we can't ignore the effects on us of factors we don't choose. That would be dishonest and self-serving. It's interesting how we talk about freely creating our successes, but usually come up with some excuse for our failures."

"I've done that."

"Haven't we all. That's your philosophy lesson for the evening."

Thinking about it later, it came to me that it would be not only dishonest but also inconsistent to say that Ken was choosing to change his life during those years, doing so out of extraordinary acts of free will, and then to say that his earlier criminal years were determined by a bad childhood. That is having it both ways.

But those years *were* caused by his early environment. If that is the case, what were the causes of his change before we got together and in the first months after that? Lots of things and lots of people, and maybe there was some free choice going on there as well as some chance and good luck.

It helps to have a Socrates, even for a short time. He is the eternal father-figure, who can be more valuable because he is not the father. He is the one to be admired, idolized, someone to guide the younger person, to teach him to question and even to make some progress toward knowing himself in the Socratic sense of right living. Ken's was an older cellmate.

"A professor," he told me. "And well off. He had really intriguing grey eyes and sort of grey-blond hair that he kept in a brush-cut."

"What was he in for?"

"He got fifteen years to life for attempted murder, he told me, because he strangled a guy in a bar fight. It turned out the guy wasn't dead, but it didn't help that his brother was the local DA. Anyway, he wrote a lot of fiction and he got me interested. I'd write something and give it to him and he'd give it back all marked up. He was the smartest person I ever met."

"How so?"

"It just seemed like he knew everything and had read everything. We had a dictionary and we made up a game. I would open it anywhere, any page, and look for a word that was totally unknown, some big weird-looking word. Then he would tell me what it meant. Every time. It was absolutely amazing. That's how I want to be."

"You're making me think of a guy I knew back in college. His name was Al, I remember, and I met him through my sister. He was pretty old, or at least it seemed like it then, and I guess he had been a gardener because he lived in an old run-down house sort of off the main road, and the place had gardening tools hanging on the walls. It was just one room with a lot of creaky furniture, everything messy and dirty, ash trays always full and coffee cups that hadn't been washed. That was one of the reasons we liked to go there."

"What did you do?"

"A few of us would just turn up in the evening. You didn't need to call and he probably didn't have a phone anyway. We'd just go in and sit down and start talking about books and ideas."

"Did he have a lot of books?"

"He didn't have a lot of anything. I don't think he was even all that well read, but somehow – at least for me at the time – he seemed to know a lot. Mostly he was just interested in talking with young people, I think. Like you're doing."

"What happened to him?"

"I don't remember for sure. Somebody told me he died, of cancer I think. It was a long time ago."

"That professor I was talking about, he got me interested in reading too. I started spending a lot of time in the prison library."

Unlike other inmates, Ken had no interest in reading law books there. The search was for self-improvement rather than legal loopholes. His reading steadily opened up a new world of impressive-sounding discourse, a world of strange words that, once mastered, had an aura of respectability and the possibility of personal empowerment in a place where power had normally very little to do with words.

Reading led to writing, eventually to starting on his first novel. Like many first novels, it took the form of a thinly-disguised biography. He gave it to me after one of our first meetings. As I might have expected, it was pretty much in the rough without the benefit of being a diamond. Still, there was a definite feel for compelling details and a force in the writing that paralleled his speaking style. Authenticity is the result of personal experience meeting up with truth and honesty and good values. In that respect the writing held promise.

Creative writing can be a release of intellectual and emotional energy as well as a way to pass the time. Whatever may have been lacking in Ken's early life, energy was not on the list. It is hard to appreciate how those years spent in small cells had restrained his young spirit more than they confined his body. For some people, the effects of imprisonment can be positive.

Famous political prisoners, among them Gandhi, have referred to their years in prison as among their better times. They can offer an opportunity to turn inward, to achieve some balance and serenity, and to allow for spiritual insights that are impossible in the outside world. It is the monastery effect, usually without the religion.

That would hardly have been the case for Ken, at least in the earlier jail periods. He was capable, like all inmates, of passing time in a numb mindlessness, but there were also times when his extraordinary energy would fairly pound against the sides of the concrete boxes. He was too young to understand what Gandhi and others had experienced in their own years of confinement. And once released, he would turn his energies into more anti-social activities on the streets of the city.

Then, sometime before we met, he claims to have undergone what he called a spiritual awakening. I do not know exactly how that happened, and there is nothing in my notes to indicate that he ever told me much about it. "Spiritual" might not even be the right word, at least not in a religious sense. He seemed to have meant it as a call to think of others rather than just of himself, in the way we would talk about later. If that was the case, he was putting himself in better company for a change.

In the years before we met, and during those years when we worked together, I had many opportunities to work with other people who were doing extraordinary things, stepping outside the normal values and practices of their society. I met them in homeless shelters, in jails and refugee camps, connected with them through feeding programs, clinics and hospices. I also sat with them on boards and worked with them, sometimes literally, on the ground. I noticed how they rarely talked about their motivations, because they were more interested in the work at hand. If they had been asked why they were doing what they were doing, they would probably say something polite while thinking that if you have to ask, you won't understand the answer anyway.

The common thread that joined these people was that they were being hopeful rather than despairing, optimistic rather than cynical. That was not a matter of naïve idealism or pious self-denial. It seemed rather to be an understanding that service to others is valuable for more than simply its role in alleviating one kind of suffering or another. It is one of the best ways to achieve that complete, harmonious self that everyone wants. If they had ever suffered from anxiety, depression, despair, boredom, or the hundreds of other afflictions that the self-help books claim to remedy, they had learned somewhere that one remedy for many of these problems is simple: do something of value for someone else. We probably should dump most of the self-help books and write some help-others books instead.

The really interesting discovery was that these people were having a good time, even if not always in a good place and even if their idea of what makes for a good time might be considered pretty eccentric by most standards. The ones I related to best were not the sanctimonious and pompous do-gooders, another category entirely. Unlike the do-gooders, they did not give off the impression that they were sacrificing their lives or undergoing terrible hardships for the sake of suffering humanity. Many of them were doing without some of the things that most people consider necessary, like hot showers and three meals a day, and some of them had committed not a portion, but the whole of their lives to their work. For them, that was not a sacrifice of anything more important. It was the core of their personal fulfillment. It was their answer to how best to live.

The reason I have taken the time here to comment on people of this sort is that in many ways Ken was the best of them. Most of what has been said here applies to him, except that he brought so much more intensity, a kind of gargantuan appetite, to his work. That difference would contribute to his undoing.

Did Ken and I talk about all this? Yes, lots of times and in various ways. The conversations were not always as clear-sighted and linear as the ones written out here might suggest. The reader needs to allow for some editing, for style even if not for content.

Enter Alicia, his six-year old niece. The daughter of his addicted sister, she was living in a parental limbo worse than that of many of the older youth he was helping. Ken decided to step in. One night he told me he about his plans to go to court, for legal custody.

"Don't do it," I told him flatly.

"I've got to, Uncle Derek. She can't go on living without a real home. You don't know what it's like for her. And I can't go on working with other kids when one of my own relatives needs me."

"How about a foster home?"

"I won't do that to her. She's one of the family."

"So isn't there anybody else in the family that can take her? What about your father?"

"He's too old to be caring for a little child. Anyway, he's got his hands full with his own kids. We're a screwed-up family, you know that."

"Do you have any idea what it's like to care for a little kid? It's 24 hours a day. You're running yourself down as it is. You say so yourself."

"I don't care. I've got to do this."

In spite of everything, he did. He managed as best he could to feed and clothe her, get her off to school in the morning before beginning another of his long days, see to it that someone in the family, or some friend, took care of her when he could not.

But he *was* running himself down, and sometimes even he admitted it. That is why I would try sometimes to get him away, even if it was not very far. We liked walking around the kidney-shaped city reservoir, a body of water surrounded by a fence of four-cornered metal bars that end in sharp points more than six feet off the ground. The macadam walkway is almost a mile long, offering views of a small forest to the east and of the city, looking calm and almost stately, a mile to the northwest. Normally we walked quickly, but I recall an evening when we actually stopped to watch the fountain in the middle, its white spray picking up hints of color from the low rays of the sun.

The shadows of the fence stakes fell across our feet in long diagonals, and it is to be hoped that the attentive reader of this part of the description will not fail to notice the prison symbolism. As he looked through those bars, Ken must have made the connection. For a quiet minute we watched the fountain, its sound barely to be heard in the distance. A few small birds circled over the water near it.

"You know what nobody really knows about this? Nobody knows how hard it is. It never stops." He was tired that night, and discouraged about something. "Man, selling drugs was hard work too, but not this hard."

"It must have paid a lot better, too."

"Yeah, money wasn't a problem then. Now it's always a problem."

Ken liked to spend money, especially on clothes and gadgets, but I knew that when he came to like himself more he would like external things less. In this case he was referring not to personal spending but to the increasing need for funds for the organization.

"Try to forget about the money. Seems like you always get it somehow, and there's more coming with every success you have."

"You know what makes me happy?"

"No."

"That I don't have to go to jail anymore."

"Let's not even think about that."

"I'll be even happier when the papers quit referring to me as an ex-con. 'Ex-con turned community activist," over and over. How about just 'community activist'?"

"It makes for better news stories, more dramatic, you know that. People who do the news have to make a living too. But I know what you mean. There's a couple of expressions that annoy me too, like 'liberal guilt'. What's that supposed to mean, liberal guilt? I don't feel guilty about anything. That's just some conservatives' way of transferring their own guilt, you know, trying to deflect it when they don't want to do something that might help people other than themselves."

"You don't like conservatives, do you?"

"It's not exactly that. Actually, I like the idea of conservatism when it comes to things like preserving traditions, like religious or cultural ones. Or core values and virtues that ought to be kept."

"Like what?"

"How much time do you have? One of my courses spends weeks on matters of value and virtue. Classical philosophy made a big deal out of virtues like wisdom and justice and temperance. Let's keep it simple. The values we ought to be talking about in these times – conserving them if you want to use that word – are things like personal integrity, dignity and decency, peace of mind, regard for others. Those would go a long way in a culture that can sometimes look pretty vulgar and shallow and self-indulgent."

"So, just those?"

"No, there's more, including my favorite virtues."

I made him wait, thinking that might give him time to wonder about what his own virtues were. It seemed that evening as though he was in a thoughtful mood, which was a bit of a change. So I said nothing as we walked again. Five more steps, ten.

"Well?"

"Courage and compassion. Confucius had those on his list too, but he added wisdom, and usually I'm not sure how far we can get with developing that one. The first two cover enough ground. Put them together and you really will change the world and bring about some justice too. The problem I mainly have with conservatives is that the hard core ones are more frightened than courageous and they certainly aren't very compassionate. I just don't like conservatism when it means trying to conserve your own advantages and privileges when it's at the cost of other people's chances for just living a decent life. Don't forget that it has always been conservatives that oppose programs like social security and unemployment benefits and even better education or health care. They opposed the Civil Rights Act and voting rights for women and just about anything you can think of that might help average people."

"Amen."

I was on a role, ranting and enjoying it. "If you look behind all this right-wing shouting and flag-waving, that's what's really going on. They're afraid of change and angry even at the idea of change because they think they might lose something. So they throw around labels like "liberal" as though that will protect them or explain everything. Anyway, that's an old problem, mindless labeling on both sides. It's hurtful, not helpful."

"I'll tell you something really hurtful. I was talking to the Chamber of Commerce last week. A really good talk. A few people were even crying at the end, and I got a standing ovation. Afterwards -- you know how stuff sometimes gets back to you -- a guy from city hall said 'Once a con, always a con.' That really hurt."

"Forget it. He was probably jealous, some second-level bureaucrat who thinks he just wasted his time listening to a little truth."

"I know who said it, and it wasn't some second-level guy."

"It doesn't matter, unless you let it."

"On the other hand, I've been telling you, there's people saying I should run for city council, or maybe at least the school board."

"I don't see why not, at least when the time is right."

"But first I need to get past that ex-con stuff. I'm thinking about writing to the governor for a pardon. So I could wipe the record clean."

"You've got lots of people who would help you with that. I would."

"Maybe I can even *be* governor someday!"

"You can be whatever you want. I'm always telling you that."

"Just seems like I could do a lot more in politics. But then I don't know."

"At first you probably *could* do a lot more. But I'll tell you what you better not do. You better not start making compromises and forgetting about the kids. You can get pulled into the system real quick, and then you get hung up on your own sense of power. Most of our politicians on any level want to hang on to their power more than anything else, that's obvious. In the end, it's ego and privilege and power. I can see you someday, a fat politician riding around in a big car and smoking cigars! You do that, and you know what I'm gonna do?"

"What?"

"I'll hunt you down and kill you."

"Don't even *say* that. You saw the paper the other day, about the guy shot on Brown Street?"

"Uh huh."

"I used to know the guy. I talked to his sister the day after he was shot. That's what I'm trying to stop, but it just keeps happening."

"Some people think it's getting worse. The thing you don't know, can't ever know, is how many killings *didn't* happen, or won't happen, because of what you're doing with those kids. There's no way to know that. But you do know you're having an effect on some kids, no, a lot of them."

"Man, that's what they keep telling me. But I wish I could be sure."

"I'm sure."

"That's easy for *you* to say."

"Right. You're the one out front. I just get behind and push some. That way, you get all the frustration. And also all that good coverage in the papers. A glory hound, that's what you are."

"I can skip the glory if I could see some results."

And so it went: ever more challenges, more responsibilities, more meetings, lectures, programs. Now his prison was his work, but this one was chosen. Even with all the frustration and exhaustion, he was putting it together and loving it. It was his turning time.

The best thing of all was Youth Day.

BUILDING BLOCKS

The universal cause is like a winter torrent: it carries everything along with it. But how worthless are all those poor people who are engaged in matters political, and as they suppose, are playing the philosopher! All drivelers. Well, then, man, set yourself in motion, if it is in your power, and do not look about you to see if anyone is watching; nor yet expect Plato's Republic, but be content if the smallest thing goes on well, and consider such an event to be no small matter.

-- Marcus Aurelius

Architecture aims at eternity.

-- Sir Christopher Wren

Up on the scaffolding one more time. Left knee first, get a handhold on the inside plank, swing up the right knee.

It is not much by way of scaffolding, just two low sawhorses holding two long, sun-bleached planks that sag unevenly and creak as I move along them. This hardly qualifies as high rise work, since I am only a little more than two feet above the ground.

The problem is to keep everything from falling off. Anna just brought fourteen more of the orange-clay building blocks, stacking them high at one end of the planks. Balancing them at the other end are the mortar tub she keeps filled for me, some bricks, the string, the trowel and the plumb. There is also a plastic container of water to freshen up the mortar as it dries out in the bright sun. That is really too much to have to work around, and it seems like something is always getting knocked off and then I have to climb down again.

Two more corners were set in place before lunch. Now their mortar has dried enough to allow for stretching the guide-string from one corner, along the whole length of the wall, to the other corner. Securing the string under several of the bricks, I make sure it is running exactly along the outside of the corner block. An eighth of an inch away. Now it can be pulled taut on the far corner and held down there with some other blocks. Ready.

This house will not be much by standards at home, but it is going to be put together correctly. Getting it right has been just short of an obsession for the past several weeks: making sure that the corners rise up straight from the ground, seeing to it that the amount of mortar between the blocks remains the same, watching that the string doesn't sag or get edged out of position.

One morning I even tore down and rebuilt a section of low wall that a neighbor had built. He meant well, but he did a terrible job, the wall sagging in the middle and canting outward when he had finished. It didn't just look bad; it would have been structurally weak, dangerous. It could also have created a problem in getting the rest of the wall straight above it.

This search for perfection is not really all that important, at least not by comparison. On the way home through the barrio in the low sun of a Brazilian afternoon, I can see that many of the little houses aren't built as well as Anna's will be. But they stand. Most of them do, anyway. Strong winds have knocked walls down now and then, but it will not happen here. Still, it is not just sturdiness that is wanted. It has become something of a point of honor for all of us that Anna's house be as well-made as possible in every way. She deserves something nice.

The house will have five little rooms, two of them bedrooms just large enough for a bed and maybe a chair. The kitchen and living room will be a little larger, and a small bathroom will be a big improvement over the outhouse they use now. They will not be able to afford plumbing for a time, but the little bathroom will be ready for it when they can. I brought its walls up to the final, eleventh row of blocks just before lunch.

It is even going to be an attractive house, with a small front porch set in to break up the front lines, and another, smaller alcove in the back. Ramiro, Anna's teen-age son, designed it, and he obviously wanted something a little different from all the other houses on their street. The government has given these families enough blocks and mortar to build a very basic house. Each is about 12 by 20 feet, though Anna's will be larger than that. Most of them are rectangular, with a simple shed roof sloping either to the left or to the right. "Half-waters," they are called, because the rainwater runs off to one side only. Some of the more affluent settlers in this barrio have, over time, added the other half, and now have twice the space along with a balanced roof. Maybe those houses are called "whole-waters." Some of the better houses even have a thin coat of mortar over the blocks, giving them a uniform, light-grey texture. There is no paint to be seen anywhere.

This next block in the stack has about one quarter of it missing. There is no point in using it, since there are more blocks than will be needed. This is my last day here, and I am determined to get these last several walls up, all the way. Anna's son-in-law Jose and some of her neighbors will put on the roof later. They would have helped more, but they work long hours at their low-paying jobs and don't get out here, far from the city, until after dark each evening. The buses are slow, and crowded.

As it is, Jose, a construction worker, had the foundation prepared before I arrived. More recently he mortared in the metal frames for several windows and the two doors. Family members and neighbors help on weekends, teenage boys shoveling sand, mixing and wheeling mortar, and the girls laughing and carrying blocks two at a time. Children bring water and more laughter and their own kind of excitement. All of that, along with Ramino's design work, Anna's mortar mixing and cooking, and Roni's errand-running make this project an argument that, when conditions are right, many people are very much willing to cooperate for the advantage of a few. There is little room on this site for competition or for ego.

Here is a better block. First I need to add water to the mortar. As usual it dried considerably during lunch, which was longer today than usual. Now I can put some mortar along the finished row and some more on one side of the block in my hand, then place the block and tap it gently into position. A kid in a sandbox never had more fun.

Every day has meant more rows of blocks put in place, and higher walls. Each morning, I first walk slowly around the four sides, enjoying the way the early sun creates new shadows from clean lines not there the day before. So it must have been for the builders of the great cathedrals of Europe and England: using the dawn sun of the changing seasons to measure in its light the emerging patterns and contours of their work. However far-fetched, it has become a satisfaction to compare this simple building with those structures, whose magnificence must in the end have been something beyond the plans or the imagination even of those who created them. In a reverse fantasy I have invented, a harmless indulgence, this simple and modern building project can be transformed into a cathedral of its own.

The foundation here, no more than a trough leveled with the back of a shovel and then lined with bricks, becomes a foundation dug 25 feet deep by medieval laborers. Under the floor of this house, a floor which will be at best a thin layer of concrete, I see the cathedral crypt with its stygian arches and candle-lit corners, storage for relics and consecrated tombs. In spaces between these walls we are building stand fluted columns that bear the stone vaults and support the triforium; instead of thin beams to support a tin roof in this place, huge arched vaults draw the eye heavenward. The horizontal slats of Jose's simple jalousie windows are replaced by stained glass caught in intricate tracery, and, from corners and flying buttresses, carved gargoyles have been placed to spit rainwater to the ground.

The cathedrals were built, sometimes over centuries, as an expression of the eternal glory of God. This house will be built in two months, to be the habitat of a family. Those purposes -- putting aside the particulars of design, size, materials, cost, labor, complexity -- are the same.

Right now Anna and her family are living in a cramped and temporary half-water at the other end of the lot. When I go in to get the big lunches Anna prepares for me each day, there is barely room to move around. Along with her stove, several beds take up most of the space. And there are boxes -- of clothes and food and cooking things -- and also bags of mortar kept dry from the rain. A rusted bed frame and mattress sit just outside the only door. One of them must prefer sleeping there when it is not raining.

There has been no place to sit inside when it comes time to eat the big mid-day meal, a plate of rice and salads and usually some chicken or other meat. No chair either, inside or outside. I sit on a plank that is set over a couple of square tin cans, and hold the plate on my knees. In the beginning I could easily have skipped lunch and kept on setting blocks, except for an unexpected problem.

"Anna's a little upset," Sister Deborah told me after I had been here a few days.

"What's the problem?"

"She says you're eating lunch really fast, and you don't eat very much. She thinks maybe you don't like her food."

"Her food is great. I'm just hurrying so I can get back to work. Could you tell her that?"

"Remember, she needs to do something for you, too."

"Okay. I'll eat more slowly. But I hope she's not using all her money on big meals for me."

"Let her worry about that."

Even simple things become complicated. For most people, helping others may seem clear as a moral imperative, but it can quickly create issues of pride and ego, of need and obligation.

The truth is that they do not need me to build this house; this work is merely moving the project along faster. There is no obligation to do it, either. But since I *am* doing it, there is a need for them to do their part. Any reasonable degree of pride requires that people not allow themselves to become victims of charity.

There are also problems of ego in a situation like this: the danger that the real motive of humanitarian action is self-regard. How can we know we are genuinely acting out of concern for the welfare of others, from a desire to serve? How much of altruism is rooted in satisfaction of the ego?

It is a familiar topic in ethics classes, and it tends to be about the same discussion each time. I summarized it for Deborah one evening, at the sisters' house where I stay and where I'm writing this in the evenings.

"People who do charitable stuff," one student will say, "are just doing it to feel good about themselves. It's ego."

"Are you saying that there is something wrong with feeling good about yourself?" I ask him.

"No, there's nothing wrong with that. But it doesn't say much about the good stuff they are supposed to be doing."

"Good stuff is still good stuff, isn't it?"

"But the question is why people do it. I'm saying it's not for good reasons. It's all ego. Kant says we have to concentrate on the motive for our action."

"Maybe it's guilt," another student will say. "They're doing it because they might feel guilty if they don't do it."

"Or maybe they want a reward," says another, "like helping an old lady carry her groceries and then she leaves you a million bucks in her will." It is almost always an old lady and a million dollars.

"So you're saying it's not possible to do something nice for somebody just because it's the nice thing to do? Didn't you ever do anything nice for your mother?"

"That's different."

"Why?"

"Because it's in the family. We're talking about outside that."

"Okay," I concede. "Who comes to mind first when you think of somebody going good acts?"

"Mother Teresa," two or three of them will say at the same time.

"That's not in the family, is it? And it's hard to think that she did all she did, over all those years, out of guilt."

Before long, somebody comes up with an answer to that too.

"Maybe it's because she was religious."

"What do you mean?"

"Like, she believed she wouldn't go to heaven unless she did all that good stuff."

"She must think heaven's pretty hard to get into," says one of the class wits.

"So even Mother Teresa didn't do good acts just because they're good acts that needed doing? Is that what we're saying? We're saying she couldn't have done what she did out of love?"

Some of them look as though they don't really want to say that, I told Deborah. Or maybe as if they haven't thought of love in that way.

"Probably we need to look at it in terms of levels of motives. If the primary motive is just to do something good, then ego or guilt or fear are secondary. Or it could be the other way around. I suppose that's a question each person has to answer individually. Or a question for the psychologists."

"I still think it's all ego, just the way we are," says the class egoist, the one who started it all.

Deborah agreed that the whole discussion seems like one that we shouldn't have to have. If something good is being accomplished, if somebody is being helped in some way and the person doing it feels good too, what exactly is the problem? I am also not happy about students' cynicism. That is a bad habit at any time but even more when it is found in the young. Like everything else, attitudes are learned, and they can also be seen as a sign of the times.

Something to the left just caught my attention.

"*Boa tarde, senor.*"

"*Boa teard.*"

It is the next door neighbor, popping up from behind the wall like a paper target in a shooting gallery. He is a steady onlooker, almost every day watching over a property-line wall that is made of these same blocks. Standing on a box or a chair, he is high enough so that he can rest his elbows on the top of the wall, one hand sometimes under his chin as he watches.

I have the uneasy feeling that this may be the man who built the wall I tore down. If so, he is the forgiving type. He watches with a smile and occasional nods that are meant to be encouraging. Occasionally he offers words, maybe of advice, which I hear but can't understand.

Here is another block with part of one corner missing, but still usable. The blocks are thin, and they are easily broken in handling. When only a portion of a block is needed, the rest can be knocked away with a few slaps of the trowel. Father Dermot told me that he once toured a factory where blocks like these are made. Mostly, he said, they were being made by children, whose hands were sometimes bleeding from the work. He could not help offering a few comments about child labor, but of course it made no difference. "Except maybe to me," he said. "Anyway, the kids want the work, their families need the money. But in a way it is not just for the money. It seemed like a matter of pride."

Matters of pride are all around, as evidenced last week while Deborah and I were walking home after an evening meeting at church. We were walking with Isabella and Gilberto, a good-looking young married couple, obviously happy with each other. As we passed under the street lights and picked our way over the diagonal ruts caused by heavy rains, they were asking Deborah questions, in Portuguese, about me.

"What is it like in the part of the city he lives in?" Isabella asked. "Does he live in a pretty house in a pretty area?"

Deborah told them I live in one of the nicer parts of our city. But she's never seen my house.

"You can tell them I have an okay house," I said, "but not a very big one."

Isabella said something in response to that.

"She's saying," Deborah translated, "that it must be unpleasant for you here, with all the dust and the shabby little houses and the streets not even paved."

"No, it's not awful at all," I said. "You can tell her I think it's very pretty here. They have wide streets, lots of beautiful vegetation, and a great climate. Tell her to look up right now at all those huge stars. We don't see anything like that where I live."

The barrio is far from the lights of Goiania, and the night air is clear. Under such conditions the stars grow vast both in number and in size. Like dinner plates and saucers that might overlap on a table, or diamonds brightened on black velvet, they peep from behind one another and compete for their share of space and attention in the firmament.

That evening, they called silently for us to reach up and spread our fingers, to gently open spaces between them so that we might peer, necks arched, into eternity.

Deborah translated again, taking so long that she must have added to what I had said. Then Isabella spoke again.

"She says that you're being very nice, very polite. But she's still wondering how you don't get depressed here, because it's not very nice."

"Depressed? You can tell her that there is no cause to be depressed by physical surroundings. Tell her there's no need to be ashamed of her neighborhood. She should be proud of herself and her husband and her friends, of all her people."

Again they talked, and we walked together in the darkness, past the half-waters sitting like little houses on a monopoly board. We nodded to the occasional night-walker, looked some more at the stars overhead, and watched that we did not trip in the deep wash-outs that angled now and then across the road.

"She understands that," Deborah finally said. "But she says she has some relatives who won't come out of the city to visit her because it's so poor around here."

"Then that's their problem, tell her," I said. "It's their loss."

Then it was Gilberto's turn.

"He wants to know how much you understand about the politics of Brazil," Deborah translated again. "About how things work to keep so many people in poverty."

"You can tell him I don't know much at all about Brazilian politics. But I suspect it's the same here as most everywhere else. Some people get power one way or another, and then they use it mostly for their own purposes. Those who don't have the power get the poverty."

Isabella spoke again after Deborah had translated.

"She wants to know if you would come to their house to visit them some evening while you're here," Deborah said. "I told her you come home very tired from building Anna's house all day."

"Not *that* tired. Tell her we'll come whenever they want."

We came then to an intersection and parted for the night. Gilberto and Isabella started down a dark lane toward their house. With a laugh, Gilberto shouted something back to me.

"He says not to come down this lane at night," Deborah said. "There's monsters along the roadside."

"Tell him I said the only monsters are the ones we put into our own heads." But they were already out of hearing.

This row, part of a long wall, is done. I kneel on the planks to sight along it, even though the taut string running straight along each block says it is fine. With the palm of my hand, I push gently on a few of the blocks in the middle of the row, and note how that sends a wobble toward each end. The row will firm up when the mortar hardens and cures. Some mortar on the point of my trowel can be used to touch up a few places where the joints are a little less than full. Now on to another row, the last one on the adjoining wall.

Two little kids run along the wall below me, chasing a puppy. Kids playing around here at night is cause for worry, because these high walls will not become firm for some time, maybe even until the roof and the joists can hold them together. I tried once to warn Anna to keep little kids away, but it is doubtful that she got the point of all my arm waving.

There is house building going on everywhere on the outskirts of Gioania and probably in every city in Brazil. There are both historical and contemporary reasons for that. In the late 1950s, the country experienced a major influx of foreign capital for the purpose of expanding manufacturing rather than agriculture. The result was rapid industrial development.

Shortly after that came a military dictatorship. Rather than making any effort to distribute land more equitably, the rulers expelled peasants from land given them by earlier governments and then gave it back to big landowners. To make matters worse, the country's population is growing fast, and as the great farms have become more and more mechanized, people are forced to look for factory work in the cities. The problem is not unique to Brazil; it just hits home when seen close up and at first hand.

This barrio was settled a few years ago by homeless people who carried out what is called an "occupation" of the land. Occupations go on all the time, the sisters have explained. The displaced people move in, set up houses of plastic or tin or cardboard or whatever they can find, and start some little gardens. It might be on public or on private land. There is plenty of land in this country, so the idea of people using some of it when they need it does not seem extraordinary to me.

In one case Deborah described, the police were assigned to drive the people out. "But the governor called the effort off when his son was suddenly killed in an accident, which these pious people interpreted as God's intervention. Like something out of the Old Testament." However, occupations aren't done by miracles. Most of them are well organized, often discreetly, and they are made to stick one way or another.

It was a different story for the people of this barrio. These people, Deborah told me, started out camping in front of the governor's mansion. "They were removed by the police just before Christmas, so that Christmas decorations could be put up. After that they moved to the banks of the nearby river, but it overflowed all the time, and the government wouldn't shore up the banks. Anna's family had a place there, but it collapsed when the water came up."

"Even the government finally realized that these people weren't leaving, so it listed each family on cards, then pulled a number of cards each day, like a bingo game, and the people were given these lots. This area had been a large farm, bought by the state."

"So these people were all peasants from the country?"

"No, though Anna's family is. Some of them were homeless city people. And now the families keep coming, moving the boundaries of the city farther and farther out."

"And how does the government handle that?"

"It gives each family 2000 blocks and 12 sacks of mortar. No, ten sacks. The other two are supposed to be for them to build their church. But those two somehow don't turn up. Also they get two doors, two windows, plus tiles and timber for the roof. That is enough for a half-water. They don't get anything for the installation of water or electricity, and they don't get any glass for the windows."

"How many people are we talking about, in this area we're in right now?"

"15,000 families in this barrio. That's about 100,000 people, by government estimates."

"So, three or four kids in each of the families?"

"I guess so. We know that a few years ago there were 10,000 children under the age of six. And only one day-care center. It can handle 50 children. There are only five schools, and only one of the schools goes as far as the eighth grade."

"No danger of anybody becoming too literate."

"No, and only one health post, not functioning at capacity because there aren't enough doctors. There aren't any dental facilities, and very few medical supplies either. Public phones were just installed recently, but no lines to the houses. Bus service out here isn't very good, so people have to leave as early at five in the morning to get to work. Sometimes they use bicycles or they just walk."

On my first weekend here, Fr. Dermot picked me up for a drive that would give me my first good look at the area while he visited with some of his parishioners. He is of middle-age, a short and wiry Irishman with a soft, accented voice that caused me to lean to my left to separate his words from the pinging of the motor. The first topic was one I have been getting used to.

"How does it happen that you've come to us here?"

"It's a bit complicated, as these things usually are. One of my students thinks she wants to join the sisters' order back home and she apparently told them about some working trips I've been on."

"Where?"

"Nicaragua, Hong Kong a few years back. And I've started making trips to Haiti."

"How do you get time off from your work?"

"I use summer breaks, and there's always three or four weeks between semesters, after Christmas."

"But you're not between semesters now, are you?"

"No, I'm on sabbatical. I already did most of the academic work I needed to, and trips like this are part of some work that relates to my teaching. Now they're also becoming research for a book I'm thinking about doing."

"Will we be in your book, then?"

"You already are."

"And you are building a house, I'm told."

"Right. When I talked about this trip with the sisters, I made sure they understood I needed some hands-on project, not just following them around doing religious stuff. Sorry."

"No offense."

"They said not to worry, they'd take care of that. So I came down here on faith. So to speak."

"And now you're a mason."

"Maybe I told them I wanted something concrete to do and they took that literally."

The barrios we drove through looked about the same to me. I kept that idea to myself, mindful of the politician who once said that if you've seen one ghetto you've seen them all -- a line that ranks high on my list of insensitive political quotes. Nearly identical half-waters lined each unpaved street. A few of the residents had added the second half, or a porch, or even a room on the back side. Some still had outhouses, but each lot had a water tank perched 15 feet above the ground on a slender concrete pillar. Vegetation was starting to provide shade and a softer, more variegated look to the areas.

They may have looked the same, but each barrio has its own story. One section we drove through, Dermot said, was an area that was leveled by a storm a few years ago, not long after the people had moved in to set up their housing. "At least in that case the federal, state and local governments chipped in to give each family just enough material to rebuild. There's hope for governments after all."

We stopped to visit a family he knew. In the yard, as we pulled in, a man's head seemed to be sitting on the ground, wrapped in a dirty handkerchief. The head turned out to be that of the husband, who was neck-deep into the work of digging for a septic tank. He climbed out, his shirt sweaty and his pants rolled to above the knees, and invited us to come in.

Inside were signs of relative prosperity. The front room contained only one chair and some tools, but one bedroom and the kitchen had fresh concrete floors. A new refrigerator looked large and impressive, if a little out of place in the hallway.

Dermot explained that I was an American who had come to Brazil to "visit and carry stones." At that, I held up my bandaged hands and they laughed in the way people do who appreciate any attempt to defuse awkwardness. A certain level of tension, or at least discomfort, might be expected when poverty confronts affluence. Its worst form would be a fawning servility: "we have only this cup of water to offer..."

That was not at all the case. While there was nothing boastful in their demeanor, the couple seemed content: they had, after all, built their own home! However modest the scale of that accomplishment to other eyes, in theirs it was major, the most visible sign that they were working their way up.

It was a comfort to be relieved of that tension. In the kitchen we sat on wooden chairs and played with a small child until the pregnant wife brought us cups of coffee on a Pyrex plate. In a custom probably brought here from Europe, it was that popular strong and dark coffee, laced with sugar and meant to be sipped slowly, a truss for social connection as much as a refreshment.

"Thank you" is *obrigado* in Portuguese, and that was my occasional contribution to the talk. Dermot translated at times, but most of the conversation was conducted in Portuguese. That made little difference. On the contrary, it gave me the chance to connect with them in a non-verbal way. A common language may be the *sine qua non* of effective international trade or diplomacy; it is definitely vital to a successful tourism industry or to fraternity in sports. For the simplest human relationships, it can sometimes be a barrier. It took no great expenditure of emotional energy, that afternoon, for me to get close to near strangers -- the smallness of the kitchen surely helped -- and it was as if a level of intimacy was achieved just because we had no language with which to threaten it.

Bertrand Russell has a piece in which he warned, in his funny and biting style, about the folly of exaggerating the virtues of the poor. He is right. Poor people can lie and manipulate, steal and betray with the same efficiency as those in better circumstances. Still, my own experiences have been fairly consistent: the less people have, the more generous and open they tend to be. Though not in that kitchen, it is often the case that people need to be proud of their generosity because they think they have so little else of which to be proud. Simplicity makes for gracious hosts and fast friends.

Sr. Margot, another of the nuns I have stayed with here, told me of how she lived once in the southern part of this country, in a town where a big dam was being built.

"There were four very distinct classes there," she said, "from the common laborers on the bottom to the management classes and the engineers on the top. The classes never mixed. There were guards on every street corner of the wealthy areas. That was partly for protection of everyone, but it also helped keep the class distinctions clear."

"What struck me the most," she went on, "was that the only houses I was ever invited into were those of the lower classes."

"You never went into an upper class home?"

"Never, not even once. I never even saw the upper classes very much."

"I'm not surprised. Marx was wrong about a lot of things, but he was right with his idea that the whole of human history is the history of class struggle."

"Do you think so too?"

"Absolutely. In more civilized situations the struggle is managed by just keeping people apart. In our own country the latest sign of that is the gated community. Heaven forbid that we would want people of different class or income to actually mix. We've also used taxation and charity to keep the lid on, so the struggle doesn't turn to outright revolution too much of the time."

"If they could mix more, maybe the classes would start to understand each other. There are things to be understood on both sides."

"That's right. This isn't a matter of everything that is good and noble meeting everything that is evil. But I think many of those in the upper classes would be inclined to be more generous if they could actually see the effects of extreme inequality. The way you see it in your work here, first hand."

"Let's hope they're generous in their own ways."

That was a charitable way to end a conversation that tended toward the judgmental, handled as a sister might be expected to do. But in our time, nuns are more than just old-fashioned symbols of charity.

The more I have talked and worked with sisters, in several venues, the more I have come to appreciate modern sisterhood. The worn-out stereotype of vicious nuns swatting grade-schoolers with rulers is a distortion from the 1940s or 50s, an unimaginative caricature that is good only for cheap laughs in plays or movies.

It has nothing to do with the lives and activities of modern sisters. The ones I know dress in jeans and work shirts, drink a beer when they feel like it, and enjoy jokes. I assume they also pray or meditate in order to carry on their work within a religious framework, but I have yet to have a religious conversation with any of them that lasted more than half a minute, as though those matters are to be reserved for other, private times. They are women who have made a choice for compassion and improvement in the lives of others. They are feminists who find their identity in efforts not for themselves but for social justice, who find their voice in the work they do. Because they are not trained or required to preach, they are free to act instead. Best of all, they can be more forceful and less compromising, because they are not constrained by the need to provide for a family or the desire for career-advancement. They are, in a word, tough. They are fun to be with, but I would not want to cross most of them.

A pause to stretch is also a chance to survey the construction site, a scene of purposeful disorder. Grey bricks and unused orange blocks are piled ready for use or lying ungathered. A 50-gallon drum, its lower third discolored by dust, contains the water used for mortar-mixing. Too wooden tables hold cooking utensils and small tools. Off to one side is the small vegetable garden, and a one-speed bike leans against a lonely tree.

In the only open space, Anna is again bending over her hoe to push dry mortar into the small pool of water, and Roni is moving toward her with a bucket. As I watch, they become multiform. They are a hirsute laborer who hands a bucket with its mixture of lime and sand and water to a mason who trowels a new layer onto a wedge of sandstone. They are two carpenters who prepare mortises and tenons for a truss that will be hoisted to the top of the cathedral wall. They become the blacksmiths forging tools, the roofers covering beams with pitch, the stone cutters at either end of their big-toothed bucksaw, the sculptors carving the figures of saints, and the window makers assembling tiny pieces of colored glass for the rose window.

Like Dante's shades, they transform and merge through each other in the noise and tumult of a project site that stretches over decades. So the immediate reality blends with the fabulous, and history absorbs the present.

Now Roni appears beside the scaffold. He seems to be introducing me to some friend of his, so I nod down at the two of them and say "boa tarde." It seems like somebody is always introducing the American house-builder to somebody else. Now and then a few people come by to watch, murmuring softly among themselves.

Roni and I communicate well. For one thing, he knows that I need a cold drink now and then, for energy and as an antidote to the afternoon sun, which by now has burned and re-burned my face and arms and legs below the cut-offs. At the moment he is asking, with gestures, if I want him to go to the store. I shake my head no. Time is important now.

Deborah told me that the price of these blocks went up two million cruzeiros between when she bought them and when she picked them up. Inflation is killing everybody, she says, and the manufacturer wanted more money. She prevailed that time, making them stick to the lower price. In a religious culture, nuns can probably exert a subtle moral pressure to go along with their own strength.

"There was a strike recently," she went on, "to raise the minimum wage."

"Did it work?"

"Uh huh. But the raises won't take effect until next month, and everybody knows the inflation will wipe out the raise by then. In the meantime, their congressmen give themselves more in one day than the average worker makes in a month. Now they want to double their own salaries."

"That makes our own politicians look good."

"And they only appear in congress about half the time they're supposed to. People are really angry."

This next row is coming along faster; the rhythm is strong. The mortar that Anna just brought, her eyes bulging as she swung the heavy bucket up onto the planks, is perfect. Rather than falling off the blocks as it sometimes does, the mortar is sticking nicely as I swing each block down into position. The blocks feel like feathers, and the trowel is flashing in the sun.

As good as all this has been individually, it needs to be repeated that a group effort is always better. Margot told me about another place she lived, where she visited a family who had a house made of sticks. "The whole place," she said, "just sticks. It leaned so badly I was afraid to go inside. The palm-leaf roof made it a fire trap. First I asked if the husband couldn't do something about the place. No, I was told, he had to work all the time, very long hours. So I organized a teen group, got some building materials together, and the kids rebuilt it in a day. They had so much fun that they went on to build twenty more." Organizing people is like a ballet in which sometimes the planning and the participation are more to be valued than the dance.

There is a pleasant empty-mindedness about this work, like being in a Zen state. Zen Buddhism works against our struggle with time, against the conflict between process and achievement in which we too often prefer the latter at a loss of the former. Since cathedrals often took generations to build, the finished product was out of reach for all but those in that last generation. All the others could focus on the process, like Zen Christians at work.

Empty-mindedness allows the senses more chances to take in the sights and sounds of barrio life, without the suffocating mediation of thought. Every second or third day, a pick-up truck with two men in it and a scratchy loudspeaker repeating something cruises the streets. A political announcement maybe -- until Deborah explained that they are selling fresh milk. Right now, on the main road just visible from here, a donkey is pulling a cart with several kids in it. It is going uphill, with a steady clopping. A motorcycle snarls past it, a cultural contrast going faster the other way.

Nearer, I can hear the scraping of Anna's hoe as she stirs more mortar. She is mixing it in a big circle near the three sinks that are the outside part of her kitchen. In the distance a dog barks, without much conviction.

In a short time now, we will have to face the sadness of saying our farewells. That has been a tacit downer all day, made more so by the understanding that we will not meet again.

The difficulties of parting started this morning, when Ramiro stopped by the sisters' house on his way to work. He and Deborah spoke for a minute, and then she explained that he had come to say good-bye because he knew he wouldn't get home in time to see me again.

"He's been saying how thankful he is, and how all of them are, that you have built the house for the family," Deborah translated." He says he just can't say enough about how nice the house is going to be, and how they all appreciate what you've done. You can probably get the idea."

She stopped then, and there was a pause as the three of us looked at each other.

"Tell him it's been a lot of fun for me, really. And that I've enjoyed the chance to get to know him and his family and all the people here. Anyway, we did it together."

That sounded lame, considering how important the moment was to Ramiro, and I hope that Deborah translated it into something finer.

Then Ramiro and I shook hands, his hand smaller but firm in mine. As he turned away, quickly, his voice was lost in the turning, and his words were almost inaudible. They did not need a translation.

"*Via com Deus*," he said.

If you can go with God, Ramiro, I can too.

It was some of the same at lunch. Because a small going-away party was planned, I had bought some small presents to give out -- a few toys and games for Anna's grandchildren and the other kids around here. Also something for Anna's children, and a little religious picture for her, to serve as a housewarming present.

Deborah came down the street at noon to join us for lunch and to translate as I gave out the gifts. Then Anna surprised me with a gift of her own. It is a little metal lamp, shaped as a small bowl with a handle curving over it. Oil must have been put in the bowl to burn through a wick.

“Anna says it’s called a ‘lampesino’,” Deborah explained. “When she was a girl in the country, these were all they had for light at night. So it’s important to her, and she wants you to have it. So you’ll remember them.”

“I’ll remember. Tell her I’m very grateful. It’s a perfect gift.”

“It looks like they painted it for you,” Deborah noted quietly. The lampesino had a thick new coat of green paint. “These lamps are usually rusty, and probably they think an American should have something that looks new.”

My own store-bought gifts seemed insignificant then. I held the lampesino in silence for a minute, and turned it over in my hand. I can learn from these people.

“I’ll get rid of the paint when I get it home,” I said to Deborah. “It should look like it was for her.”

Anna’s married daughter, a lovely young woman with a head of dark curls and an air of self-possession, had apparently been assigned to make the speech. When she was finished, Deborah explained that she had said how grateful she is as well, how grateful they all are, and that she can hardly believe that I came all the way from the United States to build the house.

“Apparently they’ve been calling you ‘the man from heaven’,” Deborah said, with the hint of a wink. “They think God sent you to build Anna’s house.”

I started to tell Deborah to say no, that I flew down here in a large jet, but I stopped just in time.

“Tell her I said that’s very kind.”

“She also said that you have given her back her faith in mankind,” Deborah continued. “Before you came here, she didn’t think there were any good people left in the world.”

“No!” I said it so sharply that several heads came up. “That’s not fair. There’s lots of people doing things like this, all over. I’ve been with them, worked with them. Tell her-”

“Hey, I’m just translating what she said,” Deborah cut in. “Let’s not have an argument about it.”

She changed the subject.

So it will be hard to get out of here in a few hours without more emotion. It is a good thing Deborah will not be here to do any translating. There will likely be a small crowd around, so the plan is to wash up, collect the water bottle and the lampesino, and get out fast.

Concentrating on this last wall can put off thinking about it. First I have to pick out a few of the best blocks and also climb down to retrieve the trowel.

Building this house is not just fun. It has been easy, even if back and arms protest every night. They are fine again in the morning, and then it is back to more blocks and mortar, the string and the trowel.

As long as the body holds out, physical work is the easiest of all. The stress is on muscles, not mind, and most muscles recover quickly. Physical labor can also be an escape from the kind of work where results are uncertain, frustrated by setbacks, and subject to change. That is some of what we were talking about a few nights ago, over a bowl of popcorn. It was a late dinner in the kitchen.

"I was thinking about Gilberto's question the other night," I began. "Remember, he asked me what I knew about the politics down here."

"And?"

"Well, I don't think I answered him very well. Maybe you can explain what I meant some other time."

"What did you mean?"

"I meant that poverty, economic injustice, is finally structural. You know, it's just a part of the social order. It's worse here or there, maybe not so bad somewhere else, but long-standing. We're not real deep into socio-economic theory with that point. It's been discussed forever. But I've been travelling around some and thinking about what I find, and it just seems that you can make whatever efforts you want toward more equality and justice, but nothing will really make any big difference. The political stuff, I mean, won't make all that much difference."

"You really think that?"

"More and more, though I don't like to admit it. Ask me next year and maybe I'll say something else."

"Have you always thought that?"

"It's probably more gradual. I remember a long time ago, when we were married, and my wife and I heard a sermon by a visiting priest -- one of the ones who come around now and then to speak in parishes and raise some money for their people. He was from South America, I don't remember which country. Anyway, he said 'The problem is not that the people in my parish are stupid or lazy, the problem is multi-national corporations. 'I wanted to stand on the pew and cheer."

"He was right."

"Sure, and it was also sort of funny, because this was in a very conservative church, and I wondered if most of the people even knew what he meant, never mind disagreeing. We had him over to dinner and had a great conversation. Yeah, he was right, but the bigger problem is that an awful lot of us have investments, like retirement money and whatever, in the same corporations he was talking about. That's what I mean when I say it's structural, part of the way things are, and it's hard to change for a better structure."

"What else?"

"Lots of things, but I'll just mention one. Five or six years ago, I think I told you, a bunch of us were in Nicaragua, during the Contra war. We were planting trees, to help them out down there. We were all very much into the revolution they were having, with lots of talk about social justice and the 'new order' and the 'new man' and other slogans. We learned a lot down there, and I don't think we were being naive. I mostly remember a lot of positive energy and high spirits about their revolution. But a few years later, things hadn't improved much, and the next thing, they had an election and essentially overturned their own revolution."

"But you know the U. S. government was doing everything it could to stop that revolution, so they never had a chance."

"Right. Our government put a lot of money into that election, to beat back the revolution. And now they're even poorer. But that's just my point. Injustice is structural, and even overthrows of nasty right-wing dictators and a lot of hard work doesn't seem to have lasting effects when those who really control things have their way. Seems like in the end they always do."

"Were you and your friends disappointed by what happened?"

"I suppose, at the time. I said we weren't naive down there, but we were hopeful. Looking back, we should have been able to predict what would happen over time."

"That sounds pretty bleak."

"I don't mean to sound that way. Maybe better to think of it as realistic. You just have to accept an overall structure that's unjust to a lot of people, and then do whatever you feel like doing to work against that. If you want to, that is. I still get little lessons in what we're talking about, the structure. Just before I came down here, for example. You know the breakfast program your people run back home, in that church on the north side?"

"Uh huh."

"I worked there during the winter months, one morning a week. I wanted to see how a feeding program works, and it was also part of the research I was doing. It's a good operation, lots of people getting fed."

Deborah swirled the kernels of popcorn around in her bowl, fast, and picked up a kernel that had flipped on to the table. "So?"

"So, one morning I had to go back into the kitchen for something. For just a minute I stood at the big window that separates the kitchen from the eating area, looking out at what was going on. I was looking straight down the long row of those tables that separate the people doing the serving from the people who have come to eat. That's when I saw what I'm talking about."

"What?"

"The volunteers, the servers, were all white, middle-class, mostly from the suburbs I assume. And the people needing food were all from the inner-city, mostly black and Hispanic. I'm not criticizing the volunteers. Especially since I was one of them. But we have it all. We live in our homes in the suburbs, plenty to eat and so on, and then we get to come into the city once a week to serve food to people who need it. We really are helping them out, but we get to feel needed and important too."

"I've heard the point before," Deborah said. "It's not the volunteers' fault."

"I'm not sure it's anybody's fault, or even a question of fault. As individuals, we didn't make this structure. It was already there. And of course the needy people didn't make it either. But we get all the benefits from it, especially that benefit of feeling good about ourselves. And they probably get to feel a little more dependent along with their free breakfast, and maybe also get to feel bad about themselves."

"So what's the answer?"

"Hmmm. Part of the answer is what you are doing here, that's obvious. Other parts of it are other projects going on in other places. Some are short term, some last, some succeed and others don't. Together they are as much answer as we can expect. We both know that people need education and jobs and medical care and self-worth most of all, not just free food. And also neighborhoods they can feel proud of."

My bowl was empty, Deborah's still half full.

"Do you want me to make more popcorn?" I asked. "I'm still hungry."

"No. Take this." She dumped most of her popcorn into my bowl.

"I agree with part of that," she said. "I've always been inclined to think that governments set up structures that keep some people poor. So they can control them. Just enough help to keep the lid on."

"Uh huh."

"But that's the main work we do here, especially with the young people like the ones you've met. The clergy shouldn't just be doing religious work. We should be showing the people how they can get into the political structure, to make changes."

"Liberation theology is alive down here, huh?"

"Sure it's alive. It's slow going, but it's working. We can see the results. What the government had to do for these barrios is a sign of that, even if it's not enough. And we had the youth working for a people's party in the last election. It was a landslide. Now the mayor has set up meetings in the neighborhoods, to listen to what the people want. We showed the young people the difference between just plain old vote-getting politics and politics that benefit the people. They never knew there was a difference before."

"You know most people are pretty turned off by politics. My students are examples of that. For one thing, it's so hard to know what really goes on. So they just think of it as vote-getting and power-tripping."

"Not here. We call it 'transformation," the work we do with them. Transforming them into power groups. There's lots of leadership around. A former bishop here was one of the best. He just died recently. Before he died, he had been asked to leave the country, go stay in Central America."

"They'd be happy to have him there, the people anyway."

"The important thing was that a lot of other clergy came out in support of him."

"And that caused problems in the church, I'm sure. It must be hard for a bishop, or anybody on the higher levels, to spend time with the powerful and wealthy and at the same time try to be sympathetic to the poor, to be on the side of socially-minded clergy that they're in charge of."

"It is. But leaders come up from below, too."

"You mean the young clergy?"

"Not necessarily. Some of our best activists are young people who aren't even especially religious. One of the really good ones was killed recently, in his twenties. He was shot so many times they said his body looked like it had a lot of measles. And he was killed on his way home from a meeting where he'd been telling the people to go slowly, not be violent."

"Well, we always see Christ as non-violent, but he sure was talking about major social changes, maybe even revolution, depending on how you read him."

"Yeah," Deborah agreed. "The Bible is supposed to mean 'good news', but it isn't good news for everybody."

That made us both laugh. "Very good," I said. "But you radicals are gonna get yours."

"We do hit the transformation theme pretty hard."

"Watch out, you'll end up in jail. No more popcorn."

"You can send protest letters through one of those amnesty groups if I do."

"I'm going to interview you now like we're on a morning talk show," I said, using a spoon as a microphone in her face.

"What's your biggest challenge?"

"To educate the people, outside of school, I mean. And by video, since so many of them are illiterate. They need to know the history of injustice, and they need a solid biblical understanding of how oppression worked back then, so they can make parallels. And we have to train leaders. Those are our challenges."

"And your successes?

She took her time before she answered.

"I think we're encouraging the people to believe in themselves, in their right to control their own lives. To demand their rights. We go with them to get what they have coming. We've also done some health education, and we're on the way to getting a clinic."

"So what's your biggest disappointment?"

"Just the frustration over the country's economic instability, which keeps the people poor and weak, uneducated, unhealthy. So they can't pull themselves up."

"Okay." I was writing most of this down. When I stopped, Deborah and I looked at each other over the kitchen table.

"You haven't asked me about my dreams," she said.

"Let's hear it."

"I dream about having part of a building, maybe part of the new church, for a library. Along with videos and lots of books so we could teach some literacy too. But mostly as a place for them to come and discuss these issues with each other. Teach each other."

"I hope you get it."

"We will," she said. "Any more questions?"

"I always have the same last question. Thinking back over your life, and the way it is for you right now, would you have done anything else, anything different?"

"No."

"Okay, end of interview."

"You like building so much, why don't you come back here next year and help them build the church?"

"Maybe I can. We'll see."

"The people would be glad to have you back, you know that."

That is not a bad idea, to come back and help build their church. For now, I am happy that I've just finished the building that I came here to do. What did Aurelius say? If you work at what is in front of you, seriously, without distractions and expecting nothing, you will be happy.

This last row is as straight as all the rest when I sight along it for the last time and then gently remove the guide string from the corners. Done.

It is both the curse and the glory of our human condition that we seek perfection in an imperfect world. There is an anecdote about a sculptor who was fitting some religious statue, beautifully carved of course, into its niche in a cathedral. But he also had shaped and smoothed and finished the back of the statue. Somebody noticed that, just as he was about to mortar it into place.

"Why did you bother with the back?" the sculptor was asked. "Nobody's going to see the back, ever."

"God will see," the sculptor said.

The late afternoon sun is sending shadows from the new walls and the old outhouse and small shrubs across the yard. Anna somehow knew just how much mortar was needed to finish, and the bucket is empty. There is enough on the sides to do some final pointing. Then I'll clean the bucket and the tools and take one last picture.

Roni has appeared again beside the scaffold. He is making signs to show that he appreciates how straight the walls are. Now he's showing that he knows I'll be leaving.

"Uh huh," I nod down to him. He smiles and pretends to brush tears from his cheeks.

"Thanks for all those drinks," I say to him, even though he can't understand that. No, maybe he can.

Deborah said she'll send a picture after the roof is on and they move in. "Then you'll know it's finished."

Building people is never finished, and no picture will record what she and the other sisters are accomplishing here. Anyone can put up block walls. It takes a different kind of effort and much more of it to raise people up and organize them and most of all to get them thinking differently about themselves.

Successful revolutions are not ones that overthrow a ruling family or an elite group and put another one in its place. The ones that succeed are the ones that gradually help people to see their own potential, to "flourish," as that idea of personal development has been handed down all the way from Aristotle. The ideal revolution is not the triumph of the have-nots over the haves; it is the one that aims at affecting social and economic relationships in a way that everyone gains. And not just material gains but a steady improvement in mind and character, a growing sense of enlightenment, for everyone. When we truly understand, we cooperate.

These sisters understand that they have to work with people, not for them or against them. And unlike most revolutionaries through history, they seem to be patient: a little change is better than none at all, and democracy is an evolutionary process.

They are not tearing down walls or putting up newer walls of resistance. They are making the building blocks.

The tomb of Christopher Wren, the builder of the magnificent St. Paul's cathedral in London, is found in the crypt. The inscription on the tomb is in Latin: "*Lector, si monumentum requires, circumspice*." Reader, if you want to know my works, look around. Look around *here*.

Roni is looking like he wants to be helpful. Maybe it is not too late to do a little empowering of my own. "Solidarity" is a word heard often in situations such as the ones I've been getting into these past years; like all words whose meaning includes some ideal connotations, it needs to be put into action. The word made material, to paraphrase slightly. So now I climb off the scaffold for the last time and gesture to Roni for some help getting the planks down to the ground. At his end, he strains to lift them off the sawhorses. Together we carry them out of the room and set them down along the back wall. Then we each take a sawhorse and put them outside too.

I pick up the mortar bucket and the trowel and indicate that he needs to gather everything else. Over at the sinks, I show that he should clean out the bucket and wash the trowel. He nods seriously and bends to his work, splashing water at our feet.

Chapter Six

"Don't forget, Uncle Derek. You'll pick me up at 6:00?"

"Don't worry, I'll be there. I'll set the alarm."

"Better make it 5:30."

"We could just start at midnight."

"I figured it wouldn't be daylight until around 5:30."

"Hey, I was just kidding."

"You gonna get the coffee and donuts? There'll be about six of us, I mean if everybody shows up like they said."

"I can go out for coffee later."

"You still got those badges and ribbons in your car, right?"

"Yes, yes, yes. I told you, stop worrying. Get some sleep."

"Minga, I'm not gonna sleep a minute."

Without any of us being aware of it at the time, the Fourth Annual Youth Day was the high point. It was an urban coming-out party, an ear-numbing, back-slapping, hand-clapping, high-fiving, hip-jiggling neighborhood jam of rock, reggae and rap, rhythm and blues. It was a social activist's dream come true, the kind of victory that erases every defeat. As usual it was Ken's idea, and most of it was his doing too.

I like to think of it now as a gift -- Ken's gift to the community and maybe even to himself. Gifts are given for many reasons, among them as atonement for some wrongdoing, or as a personal sacrifice for the sake of others, as a means to gain favor or to exalt oneself, or as a token of love. It is not quite true that the best gift is the one that seeks nothing in return; a good gift seeks recognition and should have it. The best kind of gift unites the giver and the receiver. It is therapeutic in its emotional effect on both. It is a statement of optimism about what is good in a situation and a wish for that good to continue. The best kind of gift is given with no intention to compel or even to persuade. It does not embarrass by excess or dominate by inequality. Its purity is to be found in the gratitude of the one who gives as much as in the appreciation of the one who receives.

There: a collection of thoughts on gift-giving. The reader can decide which of them best fit the description of Youth Day that follows and best apply to the motives behind it.

Exuberance should be the word most used in the description because that word -- in its association with abundance, intensity, profusion, high-spiritedness –- is the adjective around which all the other words are meant to cluster. Exuberance is hard to convey in words alone; the visual images and sounds of a film or video can do a much better job. Here we will have to do what we can with words and imagination. We might think of Youth Day as we think of the finale to a fireworks display. It is better now to focus on that finale and not on the dark and empty sky that always follows. Like the ones before it, Youth Day began very early for a few of us, when we met in the park to help Ken with the final preparations. Manhattan Square Park had been built 20 years earlier on the edge of downtown, replacing old houses and tenements as part of an urban renewal program. It was designed as an all-season recreational facility -- a skating and hockey rink in the winter, a waterfall and wading pool in the summer, along with courts for tennis and basketball. Now it needed renewal of its own: the waterfall and the lighting system no longer functioned, the observation tower and restaurant were closed. None of that would matter on this day, when the multi-level concrete amphitheater would end up holding far more than the 2000 people it was designed for.

The amphitheater, a deep dug-out, is formed of sides and steps and seating areas in angular patterns. As the morning sun warmed the concrete, some of us pulled long ropes from wall to wall, from which banners of the major sponsors would hang. The biggest banner showed five paper cut-out children, hands linked against a bright red background, announcing "Youth Day."

Shouts bounced around the pit as we attached other banners to metal railings along the walls. Two helpers helped unload and set up the huge sound system, others organized boxes of prizes, brochures and T-shirts. Half-eaten donuts, protected by the early hour from birds or squirrels, sat forgotten on folding tables. Coffee turned lukewarm. As the morning passed and the opening hour neared, I had almost to sit on Ken to calm him down.

For months he had been a dust devil; by that morning he was a tornado. Those months had gone to finding more sponsors, getting former sponsors to increase their support, developing publicity, lining up the vendors and the big-wig speakers and the sound technicians and the media coverage. Time was needed to arrange the security, to screen applicants, organize the program, and choose the performers and the judges and the prizes. A hundred decisions, some of them needing the approval of us board members, and a thousand details. In those final hours of preparation he was the harassed director, the distraught producer, the frantic choreographer rolled into one. As I write this, I realize how easy it is to put in here on paper; Ken actually did it all.

The first Youth Day had attracted 51 applications for the chance to perform. Six sponsors had contributed $1200 in prizes. Three years later the selection committee had to choose from over 350 applications for the 40 scheduled performances in four age groups. The number of sponsors had grown to 26; the prizes totaled $14,000. They included gift certificates and small scholarships, with each contestant getting some kind of recognition. Even some parents got prizes. Professional musicians were interspersed with the kids' performances, as were award ceremonies and speeches. The county executive noted, possibly with a touch of envy, that the crowd was bigger than that for the Olympic Torch ceremony the month before.

Whatever the size of the crowd, it seemed as though it far exceeded the 6000-person overall capacity of the park. With nearly everyone in motion at some point and no tickets to be taken, it would have been impossible to get an accurate count. And who was counting?

People sat shoulder-to-shoulder on the concrete steps, leaning forward, with raised knees and forearms pressing on their upper legs, with the anticipation of bettors watching their horses in the final stretch. Others sat or stood in the shade of the sycamores and maples and fruit trees planted on the grassy berms which had been formed from the excavation of the theatre.

Or they leaned against the walls, or hung over the iron railings, or picked their way, tip-toed, through those who were seated -- a sprightly swirl of colorful baseball caps and ankle-length shorts that competed with the reds and purples, the greens and blues and yellows, of the murals and banners around them. The best thing of all was that every shade of skin color was there as well.

The mayor knew exactly what it was about. "You are young, you are beautiful, you are talented," he told the performers. "You're the voice of the future, and in all these things you should be proud. Talent isn't just getting up here and dancing and singing; it's also in your heart, and you have to carry that talent back to the streets of your neighborhood. So whether you get a check or a gift, understand that the real gift is in your heart and your mind. If you do that, you will be our future."

Inclusivity rather than strict artistic integrity was the guiding principle. There were dance performances and reggae singers and rap groups with names like "Eleet Fleet" and "Born Adolescent." There were soloists, gospel singers, recitalists, orators, heavy-metal guitarists, drummers and blowers of horns. Performers took the stage variously confident, unfazed, frightened, or wide-eyed at the sea of faces washing on them.

We watched ten year-old tap dancers in three-piece suits and bowler hats, a short musical drama speaking out against black-on-black violence, a limber teenager executing a lyrical jazz dance, an illusionist in a tuxedo pulling scarves out of the air – an afternoon parade of keyboards and shiny saxophones and trombones and basses, whose sounds bounced energy and exuberance off the walls and into the warming summer sky.

The Latin Power Dance Club was four girls in short white skirts and black blouses, their long coal-black hair swinging behind them as they moved to horns in syncopated rhythms. Remarkably disciplined for thirteen year- olds, they gave off an unmistakable hint of incipient sexuality when they extended their arms straight out, wrists hanging limply, and made circles with their hips. After forming a perfect square of outstretched arms, they turned away from each other while the two in front smiled down at the crowd, enticing them to join in the clapping and the rhythms.

Those members of the audience closest to the stage clapped with their hands high in the air; others bobbed their heads to the beat and tried to imitate the movements of the sinuous hips on the stage above them.

The mistress of ceremonies had been dancing behind the group for the last minute of their routine. When they finished, she took back the mike and looked down at the crowd through dark, gold-rimmed glasses. She wore a denim shirt with long tails hanging off on the sides, giving the impression of someone walking around in a thin blue clothespin.

"Classic, class*eeek*." She leaned out as though ready to take wing over the upturned faces on the steps, and the gold chain beneath her braids swung out to them as well. "Professionals in the making." Cheers and whistles from the upturned faces. "Let's *give* it *up* for the Latin Power Dance Club! Applause over the cheers and whistles, not stopping until the girls were off the stage."

Immediately another dance group took over, two girls and a brawny young man who took the mike and held it horizontally in front of his mouth.

"First of all, I'd like to welcome everybody to this youth rally, because without the youth there's no future, and without a future there's no way to get things started. The people we have doing this today are first of all committed to God, and then to you. We want all of you to be brothers and sisters. Whether you're *blood* or not, we've got to unite as one."

"Amen, brother."

He paused, as more *yea*-aah's and *aah*-men's rose on cue in an echo of his religious fervor. But in this situation it was not prayers that he wanted. "Let's go ahead and dance now, come on!"

One of the girls took the mike and slapped her free hand on her hip. "Let's party, uhhh *huh*? Ohhhhh, you *know* it! Come on, everybody get *uuuuuuuup*!" The people in front needed little encouragement. In a moment they were slow dancing with outstretched arms making languid circles in the free spaces between them.

"Yo, the time is right," she sang in a low voice and with lips exaggerating the words. "There'll be music everywhere... ummmm *ummmmh*!"

The young man stepped to the edge of the stage, his toes over the edge, and he leaned out as though he really planned to fall directly into the crowd. "Are you having a good time to*night*?" "Not night yet," a voice called up to him. "Well, it's gonna be soon, and we're gonna *dance* all night..."

"...In the streets," the singer came back with her lyrical ad-lib, obviously inventing the words with bluesy nonchalance. She went down the stairs swinging the mike, no longer concerned with keeping it near her mouth. No matter. The dancers swallowed her, and together they became a colloid whose particles were people, a weaving and swaying and slow-clapping protoplasm moving back and forth and bringing hands together to rhythms of its own.

Then we watched a small boy in an outsized suit with short pants that reached to his ankles and whose head was topped with a pink, short-brimmed hat. Dwarfed by the speakers behind him and shifting from one leg to the other, he sang to the accompaniment of a keyboard while a local radio personality knelt to hold the mike close in front of his mouth. His voice wavered on the longer notes but was beautifully clear on the high ones.

While a crowd watches a performance it can be interesting to watch the crowd. The wide concrete sitting areas nearest the stage were full to overflowing, so I half-knelt and half-crouched in a place that allowed for an oblique viewing of both stage and crowd. It did not take long to locate the woman whom I took to be the boy's mother. She was sitting only a few yards away.

She was a large woman, of indeterminate age, and it came to me that she might well be grandmother rather than mother. What caused me to identify her -- if indeed I had -- was that her mouth was moving in sync with his own, and I pictured her on her knees, her hands on his shoulders, coaching him during the days leading up to this one. Her large breasts had once been a fleshy haven into which he, at an earlier age frightened or woeful, had buried his face. Now they swelled with the excitement of her quickened breathing.

She was transfixed. She was a modern Madonna whose brief rapture would surpass the Madonna-faces of those bland two-dimensional Renaissance religious portraits. It could do even better, because she was real. Her gaze spoke for all of us. It suggested that we were fixed in time and space among the concrete steps and the trees and the grassy berms, and that at least for now, today, nothing bad was going to happen even though bad things will happen at other times, and that there would be no dangerous differences of opinion or behaviors that anyone would later regret.

When the boy ended his song and my attention turned to others in the crowd, I discovered that the tables had been turned: I was being watched.

He was sitting one row above the Madonna and several seats to her left. In this case it was easier to guess his age -- very close to my own -- and his height, which must have been over six feet since his head was well above the heads of those around him. There was a second reason that he stood out: his clothes. He wore pressed cotton slacks rather than shorts, and shiny black shoes, as if to say that there was room for the dignity of age even at this sort of event, and his simple brown shirt above the slacks was nearly a match. Even sitting he gave the impression of being well-proportioned, suggesting a body that would have been suitable for a middle-aged male fashion magazine. In his right hand he held a white plastic cup.

Because his bearing was so like that of a soldier, there was the suggestion that he had known unpleasant things. Momentarily I pictured him standing over the body of a dead North Vietnamese soldier -- he was the right age for that war -- and if by chance something of that sort *was* part of his memory, I also felt that here he was at peace. Maybe this day was replacing those kinds of memories by the balancing joy that came from his share in the triumph of the child on the stage.

At first he seemed to look at me as if asking: what are you doing here? It was a question I could equally well have asked of him, although for different reasons. We locked eyes, though only for a moment and without expression, and then I dropped mine because by then I was aware of the possible rudeness of having watched someone too long. When I looked again, it was no surprise to see that he had not turned away.

That was the one time that I was conscious of my whiteness in that gathering. There was no fear in that, unlike how some white people might feel when driving through an all-black neighborhood as darkness falls. Rather, I felt that we had together created a contrast of race and color that was at the same time complementary. We may have been there for different reasons and we may have come there from different backgrounds, but we were there. That we would never truly know each other beyond that brief contact did not matter; there was togetherness enough in the moment.

The episode ended when he raised his cup slightly, though I could not tell if that was meant as a salute or if he had thought to take a drink and then changed his mind.

The spell was broken, and as a response to that I stood and left the place. I saw that Kyle was across the stage, looking like a human hanger for his camera equipment and taking the pictures that would appear in the organization's next annual report. He waved. Then Isaac threaded his way over to me, wearing the security badge that we had all pinned on earlier.

"You seen Kenny?" he asked. Isaac was one of those whom I had come to think of as the guards. If at other times he had been something less than welcoming, now he looked more official than intimidating, and his look fit the time and place.

"The last time I saw him, he was running up those stairs." I waved at a spot across the park. "Somebody said there was a fight. I went after him, but then I lost him in the crowd. Anyway, I didn't see any fight."

"It wasn't no *fighting*," Isaac said, eyebrows raised in a challenge to that idea: no way. "Just two guys shoving a little. The cops were right there."

"The cops are everywhere," I said.

"Guess they think *they* need to be. But we're not *gonna* have any problems today."

I walked to the side of the pit and stopped at the bottom of a stairway where young artists were exhibiting their work.

One young artist was talking to a middle-aged woman and pointing at a sketch with the lack of affectation more often found in the younger artist. Behind him the competition was spread out on tables and tripods and hung from walls. "My grandfather," he was saying to the woman. "Did it in my art class. This one," he pointed to another, "is of Martin Luther King. Showing how he was jailed, but jailed in a just cause." *Jailed. In. A. Just. Cause.* He emphasized each syllable with the intonations of a rap singer. Then he moved to a drawing of an athlete flying through the air. "This one won third prize. And that's all." He stopped abruptly, as though concerned suddenly about calling too much attention to himself.

A girl wanted to explain her abstract work to me. She pointed to a print of a guitar lying on its side. "My boyfriend's guitar," she said. It seemed important for her to explain the ownership as well as the artistry. "And this is a self-portrait, in chalk." Quickly she pushed that one aside, apparently not satisfied with it. "Here's a still-life in black and white ink. But I used colored pencil for this one." She held up a picture of a three-stemmed sunflower with the faces of pretty young girls where the flowers' centers would be. "Friends of mine," she explained.

Another boy showed me pictures of race cars and cartoon characters. He reached into a plastic bag and pulled out more of them. Then some pictures of sports heroes.

Up on the stage, E. J. gave out the prizes. "I thank God for this," one winner said as accepted his gift certificate and shook hands with E. J. "Everybody's a winner here," E. J. told the crowd, reminding them that every contestant got a camera and a tee-shirt.

"Now we've got a tie," he announced. "So you'll have to be the tie-breaker. Put your *hands* together." The shouts and applause came up to him democratically: another split decision. "You'll have to do better than thaaa-aaat." His last word echoed off the concrete as if for emphasis. So the crowd tried again and, Solomon-like, he passed out prizes to both. Then, turning to another contestant, "Where are your parents? Let's get *them* up here." The father came on stage, said "thank you" shyly into the microphone and led his child away by the hand.

I eventually found Ken myself. He was in one of the grassy areas, talking to a reporter and looking directly into the black eye of a television camera. No one could have known that he had slept only two hours in the last two days. His Youth Day tee-shirt, worn beneath wide suspenders in a red and black paisley pattern, was a bright contrast to his formal dark slacks that ended over dark shoes. As someone else might in that situation, he did not give the impression that these were the best clothes he had, and they were not.

We were far enough away from the audio-epicenter that he could actually be heard.

"Nine hours of performances," he was saying, "and that's nowhere near enough to include all the groups and individuals that applied for a chance to show what they can do. We had to turn down hundreds of kids."

The voice was more powerful than ever. It was confident in the way of one who is at the height of his power and knows that nothing can go wrong. "We're trying to save some lives today, keep them away from the pressures, the drugs and violence, on the streets."

Seeing me, Ken swung away from the TV reporter and pulled me in front of the camera.

"This is Derek," he told the viewers who would see us on the evening's news, arms slung over each other's shoulders. "He's one of our board members. We couldn't do all this without a lot of help."

There was a hint of elbow in the ribs and a tiny movement of the head. It was my turn to say something.

"It's a great day for the kids, really, for all of us here," I told the camera, and ducked out of range.

"It's all about how our young people get the recognition they truly deserve," Ken carried on for the two of us. "A chance to share their attributes with the whole city. We've got a lot of talented youth in this city, for sure. One of them has gone on to teach ballet, and another got a recording contract."

That was news to me. It was also the sort of thing that can be said without fear that someone would do some fact-checking. But I knew it was true.

I went back to watching the performances and the swirling crowd. A ten year-old played her bass guitar, thin fingers racing expertly along its long neck while her father, behind her, accompanied her on a cut-out acoustic. Two other girls in the same age category sang their original composition with a message about drug abuse, pointing their forefingers out at the audience as though accusing them of the habit as well. Three young mothers came on the stage and, fussing as mothers do, lined their children up in front of themselves as they were presented with the Special Parents' Award.

Small children, always the favorites and each one more heart-breakingly beautiful than the one before, sang into microphones they stood on tiptoe to reach. Every so often Ken would appear on stage, re-arranging something, helping someone with a mike or a prop, joking with the entertainers and the crowd. In between acts, professional musicians took the stage. As good as they were, the kids got the most attention.

"Nine hours of performances," Ken had told the TV reporter. "We're trying to save some lives today."

It is even possible that he did save some lives that day, specifically in the sense that one or two of those performers, instead of being on the stage, might have been the victim of some inner-city shootout. If that was his claim, it was not farfetched. Homicides in Rochester had been at record highs in the years just before Ken came on the scene. During the years of his activism, the city celebrated a significant decline in violent crime. The idea that events like Youth Day had a role in that decline is not easily dismissed. Two years later, the trend had reversed itself: 18 people were killed between early June and Labor Day.

That was not what he meant. He meant that the purpose of Youth Day was to allow young people to express themselves in wholesome rather than destructive ways. The method was the simple one of fostering the connection between self-expression and self-esteem. On psychological grounds there was not a lot new in that idea. The difference was that Youth Day was turning theory into practice.

Of course I had to spend the next few days writing about the experience. I knew at once that Ken was doing more than simply helping kids develop self-esteem. The real inspiration was that he was doing it through art, especially through music. When people experience music together, there is a sense that there is some beauty beyond themselves or those they are with, beyond what little bit they might personally be adding, beyond ego and all the trouble ego brings, something exceptional that is being experienced even if only for a very short time. Maybe that is true for other artists and other kinds of art, but it is much more *present* with music.

I even understood why, in that way that we understand things that come to us as dispatches from insights we thought we never had. It is because music is harmony. And sometimes, when everything else is right, music can give us a momentary sense of the ultimate harmony that is beyond the universe as we presently understand it. Justice, Heraclitus said, is "hidden harmony." It may that the justice the two of us and so many others have sought, whose absence we blame on the whipping boys of class and greed and power, is far more transcendent than simple humanity can grasp. There was more of justice in the consolidation of people in the park that afternoon than is accomplished by philosophizing or moralizing. When we harmonize we do not criticize. Harmony has nothing to do with making judgments, because judgments arise when it is felt that there is some lack of harmony in the way we act or deal with each other.

Another way of experiencing harmony can be through a belief system, finding it in one or another representation of God. It makes sense that religious exercises are so often connected with music and that some of the greatest musical compositions arose from religious belief. It occurred to me that Ken and I never talked about God or religion, not because those topics were unimportant to us but because they had nothing of immediate value about them. The things we talked about had the priority that comes from being near rather than transcendent. Probably we *should* have talked about God.

If we had, the conversation would likely have been more intellectual than emotional, and it would then have missed the point. Music gets through on a very different level. If somehow we are briefly a part of the making of that link with ultimate harmony, if we are making the music as Ken and his youth were doing that day, it has to have a powerful effect on our self-esteem, and a reducing effect on our egos. When you have even a fleeting sense of the universal harmony, ego necessarily dissolves, because ego centers us on the oneness and uniqueness of our particular being while harmony is the resolution of *parts* into the beauty of the whole. I do not know if Ken ever thought it out quite in those terms, but it seemed to me that in some way he understood it better than most. On that day at least.

Most of this has been thought out many times and more thoroughly too. What was important to me then was that we were *feeling* it, not just saying it over again. Not that I felt personally many of those harmonious connections during the day, since most of that music was not the kind I like. But I could appreciate how some of those young performers might have been feeling it, and what it had done to them.

Let's not overdo this. Even with all the high spirits and the applause and the prizes, it is doubtful that anyone -- even the young artists themselves -- would have argued that we were experiencing great art that day. What makes art great is for the critics to argue over, and there were no critics in the park that day. In any event, critics are usually concerned with the value of the artifact, the art *product*.

Youth Day was about art as process. That the artists were all youthful was central to the theme and purpose of the day, but that focus may have unintentionally stumbled on something greater, because it can be argued that the process of art is at its best in the young, and maybe at its very best in the very young. Among the first conscious acts of children are their attempts to create; on the fronts and sides of millions of refrigerators hang the evidence of that. There is something very serious about those small acts of creation, which anyone can verify by watching the child as artist.

Are they, in their total absorption, in the mindless freedom of their concentration and in the silent intuition of their choices, somehow reconstructing the harmony that they knew in another place? Art kills time. It does that just as time eventually kills art -- both the process, which has to end because every process ends – and also the products, all of which are eventually worn away. But death is not the issue. If art kills time it is because real art, on whatever level, is transcendent, and to be transcendent is to be timeless.

Finally, Youth Day itself –- from the creative benevolence of its first conception to the final act of the day -- was the best evidence of art as process. It was an engagement and a blossoming, one not restricted to the youth who took part. Even if like every process it had to end, and even if its achievement would be soon be lost in obscurity, while it happened there was light over shadow and the triumph of expression -- of the self and of the community -- in place of nullity or negativism. Because it was art it was worth more than a hundred lectures on violence or a thousand posters about the dangers of drugs.

STREET DRUGS

Arguna said: "O Krishna! You praise renunciation of actions and also the pursuit of them. Tell me determinately which one of these two is superior." The Deity said: "Renunciation and pursuit of action are both instruments of happiness. But of the two, pursuit of action is superior to renunciation of action."

-- From The Bhagavadgita

I don't know what your destiny will be, but one thing I know. The only ones among you who will be really happy are those who have sought and found how to serve.

-- Albert Schweitzer

Colum's tube of antifungal lotion is dying. He just dropped it on the ground, and some foot among the many feet around here must have landed on it, almost dead center. The greyish-white lotion is oozing out of a crack in the side, mixing with the dust. And now it's all over Colum's hands, some of it already on his shirt from where he's trying to wipe it off his fingers. He's looking a little frantic, trying to save as much of it as he can by putting a piece of note paper under the tube.

"Is there an empty jar or something around here?" he asks no one in particular.

Everybody is too busy with their own work to look for an empty jar.

"Maybe you just ought to throw it away," I tell him. "We have more."

"I hate to waste it."

"You aren't wasting it," Oliver says, coming around the table for a look. "You've got enough on yourself to keep away fungi for years."

"Maybe it'll keep the flies off me, anyway."

He is screwing the cap back on the tube, maybe thinking that will keep the lotion from oozing out the side like a tiny lava flow. Finally he gives up with a grunt and tosses the whole mess into a box under the lowest shelf. He flips his sticky hands over and back a few times as if that will somehow get rid of the stuff and then wipes them again on his shirt.

"There's a spigot over there," Oliver tells him, nodding toward a corner of the clinic. "Maybe you can wash it off."

The lotion is not water soluble, so it does not wash off. Rather it smears itself along his arms and creates tiny bubbles. Colum comes back wiping the rest of it on the backs of his hands and muttering something about sun block.

For my part, I need to get on with showing Molly how to fill this prescription. The biggest problem is just to keep a little work area on the table, which is a piece of plywood placed on top of some empty medicine chests. Right now the table is covered with jars of pills, lids, rubber bands, pens, little grey envelopes, and the prescription cards the doctors pass back to us. The four or five of us who have to work in all this clutter keep trying to claim a few more inches for ourselves.

"This one's not too hard," I say, wanting to encourage her. You can even read most of the doctor's handwriting. We've already got the TC capsules he wants, and right now we need the Salbutamol."

"Where is that?"

"See that chart hanging on the clothesline?"

"Yes."

"Can you find Salbutamol on the chart?"

She turns to it and runs her finger down the list.

"It says it's on shelf 8."

She looks on shelf 8. "I don't see it here."

"Try the shelves above and below."

She looks, but just then I see that Swedish has it in front of her on the table. I snatch it when she turns away.

"You can see that the doctor has written Sal, 4 mg, 1x2x7. That means the patient is to take one four-milligram tablet twice a day for a week."

We count out 14 tablets and pass the jar of Salbutamol back to Swedish, who has just begun to look for it.

"Most of the patients are considered to be illiterate, but the next thing you have to do is write instructions on this little pill envelope. The Indian government wants us to write the name of the drug here at the top."

"But if they're illiterate, why do we have to write anything?

"Don't ask intelligent questions. Haven't you ever had anything to do with the bureaucracy in this country? When I got here it took 20 minutes and three people just to change my dollars into rupees."

"I guess that's how it was for me too."

"Anyway, now we can shift to some drawings. You need to draw one little pill under this sort of crude picture of the rising sun."

She does, concentrating almost like a child on her first day in nursery school. She is a little woman as it is, and her small fingers wrap around the pen as if for security.

"Now draw another pill under the setting sun, but nothing in the spaces under the mid-day sun or the moon. You get the idea: this tells them when to take the pills. Now, you see these little pictures of people's faces? Circle the adult male and scratch out the faces of the woman and the baby and the young kids."

At the bottom of the envelope is a simple picture of a bowl of food.

"Salbutamol is taken before meals, so draw a line to the left of the bowl, and then an arrow leading to it."

When she is finished we count the pills into the envelope and write the patient's ID number on the back. "We'll assume he can understand all this."

"Now you can see that the last thing the doctor has ordered is Chloramphenicol eardrops. Can you figure out how much?"

"Two drops in each ear, three times a day for a week."

"Good. I'll get the drops." They are on shelf 13, the lowest, and I see where some of Colum's lotion has already been smeared into the dust beneath it.

"Now you have to draw directions on the side of the container for the eardrops, which is not easy on this small surface. You also have to deface the container by rubbing it against one those rough concrete blocks, back there behind the shelves. Try to get most of the words off of it."

"Why?"

"Because if you don't the patient might try to sell the medication on the street instead of using it."

We collect the little envelopes and the eardrops and work our way through the crowd to the interpreter, Saleem. As he nods to us, I see that his thick head of hair is showing grey strands among the black. He is sitting on a small box, and except for his head he is barely visible among the waiting patients. We will have to wait while Elaine, another of the volunteer pharmacists, explains her prescription to Saleem.

Slowly, and with enviable calm, he interprets all of it to the patient, a woman with a thin purple shawl around her head and a small ornament on the left side of her nose. What can be seen of her own hair is unevenly parted, and much of her face, above and below eyes that are blood-riven and slit against the sun, is bumpy with red pimples. She holds a baby under one arm while two small children stand beside her. Elaine is telling Saleem that the woman will receive some food as well, so all of this will take some time.

From all around us, in the tight circle, the dark eyes of women and children watch intently. Standing partly in the sun, I can feel the sweat running down my inner arms. Finally, Saleem has the entire prescription straightened out. The woman pulls up part of the front of her sari to make a little basket, into which Elaine puts the food. It is the usual food allotment: a fist-size bag of cereal, a biscuit, some nutrallah and a bar of soap. To this Saleem adds a head of cabbage, first looking and then picking the largest from a box sitting beside him.

Twisting to get in front of us, a little girl in a black dress is crying and parting her hair at the back of her head. Because I can't see what is wrong, I assume it is a cut or some kind of skin disease. Her mother starts talking to me in Bengali, pointing to the child.

"Sorry, madam, but I can't understand you."

She goes on talking and pointing to her daughter, confident that the sheer number of her words will explain everything. In the press of the crowd, Elaine almost knocks me over as she turns to go back to the prescription table. If I had stepped out of her way, I would have come down on several pairs of bare feet.

"Sorry. Hey, do you want to take a break when you're done with that one?"

"I had one already. But I think that Molly here could use one anytime soon."

We slide around people to get to Saleem on his little box, and give him our patient's ID number. As soon as he calls it out, an old woman with a basket under her arm pushes into the circle, unmindful of a few sharp looks. Saleem glances at the number on the slip of paper she hands to him, shakes his head, and shows her paper to me.

"Not right, is it?" he asks.

"No, this one's for a man. Try again."

He nods the old woman out of the way abruptly and calls the number again, louder, and then a second time. A tall man in a white dhoti comes forward, using his height and an air of dignity as weapons to move people aside. Saleem re-checks the number and hands the man's paper to me.

"Okay. This is the one."

He looks once through our drugs and then begins explaining them to the tall man. As Saleem talks, the man nods his head again and again in that odd way they all do. It is a slight twist of the head, down and slightly to the side, almost like a twitch. It is supposed to mean that they understand, I have been told. Or it can mean that they do not understand. Usually, I just take it to mean the first of these. We have been taught to make very sure the patients know what to do with the drugs we give them, but sometime I wonder.

"Saleem, be sure he knows that these eardrops go in both ears, three times a day."

As the man watches, I unscrew the dropper from the bottle and demonstrate how to squeeze out three drops. One of them falls into the dust at our feet.

"For how long?" Saleem asks.

"A week. No, tell him to use it all up."

Saleem gives me that same little twitchy nod, and then he points to something else on the doctor's card.

"What does this say?"

"Can you read this, Molly?"

"It looks like it says 'hot compress locally'.

"Thanks. Saleem, ask him if he has a bruise or sore muscles or something like that."

Saleem does, and the tall man puts his hand on the back of his neck and moves his head around. It looks like his neck is swollen.

"I guess he's supposed to put a hot towel there sometimes. Tell him to use a wet, hot towel. He can just get it wet and put it in this damned sun."

At that, Saleem smiles for the first time. As we turn to leave, the woman with the twisting child pulls at my sleeve and starts to talk again. She is pointing to the child's head and shaking her own.

"Saleem, please tell this woman that she has to go up front to the doctors and wait her turn if she wants some help."

Going back to the front ourselves, we have to step over a small boy who is peeing in the dirt. His urine is creeping slowly over toward someone's sandal. Behind him, another boy is playing with the dry soil, sifting it into one of the small earthenware cups used for drinking tea. Another child, maybe his sister, seems to want to play too.

Back at the table, Colum is waving a prescription card around.

"Is anyone doing number 67183?"

"Not me," I tell him when he looks my way." What's the problem?"

"There's a guy back there with terrible diarrhea." Colum waves the card toward the back of the clinic. "And he's making a mess of the place."

In spite of ourselves, some of us start laughing. Oliver says, "He's all yours, mate."

Before I can pick up a new set of prescription cards, one of the other new volunteers touches me on the arm.

"What's Folifer?" she asks.

"It's Folic Acid and Ferrous Sulfate, a vitamin I guess."

"But I can't find it on the charts. Where is it?"

For some reason, Folifer has not been included on the charts, and I remember having the same problem finding it.

"It's on shelf 5. I just found it myself a few days ago."

She pulls the jar of Folifer off shelf 5. It is an extra-large jar with a crack running down its clear plastic side.

"Do you want it for a child or an adult?"

She studies the card for a moment. "An adult."

"Okay. That's the right one. What's your name?"

"Trisha."

"I'm Derek. How long are you here for?"

"A few weeks, anyway," she says. Maybe longer. It would help if I knew what I was doing."

"Don't worry, you'll learn real fast. Just ask anybody."

"Thanks."

"Better yet, ask me," Oliver says. "It makes me feel important."

Trisha smiles as though she has to work up to the performance. She is short and a little stocky, and her plain brown dress looks like it has not been underneath an iron since she bought it from a second-hand store. In her early forties it seems, her distinctive features are a Slavic forehead and the nearly permanent knit of her brows. She has an air about her that suggests the protectiveness of a recent divorcee or the artifice of someone in recovery: yes, thank you, I am making it on my own. At the moment things are apparently better for her. She looks relieved and even temporarily content, and I have the feeling that the two us are the first persons in this confusing new world who have talked to her.

"When you want a break, someone can show you a little place across the street. You can get some tea and a few samozas if you're hungry." She looks puzzled at that. "They're sort of pastries, shaped in little triangles and filled with some curried stuff. Or whatever."

"Thanks again."

As she turns away, I see that the back of her dress is soaked with sweat. It is mid-March now, the beginning of India's real heat. From now until the monsoons arrive, temperatures can rise to 120 degrees, rarely falling below 80 even at night. The tar on the roads can turn to liquid, and the huge Howrah Bridge over the Hoogli River gets four feet longer in the daytime. Or so I have been told.

She is another person speaking with an accent, one hard to place, though her soft r's have a hint of Poland or Ukraine. For some reason, Europeans make up the majority of the volunteers in Calcutta. Over the past several weeks, I have worked with people, most of them young, from France, Germany, Holland, Belgium, England, Ireland and Sweden. Also Australia and Canada. So far only two Americans. That could be because the United States is so far around the globe from India.

Then again, it is a long trip for most everyone here. What is it that instills that urge for adventure and the creativity to satisfy part of that urge in a Calcutta street clinic?

Whatever it is, *some* young Americans have it. It was a student from California I watched in the beginning, at Mother Teresa's place. He and a sick or maybe dying man were sitting on a bed, side by side, and he was gently stroking the old man's head, running his hand slowly over the close-cropped, receding hair. A bowl of soup sat cooling between them. Neither one was talking. Where, or by what example, did he learn to do that?

Watching these young people -- and some of them not so young -- who have come to Calcutta has been one of the best parts of this experience. Some, they tell me, are only passing through, getting briefly involved as part of some larger travel adventure. Others are here for months or years, living in places and conditions that are not known for the comforts expected by most modern travelers. I know that because I have been in some of their digs. Some are students with medical educations in mind or already underway, others are on more of a spiritual journey. At some point they have discovered that it is possible to know the world in ways other than as it is given to us by electronic devices.

Whatever their nationalities or interests or discoveries, it has become more obvious every day that Calcutta is a mecca for humanitarian types, a city of volunteers. Most of us live in cheap little hotels or guest houses in the center of the city, and we meet each other often in the crowded streets. We share meals sometimes in the less expensive restaurants, and some of us get together in the late afternoons at a convenient outdoor cafe, shady under leafy trees and quiet behind a high wall.

New people are invariably asked the same three questions: where are you from, how long are you staying, where are you working? The scene offers parallels to the Paris expatriates of the 1920s and 1930s, allowing for some serious differences in purposes and activities.

Mother Teresa's fame and her various institutions here are a main attraction, it seems. I worked briefly at Kalighat, her first and most famous undertaking, but soon found it to be overcrowded, with volunteers more often than not standing around in anticipation of something to do. Looking for some humor in that, a few of us started making jokes about needing to take a number to get a chance at some volunteering. That others were not amused was a bad sign.

Then, through the informal volunteer network, I heard that help was more needed in this street clinic. It is one of several free clinics run by a British organization. The one we are in now is less popular because it is a 45-minute commute from downtown. Thus it needs more help.

Together, the clinics serve hundreds of people every day, six days a week, using Bengali doctors and staff and whatever volunteers they can attract. The major functions of the operation are the walk-in diagnoses and then dispensing of drugs by volunteer pharmacists. The organization also provides health education, runs a school, sponsors immunization and vitamin programs, gives out crutches, dentures, footwear, glasses and clothes, and even helps with train and bus fare for those who come from out in the country.

A very impressive operation and, like many others, it was initially the work of one energetic and compassionate person. In this case that person is a retired British physician, whom I met by chance in the hall outside my room. His age was hard to determine. A slight stoop gave him a tired look, but his voice was strong and his manner confident. He was as modest as I might have expected, and he was gracious in his thanks for the help we give.

The clinic is set up so that those of us who work in the pharmacy section can be trained quickly. In practice, we pretty much train each other. Our work is sometimes checked by people with medical backgrounds, making it less likely we have poisoned anyone. No one would want to know how badly some of us did in our high school or college chemistry courses.

Each day we meet at a neighborhood Sikh restaurant for a breakfast of coffee, toast or an omelet, and then we share a cab, squeezing in like people in a circus stunt, or we take a bus here. I have come to enjoy riding on the second level of the rattling double-decker buses. It takes me back to childhood days in amusement parks, as the bus lurches and grinds and bumps its way toward the north side of this sprawling city. We hold on tightly and slam against one another, yelling to make ourselves heard over the cacophony of Calcutta's streets: the croak of the rubber-ball taxi horns and the bells of the eager rickshaw pullers, the deafening roar of buses accelerating alongside ours, and the nasty whine of motorbikes.

Along one stretch, we can look down into the bed of the city's unfinished subway. It is being dug by hand, we are told, and work stops during the monsoon season. From the bus, we see how a few people sleep, oblivious to the noise, on top of the rusting steel girders that span the long subway grave.

"What must it be like to sleep on a girder?" I wondered.

"What happens when you turn over?" Oliver asked.

By the time we arrive at the clinic, the local staff has put up the large awning of canvas and poles that will shield us from the sun. The shelves have been re-erected and the drugs and other medications are organized. The seven doctors have taken their places on seven folding chairs. Then the people crowd in and sit on the ground to wait their turn. Some of the volunteers go to the area where vitamins are dispensed or to the corner where burns and wounds are treated. The rest of us work at being pharmacists.

Back at the table, Molly picks up the next prescription, lying where a doctor has passed it casually over his shoulder. This time it is a whole set of cards, for a family with a long history at the clinic. We look through them together.

"The mother apparently needs Brufen, a pain killer, and PCM, 500 milligrams."

"What's that?"

"Paracetamol, shelf 4. One of the kids needs an antacid, which means we will have to draw a picture that is supposed to show a mouth chewing. I hope you have some artistic talent."

Somebody else in the family needs a lotion. The drawing to show that the lotion needs to be rubbed in with a finger has been causing some amusement lately. Up until last week, the drawing was just some squiggly lines. Then somebody changed the drawings chart to try to make the picture more illustrative. Now we are supposed to draw a bent finger. But for all my attempts, I can't get it to look right. What it ends up looking like is the source of amusement.

"Does this look okay?" I asked Swedish.

She studied my tiny drawing for a moment. "No, it looks like a penis."

Oliver looked over her shoulder. "They'll think they're supposed to rub the stuff on their ding-a-ling."

Molly and I flip back through the cards and see that there is even more to do than first appeared.

"The pills for one of the children will have to be cut in half with the little chopper.

"Where do I get that?" Molly is alert, a quick study.

"It's always disappearing, but you'll find it. Don't forget to draw a half-pill on the envelope, even though that should be obvious, since the pills will be in halves. There's also an injection, but one of the nurses will do that. And we'll have to collect 13 more injection containers and little water bottles with the sterilized water. Look, this card shows that the family gets the plate with soap, biscuit and the other stuff, plus a vegetable. Also five rupees for bus fare back home. I'll show you where all that is."

The way she goes over the cards suggests that Molly is eager to get on with it. We will need to work carefully because of the chances of forgetting something from all these cards, confusing because they are also filled with notes from the family's former visits. I dread the complications that will arise when Saleem tries to make all of this clear to the mother.

"Did that guy like his shoe, do you think?" Oliver asks. His normal lopsided grin is all the more compelling because it enlivens a bony face under a mostly shaven head.

"I guess so. He didn't say."

That is another matter that has been greatly amusing him. One of my first prescriptions today was for a man with TB, one of the most common illnesses treated here. At the bottom of the card, the doctor had written, "please, please, give this man some shoes."

Oliver showed me the box that holds donated sandals, and after Saleem and I had given out the drugs, I took the man over to it. On the way I discovered that he had only one foot, the left one. His right leg was missing to above the knee. Thus I faced a small decision. Would I embarrass him by giving him both sandals? Would he be able to walk in the right-foot sandal when the other one wore out? I picked up both sandals and thought for a moment. Eventually I handed the one sandal to him and threw the other back in the box. As the man limped away, I saw Oliver grinning.

"Why'd you give him just the one?"

"I thought that someday somebody would come in here with only a right foot. No point in being wasteful."

Oliver is almost always laughing about something. He is perfect for this place, a foil that keeps the rest of us in a state of steady acceptance, using chatter and clowning to distract us from becoming the victims of vicarious suffering. It could also be that his antic character and sense for comedy are his ways of disguising the fact that he is a highly competent and dedicated nurse.

Now, while Molly starts on the prescription, he calls me away to see a young girl he is treating.

"Look at this one." For the moment the grin is gone.

The girl is about nine years old. Her eyes are set wide apart under unplucked brows, and her look is impassive. Along her arms are repulsive boils -- rolling, grey lumps spotted with white. Some of them are as big as oversized grapes. With that happy disregard for modesty that is common to most medical providers, Oliver pulls back her sari to show even bigger ones on her leg, above and below the knee.

"What the hell *is* that?"

"It's skin TB. I've never seen it worse than this."

"What can you do about it?"

"We'll medicate her, the usual. For all the good it will do."

"Can she live like that?"

"I guess she does, doesn't she?"

Oliver finds a bizarre enjoyment in showing me the worst of the ailments. At first that seemed another piece of the off-beat humor. Later it came to me that for some people a good way to deal emotionally with the suffering of others is to share it with those who are not themselves suffering but who, it is to be hoped, will understand.

Yesterday he wanted me to see a woman with a badly-burned leg. Loose red skin was peeling on her thigh, some of it dangling in short strips. She showed no sign of pain, probably having at some earlier point come to her own terms with it.

"A cooking accident," he said." The leg will have to come off."

There is no room for the squeamish around here, or the soft-hearted. It is the same for Calcutta as a whole. The city is worse than any place I have ever been, 13 million people living in congestion, relentless noise, heat and dirt, violence and corruption. If the city has a chamber of commerce, it must be hard pressed to find something positive to talk about. The adjectives most commonly found in descriptions are "ugly," "desperate," "squalid," "teeming," -- all of them by now having passed the point of cliché. Calcutta has been called an urban horror story, the most violent city in the world, a sea of meanness and misery.

At some point words fail, inadequate to describe the city that was at one time the British Imperial capitol, called the city of palaces and the second most important city in the British Empire. It is hard now to imagine what it must have been like before the British left India in 1947, before the Hindu-Moslem riots and the migration of great numbers of Hindus to Calcutta from West Bengal, now the country of Bangladesh.

It is said that Calcutta's streets used to be washed every day. Now those same streets are flooded instead, when for days at a time the monsoon rains overwhelm the tired, inadequate drainage system. That system dates from the nineteenth century, and it runs alongside water pipes that are themselves bursting with age. A few times now we have taken off our shoes to wade through wide, ankle-deep pools. A nice situation, as Oliver puts it, if you like cholera and amoebic dysentery.

Each day, the garbage from the dumpsters near my hotel is scattered by the scavengers who come in the night to look for scraps of food, or things to sell or recycle: bits of metal, plastic, paper. Whole families live on the streets we use to go to the restaurants, sleeping on piles of rags and cooking whatever they can find in little black pots. The air is fouled from their cooking fires and by the buses and taxis, whose black exhaust hangs at the intersections. The port of Calcutta is silting up from the Hoogli River, the roads and factories are going unrepaired. It has the feel of a city that began to die some time ago and has not yet noticed.

For many, Calcutta is the worst of India, an exception, but it could also be a herald of where other parts of the country are headed. It is a country with 75% illiteracy, enough beggars to fill a large European country and enough lepers to fill a smaller one. Some of the richest people in the world live among hundreds of millions of malnourished and unemployed, diseased and uneducated lower classes.

The results are inevitable. Today's newspaper, which I skimmed during breakfast, presented sufficient examples. The lead story told of two and a half tons of explosives seized in Bombay. That was enough, the paper said, to blow up half a city. In another part of town, automatic rifles and hand grenades were recovered. In a provincial town, police killed four people during a riot. The mob set six cars on fire and burned one police officer alive. On the inside pages, I read stories on the trial of a minister for corruption, a call for a commission to study child-labor abuse (ten million children in agricultural work alone, others working in firecracker factories, it claimed), a loan scam, a bomb blast, a fire at an atomic power station, and a bomb scare in a court room. The editorials dealt with the country's economic crisis, social disintegration, and the abuses of the Indian bureaucracy.

The threat of violence hangs in the air of India like that black smoke in the streets of Calcutta. Just before I arrived, an outbreak of bombings put Bombay into the international news. Then a big blast went off here in Calcutta, in a neighborhood we pass through each morning. After that our state department suggested that Americans should keep away from India for a while, but I notice that no one here has mentioned the matter.

Still, I stayed awake a long time after an explosion rattled loose window panes in my room during my first week here.

In all of this we have the reasons why there are not many people smiling in Calcutta. One of them who does is little Gita. She is a beautiful child of maybe ten or eleven, with shiny black hair that falls almost to the backs of her knees and a smile that would break the hardest heart in its contrast to the dismal scenes around her. She must live in the streets somewhere around the museum, because that is where she caught me on one of my first days here. She was carrying a small boy, like a potato sack with bare feet, over her shoulder. Her soiled sari was torn and hung in long, swaying threads from her free arm.

She had to run, her bare feet slapping on the sidewalk, to keep up. For most of a block she chattered the only English she knows: "No mama, no papa, baksheesh, papa, please papa, rupees papa, no mama, no papa, papa."

Her persistence and that honey smile got the better of common sense. I slipped her 20 rupees, about 60 cents, and hoped that no one saw.

Gita disappeared, and I was startled, five minutes later, to find her at my side again. Along with the boy, she now carried a small plastic bag. Still she was able to hold out one free hand.

"No mama, no papa, please rupees papa."

"Hey, I just gave you 20 rupees."

It was unlikely that she understood. In any case her chant went on without stopping even for a full breath: please rupees, papa, baksheesh papa.

At the end of the block, I gave her 10 more rupees and the best scowl that could be mustered against her charm. Of course another girl, of about the same age, appeared seconds later. I bought her off with another 20 rupees and almost ran for my hotel.

So I was not surprised to find Gita at my side again a few days later. This time I had a surprise for her, a 50-rupee note put aside just for her. Another day I did it again, on the way to creating a small fortune for a Calcutta beggar.

Naturally there has been a price to pay: it is now impossible to go anywhere near the museum without Gita and a few other children surrounding me, hands extended. Sometimes a woman follows behind them, yelling and throwing badly-aimed rocks; the children ignore her. This is on the way to becoming a pied-piper mob.

The other girl found me one afternoon as I was walking home from the outdoor cafe. That was a serious problem. If she discovered my hotel, an eager crowd would surely be waiting outside the door as I left each morning. I wound through side streets while she followed, chattering beside me, and then I turned abruptly into the doorway of a small hotel I had never seen before.

"You house?" the other girl said.

"Yes."

She came with me into a tiny lobby, and I was forced to go up the stairs at the back before she finally left. To be safe, I lurked in a dark hallway for several minutes, then scurried to my own hotel. Life proceeds now with the unease of the hunted: I am forced to go blocks out of the way, changing routes like a summons dodger. I am an adult playing a child's game of hide and seek.

Just as we are starting on the new prescription, Swedish shoves a card in front of my face. That is not her name, just what I call her because of the wheat-blond hair that she slips through the back of her baseball cap and the lapis-blue eyes that widen with her flirting. That genetic inheritance, along with the northern European talent for putting people politely but firmly in their place, makes the name irresistible.

"Read this one," she says in a tight voice.

Along with a prescription for 14 tablets of Isokin, the doctor has written a fairly long note.

"Patient four months pregnant. Five children. Advise tubal ligation. Says husband will throw her out of home if she has tubal, and refuses to use condoms. Patient wants oral contraceptives. Referred."

"Nice husband."

"Yeah. No wonder they can't control the population."

"We don't have those pills here, do we?"

"No, but she should be able to get them somewhere else. The doctors aren't helping much."

"What do you mean?"

"Sometimes they try to force the women to have tubals by withholding the food benefits. But that only hurts the children."

One needs to spend only a few days in India to realize that the population explosion is the country's biggest problem, a crisis that never goes away. It is a huge mudslide, rolling over itself and down the mountain, picking up momentum, and eventually burying everything. There have been attempts to control it, everything from signs on the backs of elephants and buses recommending limits for family size to vasectomy programs aimed at selected groups such as commuters going to work and free condoms offered to newly-weds. The results are obviously minimal. There is an unspoken irony, for those of us who work in this clinic, to be saving lives in a country where lives are not what India needs more of. The alternative is not something to be considered.

As we count pills into the envelopes, I am thinking about this evening's writing, to be done in the hotel room with the slanting floor and the cracked ceiling where the rain comes through, with the fan blowing hot air on my pages and the black grime on the desk mixing with the sweat on my forearms. I am thinking about a list I made of the causes of poverty. On the list -- far from complete -- were items like greed, inefficiency, intolerance, inequality, violence, dishonesty, corruption, superstition. The list was drawn for purposes of therapy and was partly the result of some bad Chinese food.

Near the top of the list was the matter of caste. For the western mind, and for Gandhi as well, caste is a slap in the face of any humanist philosophy. Happily, many of the more obnoxious caste prohibitions have faded with time; to look back at them is to find hope that humans can transcend their own foolishness. In southern India, for example, non-Brahmins were not allowed inside some temples, could not get into the inner sanctum to see the god, sometimes could not even walk on the road that went past the temple. At certain times, non-Brahmins were not supposed to take water directly from a bowl, though it is hard to know what difference that would make.

Hotels had separate areas for Brahmins and non-Brahmins. Colleges had separate eating areas for the students, while eating utensils used by a non-Brahmin would have to be specially washed. In some parts of India, a non-Brahmin had to stop eating if even the shadow of a lower caste person fell across the food. The more orthodox believer was not allowed even to hear the voice of a lower-caste person while eating. Brahmins in an earlier time could not eat food cooked by a member of a lower caste. Food was to be eaten at a certain time, facing in a certain direction. Different classes ate different amounts (*that* is worth noting). If your father was alive, you were not supposed to face south while eating.

With all of this to think about, it is a miracle that anyone ever got fed. It is not to be wondered at that modern India has had developments like the self-respect campaign and anti-Brahmin movements. There has also been the emergence of a rationalist philosophy, which really means atheism. But the anti-Brahmin movements have taken place mostly among the middle castes. The lower castes have been excluded, and even further oppressed by the middle castes when they achieved some measure of power and privilege. The age-old pecking order continues, done with only slightly more subtlety. Caste is a transparent disguise for maintaining wealth and privilege, no matter what anyone might argue otherwise.

It also accounts for an old Hindu saying: “If you see a snake and a Brahmin, kill the Brahmin first.”

A child has gotten loose from his mother and is now standing directly in front of our table. Eyes wide, he is watching as we count out the pills, possibly thinking they are something to eat. As he watches, a fly lands between his eyes and starts to crawl up his forehead. He seems to lack the energy or the interest to brush it away.

As though on a tandem bicycle, caste rides happily along with another item on the list: unproductive religions. It is impossible to talk generally about religion in a country divided among Hindus, Moslems, Sikhs, Jains, and hundreds of sects, dozens of languages, thousands of rituals and customs. All but the most grotesque or destructive beliefs of any religion need to be respected, but in our times it is reasonable to expect religions to accomplish something of value rather than getting in the way of people’s well-being.

It is not the religions themselves that are to be faulted; it is how they can easily be supported by a flight from reality. The Indian literature I read in the evenings, in poorly printed books with pages falling out as I turn them, is appalling. The myths invariably have to do with monsters, werewolves, wicked giants, fighting among gods or humans, violence and human degradation. There is rarely any kindness, decency, or even humor. The literature is filled with sorcerers, witches, wizards, snake charmers, diviners, astrologers, fortune tellers, soothsayers, phantasms, faith healers, illusionists, magicians, fakirs, prestidigitators and conjurers, along with gifts of prophecy, powers of transformation and flight, omens, miracles and mysteries. As simple entertainment that is all very well, but what does it do over time to the consciousness of a culture? What does it have to do with reality?

Metaphysics, the branch of philosophy that deals with what it means to be real, has a long history of disputes over the nature of reality. Anyone who has studied metaphysics knows how complicated those disputes can get, making interesting, career-enhancing material for books and articles and philosophical conferences. All of that is for another place and circumstance. Here, the question is one of how all this other-worldliness, religious or secular, affects this country's ability to deal with the real, everyday realities of poverty, malnutrition, disease, illiteracy, unemployment and crime. What explanation does it offer for the metaphysics of a man we see every day on the sidewalk, lying under a dirty grey blanket as people walk around him as though his existence does not share the same reality as theirs?

These realities are not unique to Calcutta, and the difference from other urban settings is one more of quantity than of quality. In any event they are not illusions. There is little to be said for governments that consult astrologers when they make their plans, especially when those plans are doomed in advance by the realities of corruption and greed. The only defensible purpose for government is the creation of plans and programs that work. What works means whatever is productive of human welfare.

What needs remembering is that it was not always this way. Indian civilization is 5000 years old. It is claimed to have invented chess and discovered the concept of zero in mathematics. Indian science was ahead of Europe during the middle ages, but behind by the time of the enlightenment -- a word, obviously, with a whole different meaning here. “Seventh century scientists,” one of their own people called them, seemingly more interested in rituals, taboos, family deities and daily pujas than with using science for people’s welfare. Those centuries of British domination and exploitation of the sub-continent can be blamed for many of the country’s problems, but there must also be a connection to an apparent cultural preference for hiding behind superstition and magic and fairy tales. That has never been unique to India; it just seems more blatant here,

There is something frightening in this. Not in a personal or physical way, since there has been nothing in the way of a threat to our safety. On the contrary, the Indian people have been courteous and friendly and helpful. But it is alarming to think that the conditions of this city could foretell the future of our own great cities, if we in like manner take refuge in fantasy in order to escape unpleasant realities.

The most popular Indian films are cheap thrillers, mixtures of violence and romance that often seem to offer the worst of both pathos and bathos. Under their huge advertisements – colorful billboards that seem almost to threaten the crowds below if they are ignored-- people push to get into new releases. Swedish and I sat through an hour of one of them recently, for the experience rather than the plot or theme, and an hour was enough. We had been told to see an Indian film not for the film itself, which we would not be able to understand anyway, but for the experience of being there. We understood why quickly enough. The audience would hiss at the villains, shout warnings to the heroes when a new and terrible danger approached, then sigh and clap at the love scenes. That would constitute enough reality to allow for ignoring the human drama going on outside the theatre.

Maybe it is no accident that India is the largest producer of films in the world. I assume the United States is the second largest. How close are we to burying our own problems under an avalanche of make-believe, whether in films or television, tabloid news or video games? Technology creates a new industry to provide "virtual" reality in its various forms. It follows that these virtual experiences have to be pleasurable and exciting ones, on the assumption that real life lacks pleasure and excitement. Any flight from reality is finally a flight from self, which in turn is a flight from others.

Is Calcutta's misery the result of a willful flight from reality, or is it the cause of it? It may be defensible to define one's own reality, but not when the purpose is merely to avoid unpleasantness for reasons of convenience, selfishness, cowardice, ignorance, or laziness. Jung was right in arguing that people cannot handle too much reality.

Some of this was better said in a poem by a major poet of the anti-Brahmin movement.

"The world is still in darkness,
Even people who believe in caste are allowed to live,
The persons who frighten people by religion are still thriving.
When will all this trickery come to an end?
Unless and until all this trickery comes to an end,
Freedom and liberty are to be equated with evil only."

And in another book, a college professor was complaining about the dirt and disarray in his office. "This place will never get cleaned," he said. Why not, it seems fair to ask, simply clean it himself?

It would take several lifetimes to master all the beliefs of the major religions and to understand their relations to reality. From what little I have learned so far, the Sikhs come closest to my own view. They believe that a government is supposed to create justice. Rather than stressing personal salvation, monastic living or worldly renunciation -- all of which are so valued in this part of the world -- the Sikhs think of salvation in terms of serving mankind. They seem not to have forgotten that the original meaning of karma is "doing"; karma is the sum of our deeds, not our fantasies. Better yet, their deity is one of kindness and justice.

Many of the Hindus in India would do better to heed what Gandhi said: "work more, talk less," offering in four words more wisdom than in a dozen books.

And more Moslems ought to focus on Muhammad's teaching: "Allah will not forgive you if your neighbor sleeps hungry." More Christians ought to think about Christ's principal message: "Love your neighbor." That means to feed him when necessary, clothe him, comfort him, and heal him. The simplest moral injunctions are the hardest to carry out because they leave so little in the way of avoiding their truth.

What would Gandhi think of this clinic? His great love and his humanitarian spirit would applaud it, of course. But he had no patience for begging and giving to beggars, if there was any way that people could be brought to work for their food and shelter. He wrote about touring a feeding program and feeling outraged at people being encouraged to beg. "I felt humiliated," he said, and added that he would rather see the poor starve than be reduced to beggary. "Misplaced charity," he called it, which only encourages laziness and hypocrisy. It is easy, he added, to give away free meals, but much harder to organize people for honest work.

He would have the same thoughts if he looked each morning at the young men standing against the broken walls of broken buildings across the street from the hotel. They have had their ritual baths under the long-handled iron standpipes that arise from the sidewalks, and probably a little breakfast. Now they will stand there most of the day, or at some place nearby, enacting a scene that is repeated daily in thousands of cities. The thought would come to anyone's mind: these young men have lots of strength and energy and also a load of boredom, while everywhere there is work to be done. Houses to be built. Buildings to be repaired. Streets to be cleaned. Crops to be grown. They stand there, and things around them fall down. It is not entirely their fault. But how to organize systems and people in ways that can match their energy to the work that needs doing?

Now I remind myself that guests should not criticize, particularly those who have not been invited. The thoughts I am recording here, on the verge of crankiness, need to remain private.

On a more positive side and apart from matters of fantasy and reality, India is considered by many to be the world's spiritual center, and some of Calcutta's volunteers are clearly here on a spiritual quest as well. One of them is Drew, who has a room down the hall from mine in the hotel of leaky roofs. A bearded, middle-aged American, he is as thin as fish line, a health-obsessed marathon runner and a vegan who, if it were possible, would live on air alone. I would not be surprised to see him appear one day in a dhoti, but for now he seems satisfied to wear a thin white Gandhi-style shirt and pants short enough to show his bony ankles over worn sandals. I like it that he is quick to mock his own spiritual search: "I'm here to trip on Indian spirituality," he says with a grin meant to assure me that he is not entirely serious.

He has been working diligently at Kalighat and it is obvious he likes it there from the stories he sometimes brings home and tells me over dinner. At least he works there on those days when he is not sick. The 104-degree fever he had the other evening was explained as a "spiritual crisis." I felt his forehead, which was burning, but I should have kept my own counsel rather than suggesting that he take some aspirin. From the look he gave me, the advice was close to an insult. Drew treats every illness with little bags of powder and bottles of white pills that he gets from a Calcutta homeopath. They are having no effect.

The two of us sometimes eat dinner with Gunther, a young German quester. Like Drew, Gunther is bright and also very spiritual. Our dinner conversations are fun and they are also infectious, in the way that more than two people can increase the capacity for saying silly things.

Last week Gunther began by talking about a rumor he heard that Christ is alive and well, running an ashram somewhere in Kashmir. If I hadn't known better, I would have thought it was the beginning of a joke.

"He wasn't crucified, then?" I asked.

"The Shroud of Turin has been studied again," Gunther told us, his voice dropping to stress the importance of the information. "It shows that the blood on his wrists isn't running in the direction it should be if he'd actually been on a cross. It runs across his wrists."

Gunther ran his finger along his wrists, while I cut into a small piece of chicken on my plate, thinking about blood and anatomy and gravity.

"I thought the shroud only showed Christ's face," I said.

"No, the whole body."

"He's right." Drew wanted to help, and he surprised me with this understanding of western religious lore.

Just then a cockroach ran across the table. Before we could shoo it away, it squirmed under the upturned edge of my dinner plate. The two of them laughed, but I was not amused.

"So I'm supposed to eat dinner with this thing lurking under my plate? You guys can do whatever you want, but I'm *definitely* not eating here again."

"Right." Drew said, "Least they can do is keep these things in the kitchen." With that he picked up my plate and casually swept the roach onto the floor.

"So this guy in Kashmir is Jesus, you're telling us?" I wanted to add that it seemed like an odd place for him to relocate, never mind the fact that he would be over 2000 years old.

"Well," Gunther said solemnly, "some people think so."

"Let's go up there and see him." I meant it as a joke, but I was not surprised when Gunther took it seriously.

"I'll go."

"Anyway, it'd be cooler up there," Drew said.

"Just think," Gunther added, "the whole idea of the 'holy land' is wrong if this is true." That part of it struck him as funny. "All those people who moved to Israel are maybe in the wrong place. They should move to Kashmir."

"The Palestinians would love that," I said, wondering at the same time why Jews who moved to Israel would care about Christ living in Kashmir, or why they would want to emigrate there for that reason or any other reason.

"Can you imagine?" Gunther said, his voice rising. "Someone would have to tell them, 'Look, you got it all wrong. You need to move to Kashmir. 'And off they would go."

"Lots of military stuff up there, anyway," Drew said, as though that was the last piece of a deal about to be done.

Whatever their oddities, they have been fun to be with. I will miss them when they take off one day soon, as they plan to, seeking to become enlightened in an ashram south of here. They will leave behind a question: do we achieve enlightenment first, so that in the manner of the Buddhist bodhisattvas we can help others to that state, or does the enlightenment come only after the compassion and the helping?

"I'm in India to blow my circuits," Drew told a newcomer as we sat over afternoon tea in the outdoor hotel garden. The newcomer was from Boston, travelling through India on a loose itinerary, he said, in the way of travelers who are wary of giving away too much of their plans. He wore his designer shirt loosely over expensive maroon shorts, and his pear shape and double chin became more noticeable as he sat down across from us at the table.

Maybe because we were tired, we did not right away offer the usual courtesy of asking his name. When one of us finally did, it seemed to me that it came out as Wally or Willy or Wooly, but I decided to leave the matter alone.

We had been talking about theology, and Drew had just finished a mild flaying of traditional western religions: too rational, too enslaving, too much dogma. And too little mysticism.

The newcomer picked up quickly on the last of Drew's points. "Do you think anyone can actually lead other people to mystical knowledge of God?" he asked.

"Yes," Drew replied, looking, for the occasion, a little mystical himself. He accomplished that by narrowing his eyes and resting his hands on his legs, palms up. Maybe some mocking going on there, but I couldn't be sure.

"Have you ever known anyone like that?"

"Yeah, I have."

"Who?"

After a long pause that seemed to be for a second dramatic effect, Drew named an Indian mystic and spiritual leader who had, at one time, founded an ashram and collected a considerable following in the states. This name also passed me by, but apparently Drew had spent some time with him.

"I've heard of him," the newcomer said. By then he was sipping his second beer, which might have made him a bit contentious. "And I don't want to question his, uh, spiritual dedication, but I remember he also owned a fleet of Rolls Royces. Does that go along somehow with his mysticism?"

Before answering, Drew thoughtfully poured me some more of our tea, leaving only a half-cup for himself. Finally he said, "That's another matter. The real point is... "He trailed off while he thought of what the real point was.

"You're the philosopher," the newcomer turned to me. "What do you think?"

"In the first place," I said, "I come to places like this partly as a change from talking about philosophy. That's something I do the rest of the time."

"But don't you think --?"Hands opening to his sides, his own palms now up but higher in the air, he looked like a coach protesting a bad call by the referee. He was not to be deterred.

"I really don't see any reasonable connection between Rolls Royces and spirituality and mysticism," I told him. "In my own view, nobody should own a fleet of Rolls Royces as long as the world has needy people. It doesn't matter if they're spiritual gurus or what they are."

"He doesn't like mystics," Drew explained to the newcomer.

"Not so much a matter of not liking them," I said. "I just think people waste time trying to get onto some other plane of existence."

"You don't believe in another level of existence?"

"Anything's possible. There might be all kinds of other levels of existence, and there's no compelling reason to think the one we're in now is the only one."

"But you don't think we can get there."

"I'm not going to argue that nobody, ever, gets in contact with some other world, as mystics claim to do. It could be. Lots of things could be. But the world we're in right now is the one that interests me, not some theoretical other one. We've got our hands full with this one."

"What about God?"

"What are you asking me about God?"

"If you believe in God."

"Sure. But you're probably asking about the usual God of western monotheism. It's what I call the linear God. He or she or it is up there, we're down here. That idea has served its purposes, I suppose, like polytheism does for other people, or atheism. I have no problem with that, especially if it helps people somehow. But with a little trying, we could be more imaginative about God, by which I mean more open to other possibilities."

"You're not an atheist, then?" For some reason he was not able to leave the matter alone, as though this was the one chance he had to discuss spiritual matters in a setting that was apparently perfect for it. It would be something for him to talk about at home: my time drinking tea with two cosmologist chaps in Calcutta. At any moment I expected a camera to appear.

Then it came to me why he would not leave it alone: in asking someone else if that person believed in God he was really asking himself. He was yet another seeker, hoping to get clarity about what he believed by being somewhere else and asking someone else. I had a vision of him holding a lantern, like Diogenes in Athens, as he edged through the streets of Calcutta, hoping in this case to find God in a thronged market. It could be that he will.

I began to like him a little for that; unlike many people, God's existence was a matter that he did not want to dodge. I also knew he was waiting for an answer and that I should not disappoint.

"Not to evade the question, let's just say that I like to tease atheists now and then by telling them that I wish we could all be that smart. To know that God doesn't exist -- wow, that's incredible! It's like all the major proofs of God's existence that we teach in philosophy classes. They're interesting as intellectual challenges, but they all take it for granted that God has to be some kind of *being*. We forget that the concept of "being" is one we have created for this world. It's the best we can do at this stage of our development. This teacup" – I held mine up – "has teacup being and we have human being. Why should God have to be a being just because we think in those terms? For me that is a failure of what I call metaphysical imagination. Let's do God the favor of being whatever God may be."

I would not have taken the discussion this far except that he asked for it. It seemed, to his credit, that he was following, even if his questing had probably not yet taken him this far. But I felt that it was time to finish.

"For me, the only logically defensible thing we can say about God is that we need to be very careful what we say. Or maybe say nothing at all."

"So what do you think God is?"

"What do I think God is? Love. Harmony. Energy. Maybe God is even some kind of higher mathematics. Those aren't new ideas. They may be the closest we can get in this world."

"How are we supposed to get close to God, then? Just by loving?"

There was an unwelcome note of challenge then, or maybe just one of disappointment. He lowered his head and took a breath and raised his eyebrows in a manner that was meant to give the question some kind of emphasis. I could see that Drew was becoming put off by all of this, or he might have been laughing. In that case he was hiding it well behind his teacup.

"People can get close to God in any way they want, if they want. Prayer, meditation, music, service -- that's a matter of personal choice. From a moral point of view, the thing we should be interested in is human well-being, including our own, right here and right now."

"That's the only thing?" the newcomer asked.

"Yeah."

"You don't believe in an afterlife?" He really could not drop it, even to the point of ignoring the fact that he was discussing sensitive matters with near strangers.

"Well, I like the idea. Most of us find it comforting. But it seems like I'm not making myself clear. There may well be an afterlife and other kinds of existence and who knows what else, but that's not what we have now. We'll find out about all that other stuff soon enough, if we find out at all, and most of us aren't in any real hurry. Right now we're in this life, which is interesting enough for me. It also offers a lot to be experienced and done, without worrying about some other life that we can't know about. One thing at a time."

The newcomer looked unsatisfied. Drew broke a biscuit and handed half to me. We changed the subject, which was just as well, since it was obvious I was not saying what he wanted to hear. He will need to uncover his mysticism at a different tea table.

Even annoying people can serve a purpose when their questions provoke one to make statements that later force some honest analysis. If there is no definitive reality, who am I to say that magic, fantasy and illusion have no place in a complete metaphysics? Why cannot religion be allowed to go beyond ritual and worship and spiritual nourishment and be given the chance to make statements not only about morality and politics but also about what defines reality? Why cannot God be whatever a believer wants to make of the idea?

Thinking about the conversation with the newcomer and the problem of reality is not helping me to concentrate on this prescription. "There is no reality except in action," Sartre said. People are waiting. The pile of prescription cards is building up where the doctors have placed them on top of the empty medicine chest. Late morning is always the busiest time.

"Did you notice the albino?" It is Oliver, appearing now on the left like a genie released again from his bottle. He never misses.

"Where?"

"Straight ahead."

Over the heads of the doctors, back in the crowd that waits on the ground, a young albino sits beside his mother. His white hair is pulled back into a small pony tail behind an out-sized head, and his pale skin seems almost to glow in its contrast with the dark Bengali bodies around him. His eyes are narrowed as he squints uncomfortably into the brightness of mid-day. He watches us watch him.

There is something unsettling in the sight. Where does an albino fit among the minor aberrations of reality? Is he the victim of some exotic condition the clinic is supposed to somehow deal with? Or is he just a minor quirk of nature, put here to show me that reality is devious, never as simple as we might like it to be?

"I've never seen one before," I whisper to Oliver.

"We need something uncommon to keep this place interesting, mate."

"Who's got the Isokin 300?" Swedish asks.

"Not me," Oliver and I say at the same time.

"Did you guys go to Boys Town on Sunday?" one of the British nurses wants to know.

"Yeah," Oliver says. "About eight of us. A smashing time, wasn't it?"

It was a good time, and it developed just after another experience that would have been exceptional under any circumstances.

That was Easter Sunday, and I awoke unsure of what to do with myself, since the clinic was closed and I didn't relish another day of wandering the unsettling streets of Calcutta. Then I remembered that two Irish women who sometimes worked in the clinic had said that I should go to mass sometime at Mother Teresa's motherhouse. Okay, this *is* Easter Sunday.

They had explained how to get there from my hotel, and even, when I was on my way there and had become slightly lost, turned up and led me the rest of the way. But somehow, after the mass, they went off in another direction and I found myself leaving the motherhouse on my own.

I was in the foyer, shoes in hand, when I noticed Mother Teresa talking to an elderly couple, maybe themselves Americans. The scene surprised me, since I tended to think of her surrounded by crowds and flashbulbs. If the elderly couple could talk to her, I thought, why couldn't I? I went over and stood behind them, ready for a private audience.

But what to say? Or rather, what not to say? There was little time to prepare, but I was determined not to fall back on any of the greetings that I assumed were commonly used by others and that had likely become tiresome to her. "You are a saint, Mother," "the whole world loves you," "you are doing God's work" would be among them.

A new opener was in order, more for her sake than for mine. The problem was that nothing was coming. Suddenly the couple stepped aside, I stepped forward, Mother Teresa looked up at me. It was the moment of truth, or in this case of untruth. Maybe it was her presence that gave me inspiration."

"Hello, Mother. I have greetings for you from Port-au-Prince."

Lie. I did not have greetings from the sisters of Mother Teresa in Haiti. The thought came to mind because I had been working with them in that country's capitol a few months earlier.

With the innocence of the sainted, she fell for it.

"Oh, how nice of you! And how are they doing there?"

Once truth has been abused, it is easier to carry on. "They are fine, Mother. I think they have some plans to, uh... paint the upper level. It will look much better." This too was an approximation, to put is nicely. But they often had made improvements to their facility in between my times there.

"Yes, it will. Very good."

Again she looked up at me, this time as though expecting more information of that sort. Or was she seeing though my diplomatic lying? It seemed that I needed credibility.

"Well... I have worked there with the sisters for a few years now, ummm, between semesters." Finally, a little truth.

"I see."

It was clear that we had reached the outer limits of any common interests. She made a small movement with her hand, something between a blessing, I thought, and a dismissal.

"Thank you, Mother."

It was fun to tell the others later in the day, adding that I could now claim the distinction of having lied to Mother Teresa, on Easter Sunday and in a convent at that.

"Or at least you are one of the few people to admit it," somebody said.

Thus began a day that had promised to be long and uneventful but that had become better as it went along, proving that negative expectations can sometimes be better than no expectations at all.

Some of the clinic's paid staff, young men who had at one time been orphans in the care of Mother Teresa, had invited the volunteers for a day at Boys Town, which is one of her projects. The hour-long bus ride into the cool, clean air and the lush greenery of the countryside was well worth the trouble of finding the right bus in the chaos of the depot. India, some of us learned for the first time, can be lovely. It can also be surprisingly peaceful and even tantalizing once the turbulence of Calcutta is forgotten.

The Boys Town compound, several acres set alongside a rural two-lane highway, showed us what can be done when people are committed to positive change. Little houses, looking fresh and cared for, were spaced along the paths. When we arrived, some of the young men were playing volleyball, while others gently took us by the hand to show us their lodgings before we sat down to the dinner they had prepared for us. Afterwards we sang some songs and lay in the grass, talking of places we have been and places we would like to go.

"Being is analogous." The mind is surely an unpredictable thing when it allows a forgotten line from a metaphysics textbook to forge its way into consciousness, here of all places. The idea is that to be, to have being, is to be part of some immediate reality. But it is never "being" by itself. It is analogous; it has to be understood by means of a comparison. Analogous to what? To whatever scene is at hand.

At this moment, we are in a Calcutta street clinic, an albino boy watching us from a crowd of sick people, behind me Swedish looking for the Isokin 300 on the shelves, to my right Molly counting pills into an envelope, and in the corner almost out of sight to the left, Oliver starting to wipe disinfectant onto the arm of a child, who stares in fright at the needle in his other hand as he makes jokes to her in a language she cannot understand.

The analogies of our being are these people in this place, now. The other day they were the friends and the peace and the greenery of the Indian countryside. For others here, reality consists of violent myths or dirty sidewalks and a pile of rags for a home.

That is such an old idea, ancient and contemporary at once. All we know is what we have around us. The past, mythical or otherwise, is only as we choose to re-construct it, and the future is constructed only from the present. That is why nothing but the present matters. Nothing but the present *should* matter.

It matters even more when the present includes suffering that can be avoided. From another perspective it can be argued that reality is nothing more than a set of attitudes toward all these analogues. If we can never know reality in any absolute way, being becomes itself a part of whatever scene, whatever analogues, we are in at the moment. It is necessary, then, to maintain the right attitude, as troubling as the circumstances of the here and now might be.

The terms good and bad, Spinoza said, have no meaning in themselves. They are only modes of thinking, notions we form from comparisons. Good and evil are found in our reactions to a situation, not in the situation itself. He was not the first person to say that -- the stoic philosophers having established the point many centuries earlier -- and he has not been the last. It is both comforting advice and a caution against complaining, but it runs the risk of inaction.

That is one of the best things about these expatriate volunteers: there is no complaining, not about the heat or the crowds or the noise or the smells or the flies. They go about their work and bring on whatever other fun they can later in the day. It is obvious that they are having a good time right now, and what is most remarkable is that there is nothing self-conscious about it, unlike people, say, in beer ads.

They really *are* free spirits, the bunch of them. They obviously have compassion, but they seem to have learned somewhere that compassion is a personal emotion and that its value is lessened when overwrought or made into an institution or a process that is limiting rather than enabling. For them, the life of compassion is more spontaneous than planned, more flowing than restricted, which is the way it should be.

It may be that what we are doing here is part of some abstract moral evolution of our species. There is that possibility. Or maybe it is not. At the very least, one distinction should be made. Basic morality, the kind followed by most people, requires that we do our best to avoid acting in ways that cause suffering or harm to other people. A higher kind of morality says that we should, when possible, act in ways that *reduce* or *eliminate* human suffering. The logic is not hard to follow: suffering is bad; certain actions can mitigate or end suffering; those actions ought to be done.

Now I need to remember that this is not a philosophy class. It is a street clinic, with lots of work still to be done. Concentrate: this is a scene in which emotion, not dry reason, is being channeled into work done for the benefit of others. Metaphysical or ethical abstractions just do not meet the demands of the particular reality of this place.

Beside me, Molly turns toward Swedish. Her movement knocks one of the prescription cards to the ground.

"Oh, I've got the Isokin," she says. "Right here."

Chapter Seven

The end of it all, as the reader knows by now, came shortly after that last Youth Day.

Writing that sentence is just another example of how this story falls somewhat short in the vital element of suspense. In a good story there should be just enough left unsaid so that the reader feels, near the end, some sense of a conflict about to be resolved. Art creates harmony through a feeling of completion; unfortunately that is not always the case with life. Still, there may yet be some changes, some resolution, awaiting the patient reader.

In any event, I do not myself know exactly when the end came, since I was on one of my annual trips to Germany.

What should have been a chance for Ken to recuperate and pick up some laurels was instead the start of a fast downhill slide. Maybe a better mentor would have seen it coming. In one way, he had warned me.

"I just can't do this again." He had said that several times when the preparations were getting too complicated, the pace becoming too hectic even for him. "I don't get enough help I can count on. People say they're gonna help and then they don't."

"That happens a lot. Get used to it."

"But I can't keep on doing it all myself."

"Well, if you can't do it anymore, then don't. You've got lots of other good things going on."

"But the kids need it. You know what it means to them. You know how many we didn't have spots for this year. I *hate* turning them down. We need a bigger park next year and two days to do it all."

The idea of a bigger Youth Day had come up before in board meetings, spurred by Ken's endless desire to expand and by our own enthusiasm for what he was doing. But the contradiction between not wanting to do it again and wanting to make it even bigger next time was, even for an amateur psychologist, another sign of the bi-polar personality. Psychology aside, he just burned out. Exhaustion is a contributing cause of depression. The only surprise, looking back, is that it took so long.

There was a larger contradiction, one that lay not far below the surface. It had to do with past and present. A firebrand youth advocate does not come out of nowhere. He comes from a particular background. In Ken's case, that background, the reason for his passion to save the youth, was never far away. This was the same city in which almost all of his less commendable activities had taken place. It was also a city full of people from his past, friends never entirely left behind. So there was always reason to wonder about the temptations that attach to old friendships and about the stresses that had to be part of a fast-track life lived partly among civic leaders and activists but partly among something of the opposite.

In the years between our first meeting and the drop of the Youth Day curtain, Ken had abstained from drugs and alcohol, faithfully attending meetings with other former users. Using was not an issue. So I had been surprised one evening at his apartment to notice a bottle of malt liquor in his refrigerator. Except for a stick of butter, it stood by itself on the top shelf, looking in its singularity like it had been placed there to invite attention. Was it meant as some sort of challenge to himself or to me? I was alone in the kitchen and for some reason I reached in and picked it up, maybe wanting to tell from its weight if it was full or empty, as if that would help me decide whether anything should be said about it. I held it for a moment, then put it back, deciding that there was something more honest than challenging about its being there. I said nothing.

We had talked about another camping trip later in the summer. It was soon clear that the camping trip was going to be hard to arrange: for the first time, I was having trouble getting in touch with Ken. It was not that his calls, which had come regularly after each new success, had dropped in number. He was not calling me at all. And he was not returning my calls.

The voices that answered at his apartment were not helpful. They belonged to the guards, who, in the end, were right.

"I'm trying to catch up with Ken again."

Long pause. "Who are you?"

"I'm... his mentor. We've met a few times."

"He's not here."

Even "he's not here, man" would have been encouraging. When that signifier is dropped, any sense of friendship falls with it. Even more, it makes it clear: you are not in this picture.

"When is he coming back?"

"Later. I don't know."

"Can you tell him I want him to call me?"

"Yeah."

Shortly after that last Youth Day, Ken left his apartment one Sunday morning and went into the inner-city.

He found two women standing on the sidewalk and went up to them. "I want to kill myself with drugs," he said. For a long moment they looked at him as though they did not understand.

Then they took him to where he could get what he wanted.

His own account: "For two days I went out of my mind with crack cocaine. Then I went to tell my father. You know, I can still see us there in my apartment, along with two other guys. All three of them sat there crying, grown men. I was the only one not crying. Nothing seemed to make any difference. After that I wrote a letter resigning from Voice of the Future. I knew it was over and I didn't want to drag the organization down with me. And I'm proud that I didn't take any of the money with me."

Getting nowhere calling his apartment, I phoned one of the other board members to confirm the obvious: Ken was using again. The good news was that he had agreed to go into treatment; he would spend a month in a downstate rehab facility.

He was there less than two days when he called.

"Uncle Derek, can you come down here and get me? I need to get back to the city."

"Okay, but why? What's going on?"

"I'll tell you when you get here."

So I picked him up, and at the front desk we both signed release papers given to us by a counselor whose look said clearly that this should not be happening. Ken tried to charm her out of that, unsuccessfully.

"The reason," he explained as we drove away, "is that they won't let me use my cell phone. It's against the rules. The second time they caught me with it was what did it. I told them I had to keep in touch with the organization. I've got a lot to do. But they said no outside calls."

"What's this, keep in touch with the organization? You *are* the organization."

"You know what I mean."

It was the last good time we had together. Western New York displays its fall foliage with all the generosity of the neighboring New England states, and that afternoon was one of the best -- full of fiery colors in clear, dry air that swells the lungs with fruity sweetness. We stopped for hamburgers and then we took country roads over surging, weaving hills and through small towns, driving slowly to make the trip last. If the season was fall, our mood was that of a spring. After a brief lapse, a momentary downturn, this would be a new beginning. Ken seemed fresher than he had been for some time. He was full of plans, eager to write some new grant proposals, convinced that he could deal with the drug situation in local therapy sessions. I bought all of it.

Just a few days later he asked me over for dinner and a video. The other company was two young women, one of them the mother of two small children who climbed over each other and us as we talked and ate. Ken was different, and at the time I could not understand why. Denial can be more than infectious; it can block both perception and conclusions.

The hyperactive personality was not directed that evening. Instead there was something scattered about his thoughts and actions, something defensive in his conversation. The behavior bordered on the obnoxious, to the extent that even the young women seemed put off by it. After a few hours I got my coat. Ken seemed surprised, like a host unaware that the party has failed until the guests start leaving.

I let a few weeks go by and then dropped in without calling first. It took several minutes and some loud knocks to get him to the door. He was having a hard time buttoning his shirt with one hand and unlocking the door with the other.

"Sorry it took so long," he said. There was no smile. "Got a woman waiting upstairs."

Neither of us sat down.

"So what's going on?" I asked. "You're pretty hard to get hold of these days."

"Well... I guess things... have changed." His voice was flat, but at least not defiant.

"What does that mean?"

"It's hard to talk about. Maybe not a good time right now." He flicked his eyes upwards, a reminder of the woman waiting upstairs.

"So when do we talk about it?"

"I don't know."

"Where's all this going, Ken?"

"Man, I don't know that either. I..." He trailed off, fingering the second button of his shirt. A long silence, while we listened to the sound of cars hissing past outside the open front door. From somewhere in the distance came the faint whine of an ambulance siren.

"What do you want me to do?" I asked him.

"There's nothing you can do. Things just have to, you know... work themselves out. Sort of go on this way for now."

It was a polite hint to butt out.

"I'd like it a lot better if you'd get some help. And stay with it. Anyway, you know where to find me when you're ready."

"I know that."

We talked around the subject for another minute, an exercise in saying nothing because there was nothing to say. Then we hugged, mechanically, and parted.

After that, nothing. Total blackout. The apartment was eventually vacated, the phone disconnected. My calls to mutual friends, and theirs to me, were pointless except to confirm the obvious: Ken had gone underground.

There was nothing to do then but to wait. It was not so much a phone call I waited for as a news item. Our media are unexceptional in their fascination with news stories about drug busts and drug-related killings. It was one of those that I began to wait for, turning to stare at the television when another story came on, or turning up the car radio. It was going to be a very different kind of media attention than we had enjoyed for four years.

Somebody had the good sense to call the board together. We began the meeting by trading what little information we had. One of the board members had seen Ken driving through downtown; he had waved and kept on going. Another, the lawyer, could probably get in contact with him through a friend of Ken's whom the lawyer was representing. That's fine, but what should we do? Since we were legally responsible for the organization's activities and financial obligations, should we disband it? To my relief, we decided to keep it alive for the time being. There was always hope, we said. But we needed to separate the organization from whatever Ken might be doing, to at least minimize any legal liability. A formal letter relieving him of his position as executive director was drafted. The lawyer could see to its delivery.

A second meeting was called to discuss the possibility of another organization taking over Youth Day. That was one positive development in the whole gloomy scenario, though I did not like the feeling that these people were in it for the money. In any case, nothing came of that.

More waiting, more attention to the local news. A period of waiting became a time for some soul-searching.

The idea of a mentoring comes from the name of the man who was a wise friend and loyal advisor to Odysseus, the wily and courageous hero of Homer's *Odyssey*. As though that would somehow make things clearer, or better, I went back to the epic poem and searched out the relevant passages. I had forgotten that Pallas Athena, whom Homer loved to call the "grey-eyed goddess," sometimes came on the scene to offer advice through the person of the aged Mentor, thus establishing him forever as the iconic advisor. It also meant that Mentor's advice had the advantage of being, literally, heaven-sent: it came from a goddess. My own advice could never have competed with that. Nor should it be expected to, after I remembered with satisfaction Socrates' statement to the Athenian jurors: "only the gods are wise."

Still, I read with interest how her advice proved valuable any number of times for an epic hero with lots of epic challenges. At one point she chastises Odysseus: "Thou are witless, stranger, or thou art come from afar." At the very end of the very long poem she calls a halt: "Hold your hands from fierce fighting, ye men of Ithaca, that so ye may be parted quickly, without bloodshed."

In the context of my own mentoring, those passages were the most interesting ones that I could find. That they held absolutely no relevance to my situation would have been obvious even to a fool. Homer's Mentor had no advice for me.

Still, I was proud to have been Ken's mentor for nearly five years, and for his part he never tired of introducing me with that title. Along with others, I had been a major player in the story of his remarkable development and his work. Mostly we had been close friends. We had shared meals, long talks, hard work, laughs, ups and downs. I had at various times encouraged him, prodded him, calmed him down, and held him up. So I told myself.

But had that really been enough? Was something missing all along? Were there things I could have said, should have said? Should I have played an even more active role in the organization? It was clear that things were sometimes less than systematic, and my work with other organizations had shown me how important it was to plan carefully and carry through fully. Enthusiasm and commitment are fine, and Ken had had a ton of each. But they are not enough. Should I have done more to keep him on track? But more of what, and what track?

Minor incidents came to mind. I thought about the time I casually mentioned having had some friends over to the house for a small party.

"Why didn't you invite me?"

"Umm... I guess I thought you wouldn't want to be there. You know, a bunch of older people and a lot of talk about work."

"I always invite you to my parties," he said simply, and because his voice was flat and had nothing of its usual vigor I knew that he was hurt. With a flush of guilt I remembered all-day picnics in his back yard, to which I was always invited, with a stern insistence that I must show up. They had been gatherings of family members and helpers and supporters, people who had mingled easily and without the discomforting scent of difference or exclusivity.

Only later did it come to me that his hurt had less to do with exclusivity and more to do with respectability. I tried then, and failed, to imagine how important it must have been for him – with his earlier background of disrespect and humiliation and rejection that came from experiences I had never had-- to gain respect at every turn and in every way.

That would have been even more so from me and the people I must have represented to him. He had been making gigantic strides toward respectability, especially in the crucial matter of beginning to respect himself, and I had told him, unwittingly, that he still had some distance to go.

Look back, dig deeper. Had I been, all along, letting Ken do all the work? There had been enough advice and plenty of encouragement and praise, pushing here and pulling there. How much was vicarious accomplishment, telling myself that I was doing something to improve the community while at the same time preserving my peace and privacy?

Mostly I wondered if I should have been more available. Generally I was there when he called and met him when he needed me. But a growing interest in what I often called my overseas humanitarian adventures meant that there were whole months when I was completely out of reach. How much had I been needed during some of those times? I thought of the time he told me how often he would come home after a busy day to sit in his apartment feeling depressed and alone. The situation was reversed: now he was the one who was out of reach.

There is little positive to be gained from guilt, I reminded myself. In the end, did any of my actions or inactions really make any difference? It came to me that what I called his flourishing, those years of moral turning, may have been doomed all along, required by some inner logic to make a circular return to what had been before. He had liberated himself, for the short term, from the tyranny of drug addiction and the seduction of crime and the shadowed threat of prison. Of those three, I knew that the drug addiction was the most powerful: he had told me more than once that an addiction to crack cocaine was the absolute worst.

As though verifying that would give me some perspective, I returned to his account of how the addiction had begun. It was disorienting to hear of a bad time, recounted on tape in a better time, and now heard again in a worse one.

"I was turned on to cocaine by this woman from Trinidad. She and her husband owned a shop on Main Street. They knew that I sold a lot of weed. At that time I was moving several pounds of weed a week and I was making so much that it wasn't even funny. I was probably making on the average of anywhere from 2000 to 5000 a week. So this woman knew I had money.

"One day I went there to purchase a couple pounds of weed and I went in the back where they had an office. They were back there smoking and they said 'Hey, you ever try free-base cocaine?' and I said 'No. ' And I saw him sitting there with a glass and a water pipe and he had a propane torch and he'd drop this little ball and it would start popping and frizzing and next thing you know a cloud of smoke would appear inside this water pipe.

"So he says 'Here, take a hit', so I took a hit and it didn't do much for me. You know, I had this numbing sensation on my lips and in my head and I said, 'Ah, that ain't shit. 'So I took off, but a couple of weeks later I came back and tried again. And that time it was like boom, like something I had never had before in my entire life. It was a utopia of everything I'd been wanting in my life. It was the sex I always wanted, the ultimate sex life, the ultimate friend, the ultimate high so to speak. I remember my head being numb, my eyes temporarily hindered, my heart pounding, the palpitations. My voice changed, like I held some of that helium in a balloon, you know, that da-da-da-duh Donald Duck kind of voice. And I was like on cloud nine. This is good shit, it was too good.

"And after that it was over with. They knew they had me hooked, so the woman used to come to my house and she would bring a gram or so with her. The next thing you know, when she knew I ran out and she knew I had money, she'd say 'Hey, you want some more? Give me two hundred bucks and I'll cop a couple of grams. 'Before you knew it I was on that shit like forty going north. I wasn't stopping. It was the beginning of the end because I found myself wanting it every day. I would discommunicate myself from a lot of people who would normally see me. I was spending enormous hours at a time trapped in a house. Anywhere from ten to fifteen hours a day. Smoking the stuff. And I did that for years... I finally had to stop when I got arrested for robbing that off-track betting parlor."

I would discommunicate myself from a lot of people.

And so I became more aware that what I had been witnessing, all during our time together, was a conflict that consisted of fighting a modern evil while holding on to a fascination with some of the sources of that evil. It was a classic struggle: on the one hand, the deep satisfaction of helping his own young people, the first experience of positive self-esteem, for the first time a life of freedom and meaning and direction, topped off by many-sided affirmation and even the rush of local fame; on the other hand, the dark thrills and dangers and temporary physical satisfactions of that other, earlier world. Darkness and light clash in an imperfect world, and sometimes darkness is the winner. The major ally that decided this battle was addiction to cocaine.

It seemed to be the time to let go, to make a fresh start. I went back to the place where I had met Ken and was assigned to another young man who wanted a mentor. He was a Latino, also with a jail record and a drug problem. Almost from the beginning our connection was a misfit, doomed by mutual apathy as much as by contrast. I took him job-hunting a few times and we walked in the park with his son, the one bright light in his life. The three of us looked through the fence of the city's new ballpark, waiting like kids for the start of a new season, and we talked about seeing some games.

But it was not working, for either of us. There was no spark, nothing like the laughter and excitement and manic energy that had spoiled me for mentoring. He cancelled one get-together, then another, and I got the message.

Stoic philosophy can be a refuge at any time. I spent an hour looking to Epictetus for help. He had been a slave. His master granted him the freedom of his body; through philosophy he developed freedom of the soul.

"Well, have you not received faculties by which you may support any event in life? Have you not received greatness of soul? Have you not received a manly spirit? Have you not received patience? What effect does anything that may happen have upon me, while my soul is above it? What shall disconcert or trouble or appear grievous to me? Shall I neglect to use my powers for that purpose for which I received them? Shall I lament and groan at every casualty?"

There were also some thoughts that could be taken as advice for a mentor.

"Why do you boast of your education? What education, man, that you have learned syllogisms? Why do you not, if possible, forget all of them, and begin again, convinced that hitherto you have not even touched upon the essential point. And for the future, beginning from this foundation, proceed step by step to the superstructure; that nothing may happen which you do not wish, and that everything may happen which you desire."

Epictetus was more helpful, but not helpful enough.

Things hoped for are most likely to happen after we have quit hoping; desires are met when we stop desiring. So it was with the phone call when it came on a spring evening.

"Hey, Uncle Derek." This time – and it was the only time -- the voice was hesitant. "It's me, Ken."

"Wow, you like surprises. You sure made me wait for this one. Where are you?"

"I can't say. Not far from your place."

"Why can't you say?"

"I just can't."

"It doesn't matter. Don't be so mysterious. Come on over."

"I can't do that either."

"What's the problem, you crippled or something?"

"Very funny. No, I'm okay. More or less. Just sort of run down right now."

"You sound okay, anyway. It's just good to hear your voice."

Keep him on the phone, say anything. The feeling was one of having a fish barely on the line -- in this case a telephone line -- maybe just the lower lip caught by the hook in one corner of the mouth, and trying to pull it gently to the surface. There was some pride, too: after more than six months, he had called me first.

We talked for fifteen minutes, about mutual friends, board members, what I was doing lately -- safe subjects. I told him he should call other people.

"Maybe," he said.

"You know a lot of us are worried about you. We're keeping the organization around, for when you're ready."

"Yeah, I heard. I don't know."

That probably was not a safe subject. "Not right now," I added. "Right now it would just be good to see you."

"I want to see you too, Uncle Derek. I've driven by your house, I don't know how many times. Even seen your car in the driveway. But I couldn't stop. Too --"

Words like ashamed and embarrassed clogged the lines between us. I pictured him driving past the house, a pathetic exercise of proximity as a substitute for connection.

"Ken, you don't seem to get it. I don't care what you've been doing."

"You don't know, man."

"No, and I don't want to know. It doesn't matter." A pause. "It never mattered before, so why should it now? You want me to start being your judge instead of your mentor?"

"I'll work on that, really. But I can't come right now."

"So come tomorrow."

"Not tomorrow either."

"Next week?

"Maybe. Soon anyway." There was not much conviction in that.

"That's a promise?"

"Man, you don't give up, do you?"

"No."

"Okay, it's a promise."

"That's better. I'll be waiting."

"I love you, Uncle Derek."

Then he was gone. The next connection came a few days later. It was the phone call from Tina, telling me he was in jail. Right after that came an item on the evening news about a murder in a drug house and that front-page story and picture in the morning paper.

TEA DRIVING

*If you pick up a man hungry for bread,
and you give him the bread, you have
already satisfied his hunger. But if you
find a man terribly lonely, this is much
greater poverty... Wherever you go you
will find people that are unwanted, unloved,
uncared for, rejected by the society, completely
forgotten, completely left alone. That is
the greatest poverty of the rich countries.
-- Mother Teresa
The highest flights of charity, devotion,
trust, patience, bravery to which the wings of
human nature have spread themselves have been
flown for religious ideals.*

-- William James

Fairy tales, haunted landscapes, exquisite stone architecture, songs of lost love and wanderlust – these are a few of the elements that create the magic and romance, the light and dark lyricism, the gothic beauty, of Germany.

The Wittelsbach Bridge is one of twenty-five bridges, some of them centuries old, which cross Munich's Isar River. From atop the bridge's main pillar, a stone Otto von Wittelsbach sits straight-backed and eternal on his stone horse, an aristocrat who watches the democratic flow of traffic below. One arm extends downward behind him, as if for balance. With the other, he pulls the head of his horse up firmly, with his own proud gaze directed slightly to the left.

The bridge consists of four spans, only one of which crosses the normal flow of the river. The other three arch above an open high-water area, a flood plain of sorts which most of the time is a grassy meadow used as an informal urban park. In the daytime it is busy with walkers and joggers, family picnics and kids playing soccer. At night, the stone arches of the Wittelsbach Bridge double as roofs, under which sleep many of Munich's alcoholics and homeless.

Ahead of me, Walter is walking quickly through the short grass of the meadow, swinging his oversize flashlight from side to side. It is his usual stride: determined, single-minded. In the beam of my own light, I see raindrops so small that they seem unlikely to complete their trip to the ground. It has been raining gently all evening, almost unnoticeably in the mild summer air.

Across the river, the lights of Munich create black silhouettes of the closest buildings, some of them hard rectangles that contrast with the soft summer foliage along the banks of the Isar. Many of Munich's buildings are attractive, both those in the Bavarian style and the modern ones. But above all they are solid. They make a clear statement about the way things are in one of the world's richest countries and strongest economies. Even here on the river bottom, the power of a major German industrial city can make itself felt.

This is one of our last stops of the evening, with only two or three to go. It is always a team of two, and tonight I am Walter's partner. What we are doing can be translated as "tea-driving," the phrase used by Walter's institution to describe the carrying of tea and food to the street people of Munich. Walter began this years ago, doing it alone while he was still employed on the railroads and before he founded the institution he now directs here in Munich.

He tells the story of how it all began to anyone who is interested. He was, in several ways, at an emotional crossroads: marital problems and middle age. It was his equivalent of St. Paul's dramatic conversion on the road to Damascus, and it happened, fittingly, in the fussgangerzone. That is Munich's busy car-free tourist and shopping area, a stretch of restaurants and trendy shops that runs from the popular fountain at Stachus to Marienplatz with its pixy-built town hall. The time was shortly before Christmas, and Walter was carrying a cake that his sister had baked for him.

"As I passed two beggars, the thought came to me that I could share the cake with them. My sister could always bake another one. As I began talking to them, it seemed that I was looking into the eyes of Jesus Christ. From that moment on my life was changed. I went home, prayed and cried for joy because I knew that through this meeting I had found my new way."

"One step after another. I began with a few sandwiches and a thermos of tea. At first my heart would pound in my chest. Would my cup of tea be accepted? But before long they were waiting for me, calling me 'Tea-Walter'. I used a bicycle, then a motor-scooter, more tea, more food. I was hard to bear the sorrow I would meet, but in some way these men took my need into their own hearts."

He invited five of them into his apartment. They slept on the floor of the kitchen and in the living room, pushing aside the mattresses to eat and washing in a basin of cold water. Neighbors were understanding, if not entirely happy, when they would find someone asleep in the hallway outside the door of his apartment.

It took two years before the right contacts in the Catholic diocese provided what he wanted most: a large house. Now, over a dozen years later and with the help of a small and very dedicated staff, Walter runs three large houses, providing a home for about sixty men and a few women, along with other services to Munich's street people. Tea-driving takes place every evening of the year, without exceptions. It is meant to combine nourishment with friendship and caring with action.

Considering all that he has accomplished and the recognition that he has received, he does not cut an imposing figure. It takes one very little time to learn that he has no interest in whatever figure he might cut. I have never, ever, seen him in anything but jeans or cheap slacks – mostly faded jeans and sometimes without even a belt. Over whatever second-hand shirt he chooses to wear is usually a dark vest with many pockets. He is slightly under medium height and is best described by the German word mollig, plump. In spite of his fascination with yet another health-food supplement and the occasional attempts at dieting, he carries a considerable paunch. That is not, as it is for so many other Germans, the reward of beer: he drinks no alcohol himself.

For all of that, he can be considered a good-looking middle-aged man. Most noticeable is the beard: it spreads out dramatically from his chin and hangs to below the clavicles, suggesting little familiarity with scissors. It is nearly snow-white, so that its lower boundaries cannot be seen if the shirt he is wearing happens also to be white.

Beyond the white beard and thick white moustache, what hair remains to him is grey and thin. It hangs, also with little care, over his neck in the back and preserves a few strands that course over the top of his head.

The eyes, dark under dark eyebrows, are the most compelling feature. They do not leave your own when he talks to you, and their impression is one of compassion tinged with a certain sadness. That is not always so: they can twinkle when he teases, as he often does. And they can flame with occasional anger.

By now we are into the third hour, following a schedule of stops that is routine and carefully orchestrated, a model of that well-known Germanic efficiency and organization. The first stop is always at a convent, where tonight a middle-aged nun was waiting inside the iron gates to trade our empty thermoses for six others that had been filled with hot herbal tea. She also handed me a large bag of oranges and a box filled with plastic containers of yogurt.

It is very important," Walter reminded me as we drove away, "very important that you shake hands with each of the people. Do you understand me?"

Walter is nothing if not considerate, and one example of that is his funny habit of repeating words or even parts of his sentences when he talks to me. The habit goes back to my first years here, when I struggled with the curious Bavarian dialect –- locally known as *bayerisch* --that even native Germans from the north cannot understand. That can still be a problem for me. The men who live in Walter's houses laugh when I get confused, and it may be that they even try to confuse me at times, for some fun of their own. "Hey, I studied German," I tell them. "I speak German. It would be really nice if someone else around here would speak German." "You're not in Germany," they remind me. "You're in Bavaria." Bavarians are proud of their unique culture, as any tourist soon finds out, and they use their version of German to protect it and to enlarge their identity.

"Yes, I understand, Walter. Don't worry, I always shake hands with the men."

"And greet each one, say something to them, yes?"

"Sure. I can do that too."

"Can you understand the dialect better now? The dialect."

"Some of the time. It depends on who is talking."

"When you stay longer with us, stay longer I mean, you will learn to speak perfectly, I think."

"Yeah, it's coming."

From the convent, we turned a few corners of Munich's downtown streets, clean and quiet on a Sunday evening, shiny black in the soft rain. We stopped at a small square, where a solitary man sat on a bench. Then as we parked, climbed out, and pushed back the van's large side door, they appeared. As if they had risen directly from the earth itself, like the warriors in the ancient Greek myth of the dragon's teeth, figures moved singly and silently toward us.

In the van, Walter handed me out two thermoses and a wicker basket of sandwiches, followed by the bag of oranges. I turned to see that the men, probably about 30 of them, had formed themselves into loose groups along the sidewalk. A few of them talked quietly; most of them stood in silence. With a smile, Walter stepped up to the nearest group and began shaking hands, and I followed right behind.

"*Gruss Gott*," he said, the first word pronounced almost like "grease." The Bavarian expression is an abbreviation for "greet God for me," or "God's greeting," something along those lines. For me it holds a pleasant old-world religious charm in an increasingly secular society.

"*Gruss Di*," the first man responded with a variation. I greet you.

I offered the same greeting and got the same reply.

"*Servus*," Walter said to the next man, another variation which probably means something like "your servant."

So we worked our way through the groups, and I rotated my greetings as the others were doing, in a rhythm of comradeship. A few of them, maybe guessing from my clothing or demeanor that I am an American, said "hello." Some of them smiled vaguely as we shook hands, others simply nodded or stared at me or away from me with watery alcoholic eyes.

Reception line finished, Walter began, as always quickly, passing out the heavy sandwiches while I poured the tea. We use white porcelain cups, being careful to place the dirty ones into one of the empty wicker baskets. No one is to be insulted with a dirty cup. The thermoses are heavy and awkward, making it difficult to control the first slosh of tea into the cups. More than once I have poured hot tea over the thumb of an outstretched hand, but no one has complained. They took their sandwiches and tea with a restrained danke, and they ate and drank in silence. The sandwiches are simple -- two slices of dark bread over a slice of salami -- and almost too dry to swallow without the tea.

As we moved among them, Walter spoke to those men that he knows, sometimes at length. My own conversation was more basic, until I came to a slender man who stood apart from the others and who addressed me in English.

"Are you from England?" The question is fairly common when they hear my accent. It was offered with caution, as though the wrong answer could cut rather than forge a link.

"No, I'm not English. American."

Under the open raincoat he wore a dark blue suit, which appeared clean and even pressed. Equally dark hair, shiny from being slightly dampened, was combed straight back from his forehead; the eyes were stern and seemed to be edged with a restrained melancholy. His thin shoulders were pulled up and back, though one tilted slightly.

"And you can speak English," I added, mostly to keep him talking.

"A little. Are you working by Walter now?"

"I help his organization every summer, for a month."

"You work for him without pay?" One eyebrow raised slightly. Then his eyes narrowed because he had caught himself in an indiscretion. The question did not suit the dignity of his temperament or the situation. It was best to get past it quickly.

"Yes. Where did you learn to speak English?"

"For five years I lived in England. Before the war."

Our conversation followed the cadence of his teacup as he raised it, in a measured motion, to his lips. In a little more than a minute I could see that it was empty.

"Do you want more tea?"

"Yes, thank you."

He nodded politely and offered me the cup left handed. The movement dropped his right shoulder a fraction, shifting the raincoat, and I saw that the right sleeve of the coat was empty and had been tucked carefully into the side pocket. He caught me looking at it.

"My arm was... do you say shoot or shotted?"

"Shot. Or shot off."

"I see. It was shot off in the war. At Normandy."

"I'm sorry." If there was any awkwardness in telling that to an American, a citizen of the country that shot his arm off, he gave no sign. We were back within the comforting framework of decorum.

"It was a long time ago," he said, as though to dismiss the incident and read my thoughts at the same time. "Our countries are friends now, yes, and you visit us here. So you and I are also friends."

"Of course. It's always nice to come here."

He nodded again and took a long swallow of his tea, his hand shaking slightly as the cup was lowered.

"With many Americans have I become known, and always I like them," he added, mixing English vocabulary with German syntax.

"That's nice to hear. How come you know lots of Americans?"

"I'm sorry, I don't understand your question. Please?"

"I said, how did you meet so many Americans?"

"After the war, I worked many years in an American army station. I was a servant in... how do you say the place where the leaders come to eat and drink?"

"The officers' club."

"Yes, that is how they called it. I have forgotten so much."

"But we don't say 'servant. 'We say 'waiter'."

"Of course. My English is not good any longer." He tilted his head ruefully.

"No, it's very good. It's a pleasure for me to hear my own language, and spoken so well."

He warmed to that, even if he was intelligent enough to know that the compliment was little more than good manners.

"Studying English was part of my training. I was professor of economics for many years. My doctorate is in micro-economics."

Mentioning not just the profession but also the specialization was meant as a way to give his biography a greater sense of gravitas. As well, I noticed the deliberate use of the present tense in his last sentence. The value of being recognized as an intellectual on the streets of Munich was not lost on either of us. But I also knew that we were getting close to a place that neither of us wanted particularly to go. He was ahead of me in changing the subject.

"It was not good for me to work in that place," he said, going back to the earlier topic. "Always I was drinking the alcohol too, when I served the leaders, the officers. Soon I drink too much, and then it was difficult to... *aufhoren*?"

"To stop, to quit."

"Yes, that is it. Difficult to stop."

The words lay prostrate between us, and we were momentarily lost in the desert of a conversational standstill. I found myself grateful that the men near us most likely knew no English. Together we stared down at his empty teacup. He pushed it toward me with what was almost a sigh.

"You -- "

"We -- "

Both of us laughed for the first time, appreciating the disharmony in the way people do when they have worked too hard at civility and then discovered a common element of the human condition: when we try too hard, things can get funny. Our conversation had been an exercise in high-mindedness, meant as a temporary fence that would isolate and protect us from this place and these circumstances. I liked that, and I liked him as well, for having wanted to build it.

"You are coming to us again?"

"I think so, if Walter wants me to. He always comes on Sundays."

"Yes, I understand that. Then we will meet once more."

"I hope so. It's been good to talk with you."

"Agreed. And I enjoy the opportunity to again practice my English. Goodbye."

"*Auf Wiederschauen*."

Walter was putting the baskets into the van, and the remaining men were handing over tea cups, impassive and private, shaking hands in the familiar ritual of departure. Some had already faded off into the night.

Back in the van, I found myself thinking about one of the Grimm brothers' lesser-known folk tales. It is about a soldier who has fought bravely for years, but eventually finds himself discharged from the army. He has no skills, no place to stay, and a brother who refuses to take him in. So the soldier resigns himself to a lonely life of wandering. Just when he thinks he is going to starve, the devil appears with a deal. The soldier will have to agree to go about his wandering without washing, shaving, combing his hair or clipping his nails. He must wear an old bearskin coat, and also sleep in it. If he needs money, however, he will always find sufficient gold coins in the pocket of the bearskin.

The devil says that if the soldier can survive in this form for seven years, he can live the rest of his life both free and rich. If he cannot survive, the devil claims him forever. They agree to the deal, and the soldier resumes his wandering. Before long, his appearance goes from repellent to loathsome: long, scraggly beard, murky face and soiled hands, nails like claws. People are repulsed. Most run away at their first opportunity, but he gets some satisfaction from giving away some of his gold coins whenever he gets the chance.

Walter breaks into my memories of the Grimm story. "Is it all right for you, doing this is all right?"

He is forgetting that this is hardly the first time for me to be doing this. Or he is concerned, with his chronic humanity, for my welfare. Or he is just worried, another condition that is common for him.

"Sure. One of those men spoke English, and we had a good talk."

"His name is Maximillian. He lived with us for a short time."

"Why doesn't he live with you now?"

"Always, the alcohol." Walter shook his head. "He is a good man, very intelligent, but not without troubles. In his head." Walter tapped his own head three times, to assist my understanding. "You must understand, some of these men prefer, they want, you know, to live in the streets. They want to be independent."

"Probably most people want that, in one way or another."

"Perhaps Max will live with us again one day. We would like him to return. Do you understand?"

He is asking if I understand his particular words, in this case, but I want to tell him that I understand more than that. He is talking about the prodigal son, or the lost sheep that was found. Maybe Max will come back to us, Walter says, and when he does we will welcome him. I know that is how Walter thinks, because I read his reference to that famous biblical allegory in a long description of the work of his institution which he gave me to read on my first day here. The impression it gave is that of a man whose services to street people are grounded totally in Christian charity. The document was studded with phrases like "our brothers and sisters in Christ" and "sharing the suffering and loneliness of the despised."

The theme of the prodigal son is also conveyed by the picture that graces some of the organization's literature, Rembrandt's painting of the father with the prodigal son. The son, clothes hanging ragged and one foot bare, is on his knees, head pressed in supplication against the father's breast. The father leans forward with eyes closed and hands spread, in a gesture of forgiveness and protection, on the back of the wayward son.

It is from that kind of inspiration that Walter gets his endless energy and commitment. Along with running an organization with a monthly budget that runs into thousands of euros, he also organizes frequent trips to pick up people's throw-aways and sells many of them at a Saturday flea-market. He ships truckloads of unwanted goods to the poor in Hungary. He keeps the tea-driving going. All this along with attending funerals for the street people, assisting with the frequent health problems of his residents, interceding for them with the social service agencies, and attending to a thousand other details, including the welfare of his staff and volunteers.

But it takes the expected toll on him, in the form of a restlessness and nervousness that communicates itself to those who live with him. "It's always hardest in the mornings," one of the staff told me early on. "That's when he wants everything organized. And he wants it all done right now." I remembered a funny old poem, heard in college.

"To live with a saint in heaven/Is all bliss and glory.

But to live with a saint on earth/Is quite another story."

The residents and Walter's loyal assistants have apparently learned to cope. Sometimes I see a few smiles exchanged behind his back when he's in his hurry-up mode, and everybody hurries just enough to pacify him. Later in the day he will calm down. The clue to his nervousness or tiredness is an occasional involuntary blinking. It occurs when there is some special problem to compound the usual ones.

There are lots of those. Gerd is sick, a recurrence of his cancer. Or Joachim has come home drunk again. Paul has been gone for two weeks, back to the streets. Fritz is angry because of something Walter said to him. Or maybe Walter is angry because of something Fritz said. I cannot always tell. One of the vans needs some repair. Hermann is late getting back with the bread he was sent to pick up. And all this when it is still morning!

Germans make almost a fetish of *grundlichkeit*, in English meaning thoroughness, and Walter adds to that a strong tendency to micro-manage. The most basic procedures need to be done in a certain way and no other. Things need to happen on time, but it is better if they happen ahead of time. He is much on his cellphone, and sometimes the calls are to confirm something that was confirmed an hour earlier, or to oversee something that has been done a hundred times. In spite of all that, I have come to admire that Walter can also be patient, when he reminds himself to be patient, and he often shows a welcome and liberal tolerance for divergence. He will forgive anything, given enough time to reflect. He knows that the behaviors of alcoholics do not normally include consistency or regularity, even in Germany.

Rex helps. Rex is Walter's dog, a German shepherd with an outsized head that gives him the appearance of a small lion. Like a lion, he moves with a flat-footed authority, and he gets the same respect. Someone told me that Walter got Rex after a man came at him with a knife. Now Rex is never far from Walter's side, sleeps in his room, and has a special spot in the back of the van. I have petted Rex many times, but always very cautiously, and I don't even think about knives when Rex is around.

There are occasional tensions and problems in the houses, but they are of the kind that can be expected when people of troubled and divergent pasts are brought together. Considering his clientele and their needs, Walter has succeeded in putting together a kind of family, lost sheep and all. Some of the mealtimes are marked with jokes and laughter, birthdays are celebrated, personal differences minimized.

Around the corner from that first stop, Walter pulled the van into a long, narrow street. Halfway along, he stopped beside a man sitting with his back to a building, his legs flat on the sidewalk. To one side were his boxes and bags, over which he had rigged a small canvas against the rain.

With a sharp twist of the steering wheel and a jolt to the right front tire, Walter drove the van up onto the sidewalk. He said I should wait. In a few minutes, he climbed back into the van and handed me two colas.

"That is Berti," Walter said as we drove away. "Always he lives there. He is blind, and he cannot hear very well. That is why I asked you to stay in the van, so he would not be nervous."

"You didn't give him anything to eat?"

"No, he never wants the tea or bread. He just likes someone to visit with him. And he wanted us to have the colas."

I pulled away each tab and handed one can across the seat to Walter.

"Isn't he going to get inside somewhere, out of the rain?"

"No, he will stay there. That is his home."

"Doesn't he get bored, just sitting there all the time by himself?"

"I don't know. He survives. And people know him, he gets some visitors."

From Berti's home we zigzagged across several more wet blocks and turned into a busy four-lane street, lit by cafes and bars. Walter pulled the van diagonally into a no-parking zone, more stopping than parking. I take delight in his indifference to traffic laws, and it is to be assumed that he gets more than one pass from the Munich police. He is well known around the city, especially in those places where police know they need to be and where his presence may have a temporary calming effect.

The next crowd was across the street, its members sitting and standing in a partially-enclosed bus stop with a sign meant to prohibit loitering. Again we worked our way among them with the usual greetings and handshakes, but with a difference. This smaller group was rowdier, several of them drunk and a few of those belligerent. Two men were jostling each other, a little beyond the point of being playful. An overweight woman wearing only a long shirt and a pair of panties watched them, occasionally joining in. She seemed alternately bemused and angry, in that unpredictable way of drunken people.

Walter moved among them and ignored the confusion, but I found myself a little nervous. Especially with the woman in the wheelchair. In her forties, she had close-cropped dirty-blond hair, and I thought of Rapunzel, in a different place and time, letting down her golden tresses. In this case the hair was plastered around a face that had once been pretty but was now alien and hard. Her voice was loud; it carried what seemed to be a practiced aggression, made more so by the rasp of the heavy smoker. Across her lap was a soiled blanket, only inches away from the cigarette that she seemed not to notice between her fingers. Ashes were scattered on the blanket, and more fell as she waved her nicotined right hand.

In her other hand was a plastic cup, holding what looked like schnapps. That was a telling sign. In this culture beer is as common as water, far more common than milk. I have heard it called things like "liquid bread," and that is only partially a joke. But hard liquor is just that: hard and, like her, callous. It is unpredictable, unwholesome, a statement about going beyond convention.

She waved away my offer of tea with an impatient gesture, and said something in *bayerisch* that made those standing around her laugh. She was, I realized immediately, the undisputed queen of this little court. She had turned her wheelchair from an object of pity into a throne, and her hardness was her power. All she lacked was her legs.

The overweight woman in the panties turned from watching the quarrel and said something to me.

"Sorry," I said. "Say it again, but slowly, please."

"Do you have any clothes in the van tonight? I need a pair of pants."

"We always have clothes, but I don't know what. We'll look when we're finished here."

She waited then and followed us back across the street when we had finished serving. Walter opened the rear doors of the van, where clothes are stacked neatly in plastic bins, and the two of them inspected various articles of clothing while I put away the baskets and thermoses. She rejected a few of the things he showed her, then decided one pair of pants fit her taste even if not exactly her size. Ignoring the traffic that swerved and honked around her, she swanked across the wet street and back to the party.

The other groups we have served this evening have been more docile. Outside a small public restroom overlooking the river, three men sat on a wooden bench and accepted our offerings almost in silence. Around the back, a young man and woman slept together on another bench, jumbled up in sleeping bags. When our whispered greetings got no response, we tucked sandwiches under them and stepped back into the darkness.

At the end of a small parking lot we served a larger bunch, men of mixed ages who were sitting, lying in bags, or standing under the protection of a large stairway. A good-humored group, they talked and joked with us as we moved among them. I felt more welcome when one of them put his face close to mine, near-sighted probably, and said with beery breath, "So! The American is with us again. *Gruss Di*!"

Another group, six men mostly of middle age, had their blankets and bags spread out neatly against the back of a loading dock, like beds in a hospital ward. One of the men took an extra sandwich, and placed it carefully beside the head of a friend who slept through our visit. Two empty beer bottles and a cassette player stood at the other side of his head.

So we have moved through the evening, probably looking like medics on a darkened battlefield, or better, like Little Red Riding Hoods with our baskets of food. We have bent over to shake the hands of men almost too drunk to raise their arms, pressed cups of tea into the hand that was not holding a bottle, talked casually to those who were still on their feet. It is clear that Walter knows all the places in Munich where the alcoholics and the lonely pass their nights. Fighting a war he can never win, he is determined that these people will not go without attention.

"It's all the alcohol addiction," he repeated at another point in the evening as though I had not yet processed the idea or needed help in dealing with it. "Most of these men simply cannot live, they cannot live, without it. I do not think we can fully understand that."

"I'm learning."

"But more than tea and bread, they need to know that someone cares for them. They do not die from the alcohol, they die from loneliness."

In the fourth year of his pact with the devil, the soldier in the Grimm fable finds himself sitting, alone as usual, in the corner of an inn. He hears some groaning, and discovers an old man in great distress. Of course the old man starts to run away from the soldier, who by now looks every bit like a monster, but finally he calms down enough to tell his own story. He has lost both money and property; now he and his three daughters – of course it has to be three in a fairy tale -- are about to be put into prison for debt.

It is the perfect opportunity for the soldier, who is happy to use some of his inexhaustible supply of gold coins to give the old man all the money he needs to pay the debts. Overcome with gratitude, the man takes the soldier to his three beautiful daughters, and says he should pick one of them for a wife. The two older daughters find him repulsive, insult him, and turn away. But the youngest one, knowing how much they are indebted to him, says she will be his wife.

With that, the soldier breaks a ring in half and gives one part to the daughter. But he explains that he must wander alone for three more years. If he can survive, he will return and marry her.

It has taken me a number of summer trips here to begin to understand what Walter says about loneliness, and to understand my role in his institution. I came to help out, I told them when I first arrived, and I explained that I am active and energetic, I need something physical to do. So I have helped the men haul furniture, loaded the trucks for Hungary, worked in the gardens, run errands in the van, driven people around, cleaned and painted. Some of this has even been helpful.

But Walter has said it over and over to me, and so have members of his staff: the main thing about my coming here is that the men see me as their friend, a valued visitor. They are surprised and flattered that someone would come all the way across the ocean to be with them. And a professor, at that; the title carries more cache in Germany, and I have given up on trying to explain my own modest place in the complicated system of American higher education. Their obvious delight, not only when I arrive but also when I have not seen one of them for a few days, shows me that every time. It is an unlikely union, all the better because of the incongruity of it.

Helmut is a case in point. He is one of the older men, often cranky, sometimes a little drunk, and occasionally contentious. He sits by himself in a corner of the television room, saying very little. His eyes suggest that what he sees around him is largely disagreeable. Something about him –- possibly the way he can make a limp look noble -- suggests that he has known better times. I picture him wearing expensive German hiking boots as he conquered twisting and rocky trails through the jagged Bavarian Alps, two per weekend.

I mostly avoided him during my first trips here. This year I decided on another kind of response: a quick personal greeting in the morning, followed by a few words of conversation during the day.

It had an effect, though an unexpected one. Last week Helmut motioned me out into the hallway. Putting his fingers to his lips, he took my right hand and slipped some paper into it. I looked down to see that I was holding 50 euros.

"What's this?"

"It's for you, a present."

"I don't need money, Helmut."

"I know, I know. But I want you to have this money."

"Why?"

"I just want you to have it," he said, almost angrily. "I just gave 500 Euros to my brother in Czechoslovakia, and he doesn't even care."

"But -- you need money for yourself, don't you?"

I tried to put it back into his hand. He waved it away.

"I don't need it. And when I have it, I just drink with it." That was followed by a self-deprecating laugh.

"How about your family? Maybe they could use it. Do you have a wife?"

"Yes."

"Children?"

"I have a daughter."

"Where do they live?"

"They live not far from Munich."

"Don't you ever visit them, or don't they come to visit here?"

"Of course not." A bigger laugh then, because the conversation was becoming outlandish to him.

"What's this 'of course not'? Why don't you ever get together with them?"

"Because I'm a bum!" That was underlined with the best laugh of all, and then I couldn't help laughing along with him.

The idea amused him even more as he thought about it longer. "I'm a bum, that's why! A bum. And a crook!" A *landstreicher* and a *gauner*, he said, and from his way of using those words I could tell that he was satirizing those who would use them in serious judgment of him or anyone. Along with the laughter there was a moral superiority in his words; they gave him not so much identity as credibility, while they renounced narrow-mindedness. They also justified his desire for loneliness.

As he moves ahead of me now through the wet grass, it occurs to me that Walter could be thought of as suffering from his own kind of loneliness. It is a loneliness bred partly of intensity and partly of his single-minded commitment. That kind of commitment separates him from ordinary people. It makes him special, but it has its costs.

Now Walter and I step into the darkness, the underworld of the first big arch of the Wittelsbach Bridge. At the end, where the bridge's massive stones curve down to become a concrete ledge, three men are lying in the darkness. All three are in sleeping bags, with the usual mélange spread on the wide ledge or on the ground: clothes, shoes, hats, boxes, cups, plates, bottles, more bottles, bags, beer caps, more beer caps.

"*Servus*." Walter extends his free hand to the first man, who raises himself on one elbow and extends his own. In the glow of our flashlights is an unshaven face under a wool stocking-cap.

"Will you have some tea?"

A grunt is taken as a yes in this case, and I quickly pour him a cup while Walter shines his light on my thermos. His sandal crunches some broken glass near the foot of the bed.

"And some bread?"

Another grunt, and Walter pulls a sandwich from his basket. Slowly, the man puts it down on the ledge and then falls back, his tea sloshing.

"Careful," Walter says. "It is hot."

The next man is sleeping hard, flat on his back. Walter raises his voice, almost shouting.

"Would you like tea?"

The man picks his head off a makeshift pillow. Blinks. Slowly turns in our direction until he is resting on his right shoulder. Blinks again, as if needing to determine if we are more than the shades of his private underworld.

"What?"

"We have tea for you, and bread. Would you like some?"

"Tea? For God's sake, no!"

His head flops back on the pillow. I suppress a laugh.

Our third client has had time to sit himself up, and he runs his fingers through his hair before reaching out to shake hands. Walter seems to know this man, and they exchange a few words while I pour tea and look for a safe place to put it.

He has just had an operation, he tells us. Feels terrible. He pulls up his shirt and loosens his belt to allow his pants to fall a few inches. We use our flashlights like police tracking evidence, and we see a fresh scar, running in a crescent down his left side. It looks like someone has used a can opener on him.

He runs his finger the length of the scar, and then points to his feet. I can see that they are wrapped in some loose bindings, but it is unclear what that has to do with the scar. We inspect all these injuries with wishes for better days, which for some reason brings tears to his eyes.

Across the rocky ground and on the other side of the arch is Greta's bed. She and I have developed a halting sort of friendship, since she likes Americans and likes to talk. Twenty years of working for an American business in Germany has perfected her English. Although I have never seen Greta standing up, it is obvious that she is tall. And also extremely thin. Her cheeks are pulled into hollows under high bones and sunken eyes, and her long arms and legs seem longer for their lack of flesh.

We visited one afternoon last week when I was in this part of town and decided to see what life under the bridge was like in the daylight. She was lying that day in her usual position, head slightly elevated, legs straight out and covered with a sheet as though practicing for her own funeral. She put down a magazine as I approached, and smiled with yellowed teeth.

"So you have come," she said. "That is nice of you."

Greta's English is always very precise.

"Hello, Greta. I was in the area and I thought I'd say hello. But I wasn't sure you would be here."

"I am always here. Except when I take a little walk over there." She swept her arm toward the uneven grasses of the high-water area, where two people were jogging and a man was walking his dog in the sunshine.

"How far do you walk?"

She shrugged. "Just along here, and only for a few minutes. My legs are not good yet."

"What's wrong with them?"

"Something... I do not know exactly how to explain it in

English. My stomach is also bad. I am not sure how you say that either."

"Do you have some pills?"

"Oh, sure, right here. She leaned part way out of her bed, ignoring the magazine that fell to the ground, and fished among some items in a cardboard box. Then she held up a small bottle of pills.

"Okay, but it looks to me like you need to eat some more. You're way too thin"

"I eat a lot," she said defensively. "But it does not help." She pointed to a man sleeping a few yards from her.

"See that man? He is very good to me. His name is Johannes, but we call him Hansi. He brings me lots of food every day."

"I'm sorry I couldn't get to your picnic."

Greta had invited me to join her and the bridge people for an all-day summer party, but I missed it. "Did you have fun?"

"It was very good, really fun. A few days before, I was thinking it might be too noisy and, how do you say, rowdy, and I thought I would go to Walter's for the day, to get away from here. But I did not, and now I am glad. We had music all day, and games. And some of the people even put on some little plays. It was all organized and a good time all day."

"I don't think that could happen in my own country, the homeless people having a picnic. It's like you have a little community of your own down here."

"Is it really?" she smiled at the idea and looked momentarily coquettish, like a woman aware that she was in bed and talking to a man. "Last year we even had a football game -- you call it soccer, I think -- between our people and some from another area. And Walter's place got tee-shirts for both sides, with names on them."

She put her hand to her mouth, suddenly reminded of something, and then reached under some clothes for a letter. "Look, this is from California. Have you been there?"

"A few times, yes."

"I have some friends there. I have visited them before. They want me to come and live with them. A beautiful home. And they say they can get me a job there, in an office."

"Are you going?"

"Yes, of course. But first I have to become healthier."

"When do you think you'll go?"

"I think next year. They really want me to come. And it is lovely there. The ocean is not far away."

"How do they write to you? I mean, there's no address here, is there?"

"I gave them an address of a girlfriend of mine, her apartment. That is where my sister contacts me too."

"You have a sister here? You mean she lives right here in Munich?"

She lives near here. And she does not know that I live here under the bridge."

"Does it matter?"

"Yes, to her it would matter. She is very..." Greta gestured vaguely. "How do you say a person who lives very high --?"

"Probably you mean 'high society'."

"Yes, that is it. She lives very high society. And she would be angry with me if she knows that I live here."

"Couldn't you move into your girlfriend's apartment?"

"But I like it here better. People are nice to me here. And it is a better time here."

Now, on a rainy Sunday evening, I am finding Greta exactly as I always do, and her look is again welcoming in the circle of the flashlight's beam. The bed next to hers is empty, and beyond that a man sleeps on a pallet, one arm hanging to the ground. More bottle caps dot the ground in front of the beds.

"It was very nice to have your visit last week," she says, gently.

"My pleasure, really. But it was a little different to be here in the daytime."

"Not much changes here. There are more people at night, and it is sometimes a little noisier."

"You'll have some tea?"

"Yes, please. Put it --." She looks into a plastic cup by her bed, places it upside down with a giggle, and points to another, sitting on a box out of her reach." -- in that one."

The ground slopes, and the cup is about to tip over. "Maybe it is better to put it there," Greta suggests. She then points to another small platform that seems to belong to the home next to hers. "And could you fill his cup too? That green one. He is gone now, but he will be back soon. At least I think he will be back soon."

"Sure." How have you been? Are you still eating so much?"

"Oh, of course. You can see how fat I am becoming."

"I just don't want to come here and find that you disappeared completely."

The idea of disappearing apparently triggers an opposite one, and Greta modestly adjusts a slipping strap on her thin night shirt.

"That will not happen. I am feeling better these days."

In the shadows, Walter has moved around us while we have been talking, and he is now handing sandwiches to people further on.

"It looks like I can't visit long tonight." I say. "The boss is moving on."

"That is all right," she says. "When are you going back to America?"

"In a couple of weeks. But I'll come back next year, and I can see you again then."

"No, not here. Remember, I will be in California."

"That's even better. Maybe I'll see you there someday. We can keep in contact." I doubt that we are fooling each other.

"Can I have your address in America?"

"Sure. Where can I write it?"

She twists around and pulls a notebook from behind her pillow, turns pages until she finds a blank one. Then she uses my light to dig around until she finds a pen.

"Write it here, please."

Putting the flashlight on the little platform, I print my name and address and return the notebook to her.

"I'd like to hear from you, whether you're in California or here. And I'll write back, don't worry."

"That would be very nice. Good night."

Walter has finished handing out sandwiches and is heading toward the abutment that separates the first arch from the second, so I quickly pour a few more cups of tea and follow after him. Around the corner of the abutment, we enter a scene that is always a favorite of mine. The people who live under this second arch have created something straight out of *Les Miserables*. They are lying on mattresses, or sitting, or standing in twos or threes. Others are sleeping, talking, laughing, eating, smoking, drinking -- all this among a jumble of bags and boxes and old furniture. It looks like someone has dumped the entire contents of a thrift shop under the arch, and some of Munich's citizens have burrowed into the pile. In a few places, makeshift partitions create the semi-seclusion of little cubicles, but otherwise they live in this jungle with apparent indifference to privacy.

A large puddle, almost a pond, has formed in the lowest area, under the high point of the bridge's arch. Apparently it has been designated for chairs. They lie in the water in every possible position: ordinary kitchen chairs, an overstuffed chair, a child's high chair, two wheel chairs, a desk chair, several broken lawn chairs, and a canvas camp chair. The impression is of a mischievous attempt at street art.

In front of one large mattress, a man and woman are cooking something on a camp stove. Further on, I can see a bulging and twisting under some blankets that cause me to turn my flashlight away. In some places, candles make quivering shadows on the upward curve of the arch, like a hint of bats in the night air.

The oddest thing about this scene is that these people are watching television. Color television. It is a medium-sized set, old but working well, that has been thoughtfully positioned in the center of the viewing area. The program, as usual, is some old American western, a genre often in favor. The volume is high, so that we have to compete with gunfire and excited cowboy dialogue in German as we move around furniture and reach over mattresses to shake hands.

On my first visit here, I was puzzled as to how electricity is brought to a television set under a bridge, and I threw the beam of my flashlight around the set in a search for wires or batteries. Eventually I noticed a gasoline-powered generator sitting in the grass outside the arch, its throbbing muted by the nearer noise of the program.

Walter is oblivious to the fact that he is blocking the view of some of them as he stops to hand out sandwiches and talk. I try to crouch on the ground to pour the tea, and otherwise keep moving. It is difficult to see very much, since I have to put my flashlight down, and the thermos tilts dangerously on the sloping stones when I place it there.

A young man appears at my side, holding a can of beer. I think he has been watching us with more than the usual interest.

"What is your name?" he asks in very clear German. It is right away obvious that he is not from Bavaria.

"Derek. And yours?"

"I am called Jan." He pronounces it "yahn." It is the universal male name: Jan, Juan, John, Sean, Jean, Johann, Ivan. Because it is also my own first name, it creates an immediate bond.

In the wavering half-lights of the candles and the flicker of the cowboy movie, I can see that Jan is in his late-twenties, and he is in better condition that most of his nocturnal friends. His striped tank-top looks almost new; outside of it hangs a silver medallion that catches what light there is as he moves. It seems that he has missed a few shaves, though possibly that is meant to be stylish. The left side of his head has been shorn down to a stubble that reaches about two-thirds of the way to the crown. The rest of the head is covered with long brown curls that dangle over his collar and his right ear and half of his brow, and they swing to cover his right eye when he turns to look at me more closely.

"You aren't speaking with the local dialect," I tell him. "Where are you from?"

"I am from the former DDR, -- it comes out day-day-air in the pronunciation of the German alphabet -- East Germany. And you are an American?"

"Yeah. I've heard a lot of East Germans are coming here."

Jan nods. "We are looking for work. Three of us came together last year, and we are staying. It's much nicer than East Germany."

"Did you have a job there?"

"Yes, I was a mechanic."

"And do you have a family back there? A wife or children?"

Why do I keep asking this question?

"No, I had a girlfriend. With not enough to do." He smiles at some memory, a chord that reverberates from north and east of where he is now. The chord has been struck and for a moment I think he may share the memory. He does not.

"That is why I am here, for a better life."

I wonder in silence how sleeping under a Munich bridge qualifies as a better life to Jan.

"And have you found any work here?"

"Not yet. But one of my friends has." Jan gestures over his shoulder at several shapes in the darkness." That one. We are living on what he earns."

From the pocket of his jeans, Jan pulls out a flattened pack of cigarettes, nearly empty. They are the popular and inexpensive Czechoslovakian brand, not noted for their mildness.

"You want a cigarette?"

"No, thank you."

Loose tobacco strands project from the end as he places one in his mouth, and tiny embers fall as he lights it. In the glow of his wooden match, a gold earring shines on the shaven side of his head.

"These are not very good, are they? American cigarettes are better." Jan takes the cigarette out of his mouth and studies it. "A lot of things are better in America."

"Well, some things are. But we have our problems too."

"Do you have homeless people?"

"Sure, lots of them. But ours do not seem as -- what can I call it -- sociable, most of the time."

Jan smiles at that, and with a quick wave of his hand he brushes some of the pesky hair from his forehead. He starts to ask another question, but now we are interrupted by another man. He is holding a small plastic yogurt container, one of the ones we have been handing out through the evening. He is swaying dangerously and he is trying, in that way that drunken people have who must try too hard to do anything, to look aggressive.

"Look at this," he says to me, pointing to the lid.

"What about it?"

"Look at the date. Right here."

The thin lid is torn, right through the last number of the final sale date. Even in the direct beam of my flashlight, it is hard to see the number clearly.

"It says 'No sale after July 23'." His voice is rough and belligerent. "That's four days ago."

Jan takes the container from him and fits the torn pieces together.

"No," he says. "Look. That's July 28. Tomorrow."

The man is not convinced, and it is clear that nothing will convince him, wrapped as he is in the obstinacy of his anger. There may also be some shame, to the extent that he may be aware that he is making a fool of himself. For the first time this evening, I have a sense of trouble coming.

"It is, man," Jan says.

"I dunno. It still looks like a three to me," the man says. "I don't want no bad food."

He takes a step toward us and then he blinks, like a person who needs to assess exactly where he is and what is happening around him.

Jan also takes a step forward, so that the two of them are inches apart. His hands are loose at his sides.

"Relax," Jan says. It is a command more than a suggestion.

The man blinks again, his eyes narrowing with a question he cannot wrestle into consciousness. His gaze goes from Jan to me and then back. His eyes widening, as though just now discovering a welcome compromise, he flips the yogurt container onto the ground and walks away.

"Thanks for the help," I say.

"That's okay. He's just... you know."

For a moment he looks down at his feet, and I am surprised that he seems embarrassed by the scene.

"I guess I'd better pour some tea. I'll probably see you next week."

"I'll be here," Jan says.

Deeper in the shadows, Walter has started a conversation with another man, who is half-sitting and half-lying on his mattress. They are examining the man's flashlight, which apparently is broken. The man shakes it and slaps it against his palm a few times. Finally Walter hands his own light to the man, shakes hands, and comes in my direction. Somebody turns up the volume on the television, and cowboy gunfire echoes from the arch over our heads.

Now Walter stops at another mattress and right away begins a serious conversation with its occupant. It looks like they are going to talk for a while, so to pass the time I watch the rain drip off the edge of the arch. My thoughts drift back to the man in the dark suit, the professor of micro-economics who holds calmly to his dignity in a world of drunkenness and handouts.

That makes me think of my own recent handout, an incident they are still laughing about in the houses.

It happened one afternoon when I drove to the convent to pick up food. The sisters prepare large kettles of soups and stews for the houses, and picking them up is a regular errand. That afternoon, as it happened, I was asked to go alone. A little unsure of myself, I put my lines into perfect German as I drove through the gate and up to the door of the convent.

"Good evening, sister," I said to the elderly nun who let me into a foyer that had little furniture and no dust. "I've come to pick up the food."

Her eyes went quickly over my work clothes.

"Very good. Wait, please."

Within minutes she returned, holding a single sandwich. With an encouraging smile, she handed it to me.

"I hope this will do."

"Uh, I'm not really hungry, sister. We just ate. But thank you."

"I see." With another smile, she turned and left.

Turning the sandwich over in my hand, I paced the foyer. Apparently she thought I needed a snack while I waited for the boxes and kettles of food. Some time went by. Eventually the elderly nun returned to the desk, looking surprised when she saw me.

"You are still here?"

"Well, yes. I'm, uh, waiting."

"What else do you need, then? Are you also thirsty?"

"No, sister, I'm not thirsty."

"Perhaps you need to sleep. But we don't -- "

"Sister, I'm not hungry or thirsty or tired. I'm here to pick up the food, for Walter's house. Do you understand? The house at -- "

"But what do you want, actually?" Her tone mixed confusion with annoyance, possibly even a bit of fear.

"I think we need to start over," I said, as the awkward truth hit me: I was another beggar at the door. And why not, wearing those clothes, speaking haltingly? Not just homeless and hungry, but probably drunk too.

Her confusion naturally undid my rehearsed German, and we had to go around a few more times before I had the idea to ask for another nun there, one who knows me. With her help, the old nun finally got it right: he's from America, works with Walter, the food is for the *houses*.

"I've made a terrible mistake," the old nun said.

The men teased me about it for days. "The beggar from America," I'm now called.

Walter is finishing his last conversation, so it is time to go. Without his flashlight, he is forced to follow me back across the grass, which has become noticeably wetter. Out from under the arch, we can hear the swish of traffic on the bridge above us. We walk in silence.

The faces of the evening slide, in no particular order, through the raindrops. First, Greta, who is going to California as soon as she is healthier. Jan, looking for a better life. The queen on her throne and the woman who needed pants. Dozens of others with whom I did not talk, coming out of the cardboard boxes and the beer bottles of their lives and then returning to their sleeping bags and invulnerable privacy.

"*Wilde Gesellen.*" It is a German folksong I learned in college. Scattered lines from it sometimes come to mind when I am in these scenes.

"Wild fellows, blown by the storm wind,
Princes in rags...
Fiddle, gown in colorful splendor, you'll meet no birds
More beautiful...
Even if they mock us, for us the sun never goes down."

That is the romantic side of these scenes. There is more to that side than is generally understood, because romance is more than escapism or a gloss for sexual love. It can be an accompaniment that creates nobility and gallantry out of disgrace. It can turn dull shame and bitterness into its own kind of rag-tag splendor.

The soldier in the fairy-tale survived the last three years of his wandering, much to the chagrin of the devil, who was forced not just to hand him over but also to clean him up when the seven years were done. In a fine velvet coat and a coach drawn by four horses, the soldier returned to the house of the old man, where the two older daughters suddenly found this handsome stranger to be very marriageable indeed. Ignoring them, he produces his half of the ring, and the younger daughter throws herself joyfully into his arms. The two older daughters are not at all happy, but everybody else is.

Walter is looking down at his feet as he walks through the grass. Above him the bridge is darker now, the light from its few stanchions dimmed by the rain and the lowering skies. Otto von Wittelsbach, in the stony solitude of his aristocracy, watches the cars that we can see but not hear above us, unaware of the actual lives playing out below him.

I realized that I had missed someone.

Michael was not under the bridge this evening, which is our loss. He is the alcoholic as extrovert. He is jovial in an unaffected way, and as he talks, he leans close in his excitability and holds his cigarette politely to the side. He is always glad to see us and always grateful for his sandwich. Michael even works occasionally in one of Walter's houses, and I asked him once why he doesn't live there too.

He gave me a zany smile and flapped his arms in the air.

"Because I want to fly like a bird," he said, a wild fellow.

There is the problem, and it is an important one. Some of these men and women have made peace with their addiction and can live reasonably well in Walter's houses. There they have private rooms, hot meals, a few hours of work done partly to provide a sense of worth, and even a modest allotment of beer, enough to keep most of them content. Except for the morning work period, they can come and go as they please.

Others cannot live in the houses, because to them freedom is more important than anything else, even if that freedom means sleeping under the bridge or sometimes under trees and on benches in the rain, asking for spare change in the tourist areas, and being partially inebriated much of the time. It may be that part of their idea of freedom is to accept the necessity of their addiction -- "I'm an alcoholic" they will tell me without guile, because that explains everything -- and to make a defiant romance out of the commonplaces and consolations of their lives. Another part is to claim freedom from both guilt and innocence, escaping this additional duality to make sure that they alone will be in charge of who controls their world. Or does their need for freedom have something to do with ghosts who follow them from pasts that can magnify memory, chasten, even destroy?

Better than anyone, I think, Walter understands their conceits of freedom, even if he does not always appreciate or approve, and he subscribes, in the best liberal tradition, to the German motto of *leben und leben lassen*, live and let live. From that starting point, he wants only to make their lives in some ways better. And thereby to make his own better. He knows that if you love them they will ease your pain.

There is a poster in the front hall of each of Walter's houses. It quotes a letter from St. Vincent de Paul, another friend of the street people, only better known. It is written to one of his young helpers, someone named Jeanne.

"…The more ugly and dirty and unjust and coarse they are, all the more you have to give them your love... On account of your love alone, and only for the sake of your love, will the poor excuse you the bread that you give them."

"I'm a little tired now," Walter says from behind me, in a voice uncharacteristically soft, or weakened by emotions that he has learned to control in front of others. We are walking on the dirt path that angles upward from the meadow to the parking area. The rain drips lightly on us from dark, soaking branches.

"Could you drive the rest of the way tonight?"

Chapter Eight

We were sitting around the picnic table one evening in Munich -- Walter and a few staff members and I -- when I told them the main parts of the story, right up to the latest developments. It was probably hard for them to fully understand that side of America, since most of what they learn comes from films and TV programs that have very little to do with our realities. Still, they know quite a bit about life on the underside of their own city, so they had a few comments and questions when I finished. Walter, ready as always to go after the lost sheep, made the comment that stuck.

"Reach out to him again," he said. "Sometimes it takes just one more try."

That is easy to say but hard to do when the person keeps disappearing. Ken did not go to Tina's place as planned, after that morning of the breaking-in and the drive-by of the gangster car. He went wherever he would go when he did not want to be around people who might remind him of what had been and of things that had been left behind.

Then he turned up sometime later, by means of another phone call. He was living in a different neighborhood and must have been watching for me, because he came out of the house immediately. Since I was not invited inside, for reasons I could guess at, we stood out on the sidewalk, leaning up against my car.

"Is this place a drug house too?" I asked.

"Naw. It belongs to a friend of mine. He's in jail, I'm just sort of house sitting. And that other house wasn't a drug house either."

"No?"

"I was using, but what was going on was that people, mostly white people from the suburbs, would come into the city and ask me to cop. I would go to the drug houses and get the drugs and we would come back to that house and get high. So I was like the go between, copping drugs for them. I wouldn't exactly call myself a dealer 'cause I wasn't actually selling the drugs. It was a way of supporting my own addiction because the money went to get my own drugs. Some of them would use the drugs in my house and others would just pick them up and leave."

The distinction seemed unimportant to me. More than that, his explanation was just making specific some of the generalities we had traded many times, sounding often like talking heads on a television special. We had long before agreed that the war on drugs, with all the busts here at home and the military excursions in South America and the well-meaning rehab programs, was a losing proposition. As long as there is a demand there will be a supply.

We knew that our state was known for some of the harshest drug laws, which put a lot of people in jails and prisons while others fill their places in the neighborhoods, like driven rats setting up new nests. We also knew that two-thirds of those arrested for drug offences were black, but as Ken would say, "Those are just the ones who are *arrested*." Drug addiction cuts across cultures and social-economic classes even if we don't want to admit it.

We knew statistics claiming that 60 per cent of all the cocaine produced in the world is consumed in this country. We suggested that one reason was that we have the money to spend. But we also suspected that another reason is that we have a lot of people who do not like themselves very much.

It was all old news, and some of it went through my mind as we stood there, neither of us sure what more there was to be said -- not of those generalities but of the specific instance that was now separating us.

A baseball cap, one side of the brim slightly torn, was pulled low over his face. I reached up and raised the bill a few inches.

"Are you growing a beard, or just trying to cover up that skinny face? You still need some weight."

He felt the stubble on his cheek, then shrugged by sinking his head into his shoulders while pulling them almost straight back, like someone trying to loosen the upper vertebrae. Slowly he unwrapped some chewing gum, rolled up the gum before putting it in his mouth, and crumpled the tin-foil wrapper before swatting it into the air with a flat palm. The tiny packet caught for a moment on the breeze and then rolled across the sidewalk and stopped at the edge of the lawn.

The gesture annoyed me, not so much because it suggested a small disdain for the appearance of the neighborhood but because there was something adolescent about it, a small show of defiance that was not worthy of him, or a reversion to a time that was being remembered with perverse affection.

I unzipped the top of my jacket to show him that I was wearing one of the old Youth Day T-shirts.

"It's getting pretty worn out," I said, showing him a thumb-sized hole near the bottom seam. "Do you have any more?"

"Somewhere. Not here."

"That's one of the problems," he said after spending some time watching a car pass slowly by, the driver staring and then averting his eyes when he saw that we were staring back. "I got bored with Youth Day. And I wasn't happy with the organization sometimes. You know that better than anybody."

Given his extraordinary drive and the corresponding need for ever more validation, it was no surprise to hear about boredom. We seek always to be satisfied with ourselves, but few of us have the confidence to achieve that fulfillment without the praise of those who are close to us. It also came to me that happy people generally do not need a great deal of change. It is the unhappy ones, usually themselves unclear about the source of their special unhappiness, who often seek... something else.

"Yeah. For some people the fun is putting things together. Once that's done, it's not so much fun to keep them going. Others are better at that. As for boredom, maybe you ought to be more like most people. Just get excitement out of the usual stuff. Or maybe you could take up rock climbing or bungee jumping. Thrill seeker."

He smiled at the old allusion.

"You know," he said, "I should never have taken that money."

"What money?"

"The $50,000. You remember, the big grant I got from the city. It meant I had to do stuff they wanted done for the kids, along with everything else."

"We really needed that money then," I said. "I mean, for the organization."

"Yeah, but it compromised me in a lot of ways. For one, I had to stop opposing that new ball park. It was a done deal anyway. Then they made me pull back from running for school board -- they already had their slate of candidates, they said. Mostly they didn't want me doing certain things, saying things."

"They actually told you that, directly?"

"Sure they did. The mayor and I really had it out once about that. Right in his office, yelling. 'Don't forget that we're helping you out,' he said, meaning the money of course. Besides that, the money made me complacent."

"It's hard to imagine you being complacent."

"Well, I was, and it bothered me a lot. As for being a thrill seeker, yeah, it seems like I always have to have the extremes. The way things are now, or else all that stuff with the youth. It's like living in two worlds, but not being happy in either one."

"You know which one you were happier in."

He knew there was no point in arguing that. "Life's a bitch," he said instead.

That angered me. "That sounds like some dumb bumper sticker. Anyway, it isn't. It's just the way things happen sometimes. Everything else is your attitude. Anyway, I always told you that you couldn't handle your own success."

That point at least hit home somehow.

"Those were the best years of my life – a nice home, brand new car, a savings and checking account and a career that could have went anywhere. And I just threw it away. I purposely did it, and a lot had to do with -- because, when I got involved with community activism and working with youth I did it because it was something I felt I had to do. And a lot of people came into play where I started to get polluted, you know, seeing my name in the media, being in the news, being asked to speak at big functions. So what it was about wasn't the future and it wasn't about the kids anymore. It was about me and I started to feel that and I didn't like what I was feeling. And I actually hated it and I said, 'man, I'm starting to feel miserable, not good anymore about my work. 'And I said, 'well, the hell with it, I'll throw it away. 'And that was stupid because I should have sat down and said to myself, "how can you contain your ego, go back to what you know is wholesome and right?"

"I was happy about what you were doing, so I let it go. I should have said something."

"Not your fault. We're all our own men. A lot of people said they should have come to my aid. One of them told me I was suffering from bi-polar disorder. I could see those tendencies when I would have my ups and downs. I got a thrill – my job became my substitute for my drug abuse because I was working 10-12 hour days, running myself ragged. And when Youth Day came off it was like a high, when it was so successful. It was like 'wow, I'm great. 'And I was always searching for something bigger or better, when small is okay too. I've always been a grandiose type of person, and that's a danger."

This was turning into one of the best conversations we had had in a very long time, even if it was out on a chilly sidewalk and most of it should have been said long before. So it is that self-knowledge, and with that the work of a good mentor, can come too late. Still, he was on a roll, being honest with himself and me, and I wanted to keep it going a little longer, even if that meant some repetition.

"You didn't have to totally disappear after that last Youth Day, you know. Why did you?"

"I wanted to escape from everybody, basically, and I wanted to leave my past behind. Because I had become very dissatisfied, using a kind of self-serving mentality. What started off as a humble and righteous venture became one of a polluted and missed opportunity. I became an opportunist and I didn't like that about me and thank God, too, that I have a conscience about stuff like that. Even though I did it the wrong way. I handled that egoism and grandiosity the wrong way. There were other ways of doing that, now that I look at it. Here I was this person teaching alternative lifestyles from drugs and I was an oxymoron, the epitome of a hypocrite."

"So you had to go the whole opposite direction?"

"Yeah. It would hurt me more to see one of my students or someone I had counseled to see me in the streets. So I came out at night, like most partying people. I went in search of my drugs at night and I stayed in during the day. I avoided anyone who cared and who loved me – my family, you, the rest of the members of the board who were also my friends."

Here he stopped, and stopped in a way that said there were limits to this sort of conversation, to confessing. So I said nothing more, waiting for him to go on.

"You know what would really be good?"

"What?"

"To go camping again, like that other time. Do some fishing."

"Then *I'd* be the one who's bored. But I can handle it. Anyway, we've already talked about that. Just say when."

We fell silent again while a woman walking a small white poodle maneuvered around us. She gave us a wary sidelong look, probably hurrying home to alert the police to a drug deal in the making.

"The 'hood, I know it's not right there," he said. "Like the things I do. And see. Like that guy's brains coming out. And you know I almost died myself from that overdose, last year. I told you about that. My girlfriend found me lying in my own feces. Next thing I was in the emergency room, stuck full of IV's. Aspirated pneumonia. They said they didn't think I would make it. Of course I went right back to the drugs after I got out."

That flair for the dramatic would have been laughable if it hadn't been so predictable. Instead it was welcome, a reminder of the early times and a suggestion that some things at least had not changed.

"With all this nasty stuff going on, and everybody knowing about it, why don't they just lock you up?"

"It's not that simple."

"What does that mean?"

"It would take too long to explain, the legal complications. Anyway, it doesn't matter right at the moment."

"So where's all this going?" I asked, and remembered having asked the same question at a different time and place.

"I don't know. But the funny thing is, you know, I still want to help. There was an accident last night, two streets over." He waved his hand and pointed to the right. "I ran over there, pulled this guy from the car. He wasn't hurt much. Then I restrained the other guy from leaving until the police came. That felt good, like I was doing something."

"Okay, but I'd also like to see you start helping yourself again. It's kinda past time, isn't it?"

"That's a problem for me. Not helping myself. I still care about people, don't want to hurt anybody. I don't want people getting upset over me."

"You can't stop us from doing that. But you just said it: you want to help. So do your friends. Wanting to help goes both ways. Sometimes accepting help is harder to do. I've found that out myself a few times."

"No one can help me. I told you that before. I've got to help myself on this one."

"So help yourself. Start thinking about what you really want. But remember, nobody has more support than you, and you've earned it."

"Every night I'm thinking about you and other people, looking at pictures. Like those pictures of us camping. I still have those. But I can't look at any pictures of Alicia, or my father."

At that, we both stopped talking. I zipped up my jacket as a little wind blew down the street, carrying a few dry leaves and scraps of paper.

"Problem is," he said, "I still don't know who I am. Still looking."

"Some people spend their whole lives doing that. I guess that's okay for them. But you can do better than that. Anyway, we're not rid of each other yet, seems like."

Failure can be hard on a person in ways that only the person knows. It can be equally hard on friendships, as we had been discovering. The difference between us was that Ken had known when to stop, something that not everyone knows to do. There was a clear sense of integrity in that. Even when you are doing the right things, it is time to stop when those things are not good for you anymore. Otherwise you start hurting yourself and then you start becoming resentful. From there it is only a step to becoming ineffective.

In contrast, I was not as willing to let go. It seemed that while he at one time had a good thing and then did not want it anymore, I still wanted it *for* him. Along with that was the idea that, if I could persuade him of how good it still was, that would make it good. Not then but later I asked myself: is it because if you let go you are admitting that the whole mentoring episode was a failure? Or is it that you think the achievements of the past five years can be repeated, that things do not have to change, or that someone who wants something you don't understand can be made to want what he does not want?

What I could understand was just how much the energies of social activism could be drained by lack of enough support, of how the spirit can become numbed by doing too much while others are not doing enough. Praise is meant to sustain the spirit but it does not translate easily into help and action.

"I'll call you," he said.

He was back in court when I saw him next, a few of us appearing with him in support. It was one of several appearances on the charge that had put him in jail after that long period underground. He had been pulled over for speeding. It wasn't just that he had already had a few speeding tickets. The arresting officer reported seeing him and a passenger lean into the back seat. A K-9 dog uncovered drug paraphernalia. Along with that was a loaded 9 mm pistol with a loaded clip and allegedly some traces of cocaine.

"It wasn't even my gun," he told me later. "It was in a backpack in the car. Not even my car."

"Whose, then?"

"A guy I know. I was just using his car."

"Where is he now?"

"I don't know."

I found myself impatient with that kind of answer. There had been a time when my questions got long and honest answers. Now the responses bordered on the defiant. Either that or they harbored a suggestion that none of this was my business. He must have picked up on that, since he went on.

"He's somewhere. But they're wrong about that coke. There wasn't any coke in the car. The whole thing is so legally bogus. First of all, that car had a state of the art radar detector. I was going 47, and they claimed I was going over 50. They only pulled me over that night because I had a white woman in the car with me. Everybody knows the cops are racist."

I wondered to myself if a disagreement over a few miles per hour made any difference, and whether police really could see a woman's skin color in the dark. But it seemed pointless to start a cross examination. So I said nothing, letting the silence do the work for me.

"The cops took two sets of fingerprints," he went on, "and neither of them were mine. This whole legal process is being speeded up. They're railroading me, trying to put me away for being too outspoken and too challenging."

That last would be impossible to prove or disprove, and we both knew it. In any case it didn't matter. Felons are not supposed to be driving around with a gun in the car, no matter whose car it is or anything else.

"This isn't real helpful right now," I said, "but I've got to tell you. I'd rather see you go to prison for a while than end up dead, which is the direction you *were* headed in."

He could not argue that.

What followed then were months of legal maneuvering. Although he pleaded guilty to a misdemeanor illegal-weapons charge, he tried later to claim that he had been high on cocaine when he entered that plea. No success. His lawyer managed to get him out of jail for a time on some sort of good conduct release while the legal maneuvering went on. It got pretty complicated, and the most I could do was listen when he explained the ins and outs, the next moves. Most of it seemed like grasping at legal straws.

At one point, sitting over breakfast in an outdoor cafe, he told me of a possible deal.

"Tell me what you think of this, Uncle Derek. There's a chance they might offer me an out if I would go to work undercover for them."

"How?"

"They know I've got a lot of contacts in this city, that I know a lot of stuff they'd like to know."

"Are these people *serious*?"

"Well, could be. I don't know yet."

"Not a great idea, considering how well known you are in this city, on both sides of the law. Unless you want to go live in some place like Easter Island when all the busts are over."

Happily, nothing came of that deal.

At least his being out of jail gave us a chance to spend some time together again. We met for a few meals, took our walks, and I even took him to jail to visit the young woman who had been in the car with him on the night of the arrest.

Through some legal maneuvers that were unclear to me, she was in jail while he was out. In another time that might have been funny, but nobody was laughing about it then, least of all the woman.

We talked the situation through again and again, turning over new possibilities like geologists with a pile of promising rocks. Each time I saw him, it seemed that there was another twist to the tangle of legal strings. In my own mind, none of these twists seemed to be in a clear direction away from the inevitable.

Aside from the legal talk, the conversations just were not the same. He may have thought that nothing had changed, but there was to me an unreal quality to the talk and a growing distance between us. It may have been the sense on my part that we were doing no more than going around one more time, saying the same things. Or it was a loss of patience on my part, a time of doubting his sincerity even if he didn't doubt it himself.

"It's amazing," he said one time too many as we took yet another long walk through a suburban park, enjoying the crackle of dry leaves under our feet. "People are still behind me, still supporting me." He named some of the old names and grew excited as he gave me more details.

"That's great." I said that without enthusiasm and thought back to a recent phone conversation with a wealthy supporter who told me she was through with the whole business. Her tone and some of her language suggested that she included me in that too. There was little point in repeating the conversation. Instead, I hinted at it. "But you can't expect these people to keep supporting you forever. There's a limit to people's patience." I meant my own as well, and he knew it.

"You're right," he said, almost too quickly. "But there are some differences. For one, I've got those pills now for the bi-polar stuff. Thing is, they have some nasty side effects, like they make me dizzy sometimes."

"Better tell the doctor about that. Now, what's the other difference?"

"I'm more willing to let God take things wherever. I've been reading the Bible a lot, and other books too. It's really changing things. Letting God into my life more, admitting that I can't do it myself. You wouldn't believe what a difference that makes." He clenched one fist and shook it in front of himself. "It's like getting rid of yourself or something."

That was not entirely a new development. Over the years he had been involved with a religious group, I knew. During this last brief attempt at re-building, or at least at escaping time in prison, he was involved more than ever. I had my doubts about that too. Not that the group wasn't supportive or genuine. The question was whether Ken was still far enough above the surface for it to make any difference.

Along with my own doubts and impatience, there was another obvious difference in our conversations: we no longer talked about his work with the youth. Not only did we avoid referring to past successes, with good reason, but we also said nothing about future plans. Before, that had been the promising focus of most of the talk. Now, the only interest was in what might be useful in staying out of jail, first, and dealing with addiction, a far second.

He stayed a month or two at a downtown rehab center. When I went for a second visit there, they told me he had left for a different one. "A falling out with my counselor," he told me when he called to explain. The next place was no better. At one point I helped him move a bed and some belongings into a cheap apartment that reeked of mildewed wallpaper. He was out of there almost before he had moved in.

It was not just that the places to stay were no good. Nothing was any good. It was one straw after another, one more anemic attempt to convince himself and me and others that he was dealing with his problems, or that his attorney would somehow come through. Eventually, after he stopped attending the last of those rehab programs, the judge ordered an arrest warrant. He was picked up the next day. The court appearance came not long after.

The next headline said, "Ex-con Crime Fighter Sentenced."

The judge referred to the various letters of support Ken had received and offered his best wishes. "You've got a lot going for you," he said. "You've got some big issues to address, though. You know what they are."

The assistant district attorney offered the opinion that Ken had done a great deal of good for the community. That he let people down, the DA said as though as an afterthought, "was a shame."

"He has done a lot in his life to contribute to this community," Ken's lawyer added. "I'm sure he can do that again."

The mayor's office was not available for comment.

When it was finally over, he was given five years.

LITTLE THINGS

The origin of all human evils, and of baseness and cowardice, is not death, but rather the fear of death. Fortify yourself therefore, against that fear. In this, let all your discourses, readings, exercises, tend. And then you will know that thus alone are men made free.

-- Epictetus

Death is the true inspiring genius, or the muse of philosophy... Indeed, without death men could scarcely philosophize.

-- Schopenhauer

This one is blind, although I didn't realize that until I noticed one of the other men leading him back inside. He has been waiting, along with a couple of flies that move lazily aside as I sit on the edge of his mattress.

"*Bon jour.*"

"*Bon jour, m'sieur*," he answers with a trill of cheer in his voice, like someone happening on an old friend.

"*Ou vle febab*?"

"*Oui.*"

Asking, in the simplified grammar of Haitian Creole, if he wants a shave is not even necessary, since they never decline. Even before being asked he was rubbing his palm on the stubble of his chin, offering more evidence of the peculiar vision and supersensory hearing of the blind.

He is already up into a sitting position, so that he can help tuck the towel into the neck of his hospital gown. The gown is fresh and clean, with a logo indicating that it was donated by a hospital in Ohio.

I splash a few drops of cold water on his cheeks and try to get some under his chin as well. It is hard to get enough shaving cream into the deep hollows of his face and the lines around his mouth. As we begin, I have to pull his skin to stretch it, not easy with hands that are wet and slick with shaving cream. He tries to help by bulging out his cheeks, extending the skin around his mouth with his tongue, and tilting his head back.

We are in one of the several large rooms that make up Sans Fil, one of Mother Teresa's homes for the dying that are found all over the world. Sans Fil is one of several facilities in Port-au-Prince run by her sisters. Besides ministering to the very sick or dying -- their primary task -- they also operate a walk-in clinic on certain days along with other programs. It can be a busy place. Sometimes we have to pass through a tight crowd of women and children waiting outside the main gate. The black people predictably move aside in deference to the whites, and the guard slams the heavy metal gate in their faces with an officious clang after we have squeezed through.

It was Michael, sitting across the dinner table at the boys' home and guest house where we stay, who suggested that Sans Fil would be a good place to work. As usual, he was right.

Now it is years later, and there is a pleasing nostalgia in coming back here. Some time ago, I changed venues and began doing the same work at a hospice for men only, run by the brothers of the Missionaries of Charity. Their area is known as Pele -- named for the soccer star-- and it is one the most destitute in a city scarred by destitution. Smoke from piles of burning garbage sometimes swirls across the dirt roads, stinging the eyes and distorting the human shapes that move through it. The effect is like a scene out of Dante. Alongside the canal, pigs root in the garbage that floats sluggishly for a few yards before piling on itself and stopping and then, as if falling back on a will of its own, gathers just enough force to continue. Shallow puddles in the road turn to mud at their edges and from there to rocky walkways that lead into narrow alleys.

There is much of humanity to see and hear in Pele. As I turn one corner, the voices of children chanting their lessons come sweetly over the wall of a school. At another corner, women gather beneath a water tower to fill their white five-gallon buckets. They strain to hoist them onto their heads when they are full, and some of the water sloshes over their thin shoulders as they walk away.

Men move past pushing wheelbarrows or carts, while others watch from the shadows of one-story stucco buildings.

It is gratifying that so many of the children now know me there. They come running, one or two of the boys sometimes naked and the little girls wearing dresses full of holes or held up by one torn strap. I kneel for a minute in the dirt and talk with them while they smile with tiny teeth and stroke my arms as though to remind themselves that white skin feels no different. Then several of them take my hands in their little fingers and lead me to the door of the hospice, either pretending that I need help or honestly forgetting that I know the way. If there aren't too many of them, I quickly slip each a piece of candy, then duck inside. A gunny sack of candy would not be enough to go around.

The main reason I'm here at Sans Fil again is that some new people staying at the boys' home needed help finding the way here. Now and then Michael asks me to bring new people along. The student who came with me on this trip also wanted to work here. It's a better place for her since it has women residents.

So it is a day for memories, going all the way back to the earliest time. Michael assigned Antoine and Maya, two of the older boys at the home, to guide me to Sans Fil. Even they seemed confused once or twice as we turned and returned through the streets, not always clearly marked, of Port-au-Prince. The last part of the route was through a marketplace where women sat beside colorful piles of fresh food, neatly stacked, or behind tables covered with toiletries, canned goods, and blackened fish.

First impressions are the best because the senses are more alive to new experiences. Some of the streets looked then like makeshift flea markets. The corner before the gates of Sans Fil was, and is, one of the more crowded and noisy. A car or truck trying to get through needs to honk and wait for women to free the road by pulling their baskets a few more inches back into the crowd behind them. Horns blare in varying pitches and people yell in frustration. Without enough care, fruit can be squished under tires. Anger flashes and just as quickly turns to laughter.

Following the boys that first day, I found it difficult to slide politely through the crowds while trying not to jostle women carrying their large loads. They are incredibly graceful in their cheap sandals and simple dresses, so much so that the outsider feels awkward in comparison. It is better with practice: a slow, learned dance.

Not far inside the gates of Sans Fil, a sister in the blue and white sari of the Missionaries of Charity came toward us. After everything, this is the right place! I gave Antoine and Maya some change and sent them home. The young nun was carrying a basin of soapy water under one arm, and her gentle brown features, fresh and pretty in the morning air, were obviously Indian.

"Good morning, sister. Do you speak English?"

"Yes," she answered mildly, "a leetle."

"I understand that people can work here."

"Oh yes, we have much wurk to do here. When do you want to begin?"

"Right now."

The eagerness must have amused her, because for the first time a slight smile crossed her serious young face.

"Come with me," she said.

Sister Maurice took me along an outside corridor, where men sat on wooden benches or in wheelchairs. A small room with neatly-arranged shelves holding bottles and boxes gave some relief from the sun of the yard. In the middle of the room was a table, nearly covered with medications and papers. She showed me where the lotion bottles and shaving things are kept, then handed me some latex gloves. Pointing to a basin and pitcher of water, she cautioned me to wash carefully when I finished for the day.

Then she led the way back along the corridor to the doorway of a room that was filled with men sitting or lying on simple cots. She motioned toward them.

"You wurk here," she said. "Give massage."

"Okay, sister. Uh, how should I, that is, how do --?"

"Yes, that is right. Give massage."

She smiled once more and when I turned to thank her she was gone, vanishing in the morning air like an undersized fakir in a sari, and I wondered then if her spirituality somehow allowed her to dematerialize at will. In any event the training session was clearly over. It was time for some wurk.

She appeared only seldom after that, as was the case with the other sisters as well. As far as I could tell, there were four or five of them altogether, a small staff for a busy operation. Sometimes they could be seen slipping into other rooms, or into the room where the supplies are kept. Often, during that first summer month, I worked by myself in this room for hours at a time.

The room is a large rectangle of concrete walls and a concrete floor, holding about twenty-five cots. A few naked bulbs hang from the high ceiling, but the power is at best intermittent in Port-au-Prince. The light we work by comes from slatted windows on two sides and from the open door.

Although most of the beds are occupied, the silence is noticed most, particularly as that silence contrasts with the noisy streets outside. It is the protective and private silence of the dying. At most, there are shuffling sounds as men move in their beds or make their way toward the bathroom in the back. Those who are ambulatory prefer to spend time in the outside corridor and the better air, which accounts for the empty beds. It is fair to assume that some of them are in pain, but their pain is generally borne in silence. "God speaks in the silence of the heart," Mother Teresa said, "and we listen."

My patient in bed number seven is feeling his chin, which I have just dried with the towel. Some inspection shows that a few whiskers on his upper lip remain. That is taken care of easily enough.

"*Preske fini*. Almost done." The use of both languages is for practice.

"*Dako*." Agreed. He nods and smiles happily.

Now comes the part they all like best. I take his right hand and pour a small puddle of after-shave in his palm. Immediately he slaps his palms together, sending errant drops onto his gown. Then he runs both hands over his face, his neck, even his close-cropped hair.

The after-shave was an inspiration, even if slow in coming. The men love it, the way one can learn to love a small thing that is normally unknown, and they call it "parfum." Visiting wives and mothers are eager to have their own palms filled, even if shy about asking. They slap it happily on their necks and under their arms.

One young patient from the room next door stole the bottle once, trying to hide it under his gown as he spun away in his wheelchair. Some of the men yelled "vole!" thief, and pointed righteously as I chased him down the corridor. He pulled it from beneath his leg and gave it back with a sullen look.

Over at the other hospice last week, an old man who maybe has never experienced after shave started to drink it. His cupped hand was almost to his mouth when someone called out a warning. I slapped his hand away in time, splashing the liquid down the front of his gown and avoiding what might otherwise have been history's first recorded instance of death by after-shave.

Now we are finished. It is a treat to talk to them when I can, though it is not certain that they understand.

"*L'ap boule*? Does it burn?"

"Oui." He laughs with a gurgling sound.

"But it feels good, huh? *Santi bon*?"

"*Oui, bon.* Is good."

"That's right, 'is good'. You speak English, don't you, you old rascal?"

"Yes, is gooouud." He says it with greater conviction, now that I have acknowledged his fluency.

His eyes stare at the wall behind us, caved-in sockets under thick white eyebrows. Then he sinks back onto his bed, left arm pressed at the wrist to his forehead in a familiar posture, as though he is trying to remember something.

"That's it, my friend. I mean, *fini, z'amni*."

"*Oui, fini. Merci, m'sieur*."

"*Ou merite sa*." You deserve it.

The bed beside his is empty, so I move around it to bed number nine. When I first started working here, that bed was covered by a thick wool blanket, a counter-intuitive sight for a room stifling in Haiti's summer heat.

Then I noticed that the thick blanket sometimes moved: someone was under it, setting a new world record for thinness. Later one of the nuns lifted a corner of the blanket and give him something, maybe a pill. A few days after that he was gone.

Now a different occupant of bed nine is also sitting up and waiting. A taller man, maybe a little younger, he is noticeable for a large bulge in his abdomen that would be of interest to an oncologist. He pats his forehead with the ends of two fingers.

"*Maltet, dokte. Ede'm souple*" He wants help for a headache.

"*M'regrete. Mwen pa dokte.*" Sorry, I'm not a doctor.

There is probably little that could be done for him even if I were a doctor. In any case, the sisters have already come through with the day's medications.

The first thing we need is to fix the top laces of his gown, which appear ready to strangle him. They are bunched together in several knots, which my hands, still slippery, cannot undo. To help, he reaches back with one hand so that our fingers become entangled as well.

Across the room, one of the men is struggling to get off his bed. He rolls onto his side and grasps the bedframe. Slowly, carefully, with the formulated moves of the elderly and infirm, he pulls himself into a sitting position. Then even more slowly he gets to his feet and takes about five tentative steps toward the door of the bathroom. The sound of urine splashing on the cement floor under him follows, missing even the bathroom door by about eight yards. He backs up the same five steps and sits down contentedly on his bed.

Death comes most commonly in the night. In the morning, a van may pull into the courtyard. The driver and his helper go behind a low wall and pick up the canvas-and-pole stretchers. The skinny arms of the corpses dangle nearly to the ground and sometimes swing as the bodies are placed into the van. They are taken to the common grave outside of the city. Then a phone call to the city hospital: we have space available.

While the MC sisters are providing a place in which to die with a measure of comfort and dignity, other people and other organizations are providing help to Haiti in the form of orphanages, schools, clinics, hospitals, feeding programs, cooperatives, agricultural projects, environmental initiatives, or help with small businesses. This is a large and amorphous assemblage, getting larger.

In the developing language of humanitarianism, the phrase "non-governmental organization" has emerged to distinguish these efforts from those of actual governments in poor countries, which often have no programs of any value for the marginalized. NGO's can be secular or religious, they may be of long standing and large, or newborn and tiny. They grow like sugar cane in Haiti for at least three reasons. The most obvious is the history of traditionally inept, corrupt, and uncaring governments. The country's well known poverty is the next. We joke that the country that used to be named The Republic of Haiti is, thanks to endless repetition by the media and fund-raising NGO's, now officially known as Haiti the Poorest Country in the Western Hemisphere. A third reason is that Port-au-Prince is little more than an hour's flight time from Miami; one can confront extreme poverty without flying all the way to, say, Africa.

As the worldwide gap between rich and poor has become larger, humanitarianism has become big business. The larger NGO's have impressive budgets and they employ large numbers of people. Some of those people are on the ground, working on behalf of desperate Haitians. Others are noted for driving around the city in large white SUV's, with windows rolled up to preserve the air conditioning, or for sitting by the day in the city's best hotels and drinking rum punches.

It is hard to know which NGO's are making effective changes in the country and which are not. Given their numbers and growing influence -- an influence that is greater in many areas than that of the government --there is reason to wonder if too much of their work may be gradually robbing Haitians of both self-respect and the motivation to improve their conditions by their own efforts. This is not a simple question, and it is not helped by generalizations. Many Haitians would be happy to live in a situation in which they can expend their own talents and energies to make life better; others are equally happy to let outsiders do the work.

Another memory: working occasionally that first year in one of the very smallest and least heralded of all NGO's, before that acronym had even come into common usage. It involved helping a young American nurse in Cite Soleil. No account of time spent in Haiti is complete without mention of this part of the city, two square miles of flat waterfront that is home to an estimated 200,000 people living for the most part without running water, electricity, or toilets.

Narrow alleys lead off the main streets into a maze of shacks made of corrugated tin or cardboard or concrete-block where women squat to wash clothes in large plastic pans and children play in the mud and the rubble.

The route to the clinic passed along another canal, one of the many that carry rain and much more off the hills that rise steadily from the bay and make up the city of Port-au-Prince. The canal was also clogged with garbage of every possible sort, half sunk or floating in dark liquid that was more sludge than water. During the rainy season the canal would overflow, diverting the canal and its contents into the shanties that sit barely above it. Some of the houses showed dark water stains a foot or more up their sides. People would have to sleep standing up until the water went down.

Eventually an organization built low cement walls atop the dirt banks, and the water is now contained in the canal. That was a welcome improvement, but there has been no change in the canal's contents. Uncollected garbage is one of the first impressions one takes of Haiti, and one of the last.

While I sorted medications for diarrhea or infections or pain, the nurse looked down throats and treated wounds and spoke softly in Creole to the women who would came, one behind another, with their sick or broken children. Two Haitian men assisted her in keeping some order, mostly by blocking the door to the examination room until it was free, at which point they would shout "yon lot moun," another person, in case no one within a hundred yards was aware of that development. Eventually even this simple system would break down, and the room would fill to overflowing. Then the temperature would rise even more in the airless space and the sweat would roll down our faces and drop off our chins onto the table. Finally someone would plug an old fan into a socket whose wires ran right out the room's only window. The electricity was being pirated, the nurse explained to me.

Port au Prince is a city of extremes. A person, if so inclined, can serve food to hungry people in the afternoon and later enjoy their own dinner at some place like the Oloffson Hotel in the evening.

The most famous watering hole in Haiti, the Oloffson is a remnant of Haiti's better days, when it served as a residence for luminaries such as Humphrey Bogart, Lillian Hellman and Graham Greene. Or a person can drive up into the mountains to admire the pink and white homes looking down on the city like forts, with their high walls topped by shards of broken glass and their wrought-iron gates. Directly below them, and sometimes up against them, the shanties of the poor cling to the sides of gullies.

Or the morning can be spent at some place like Sans Fil and the evening out on the town, like last year when I took some new arrivals to one of the casinos above the city. We enjoyed watching a paunchy mulatto scatter $100 bills on the blackjack table, naturally hoping that he would lose. That morning we had done some physical therapy on a child who was entirely paralyzed, presumably from end-stage MS. His little face was fixed in a permanent grimace, lips pulled back over the teeth. Flies crawled freely over his teeth and gums.

It seemed then that no scene could be more appalling, but something else always comes along. Like the dying baby over at the brothers' clinic in Pele. He was not quite a baby, more likely a very young child whose last struggles for life had warped his face into the hollow cheeks and taut canvas-skin of an old man. He was lying on the bed making what sounded like faint hiccups in his last few attempts to draw breath. What was left of his flesh was drawn so tightly over his skeleton that he seemed, as we watched, to be shriveling into himself, like a drop of water, in slow motion, on a griddle.

A young blonde woman from Holland sat beside him, her left hand lying gently on the tiny body. She looked up and shook her head once, almost imperceptibly. Her look said: AIDS baby.

"Where did he come from?"

"A woman came to the gate an hour ago and handed him to the guard. Then she walked away."

"Way too late."

She shook her head again. "I'll stay with him until he dies," she said. "He shouldn't have to die alone."

Oddly, the one scene that comes back most often is that of a little girl I saw in Pele. Maybe a four or five year old, she was sitting on the ground with her back to me, listlessly hitting a small jagged rock against the side of a house.

In comparison to disease and hunger and death, what could be so upsetting in that? It is just that a little child should have a toy, in her case a doll. It is a fundamental rule of the universe: every little girl should have a doll. For that matter, so should every little boy. I thought of the dozens, hundreds, thousands of dolls lying unused in children's bedrooms back home. Most kids, my own young granddaughters included, would be willing to share one of them if they were told the reason. Or I could bring her one myself, except that an older child would take it away. Then she would have a broken heart to go along with that rock in her hand.

So I just kept walking, that day. But the image did not go away. Now, against my own expectations, I include dolls in the duffle bags of clothes and medications that we bring with us on these trips.

Whoa, hold everything. It is way too easy -- an unhealthy habit all too common in small minds -- to focus on negative memories. Wallowing in the misfortunes of others is not the reason why most people come to Haiti. Or if it initially was, there is a turnaround. The attraction soon becomes the spirit of the Haitians.

We love to look at the Haitians in their clothes that are used but often still bright in their sun-soaked colors, and we are amazed at how they keep clean in spite of the dirt around them. On Sundays they put on the best of those clothes for church, the women flowing in flowered dresses and the men straight-backed and dignified in dark suits. Even the little girls look serious in their lacy white dresses and pigtails tied in white ribbons. The families are in church for hours, singing with their heads thrown back and swaying with their arms in the air.

Spirit is not reserved for Sundays. It is everywhere in the streets. It is a constant joy to walk down the long hill in the morning, saying hello to anyone who looks and to some who do not, and then getting their surprised, happy smiles in return. A *bon jour* merits a *salu*, with the "yew" sound drawn out through pursed lips to stress the pleasure of connection: *saluuuuu*.

The tap-taps are crowded, and we squeeze even more people in as we make our way downtown. People sit on each other. They hang on, sometimes half in and half out, with tenuous holds on to whatever is at hand. Someone will have a live chicken under one of the benches, or cardboard boxes on the roof. One time it was a small refrigerator strapped on top, and its weight began to collapse the thin aluminum roof struts until, alarmed that we would be squished, some of the men in the cab got out and somehow re-positioned it.

My first impression when I began to ride the tap-taps was that everyone must know everyone else in this city of several million, because people actually talk to each other in the tap-taps. The topics are the universal ones: politics and the weather. In this country there is rarely any change to be discussed on either topic. No, I found, they do not know each other. They have discovered that conversation is a way to make life more endurable as they bump and lurch through the streets.

A shadow is blocking part of the light from the single doorway to this room; Jenny is standing in its frame. She hesitates.

"You can come in."

She comes over to the bed. "I just wanted to see what you're doing."

Jenny is one of those lovable extroverts, the lovable part being a condition that is not always the case with extroverts. She has the natural confidence and compelling presence that seem made for the stage. She also has the beauty for it, with wide-set dark eyes and a trace of dimples to complement the allure of those Mediterranean features that show themselves to best advantage in a woman's twenties. She is 21.

"About the same as always. How are things upstairs?"

"It's great!" The youthful enthusiasm that carries Jenny through the day has been ratcheted up several notches by the spirit of Haiti.

"There's a couple of girls up there with me, from Iowa. They're showing me everything."

"What have you been doing?"

"Lots of things. Helping the women wash their hair, and then we fix it. We were just doing this woman's nails, because one of the girls has some nail polish. She's really, really sick, but she's sooo sweet! It's just that we can't talk to them very much. Tell me again how to ask someone's name."

"You can say '*kijan ou rele'*. And then say 'mwen rele Jenny'. Or just point to yourself.

She repeats that a few times. "How about 'do you have kids'?"

"*Ou genyen pitit*?"

"Okay, then we can use our fingers." She waves hers and smiles with perfect teeth.

"Right, there's lots of ways."

"You know, it's not so bad here."

"Maybe I made it sound worse at home. What did you think?"

"I don't know anymore. But it's just... hard to explain. It's like it changes things."

"It does. You'll have lots of stories to tell at home."

"Really." She points to the man lying on the cot across from us. "What's wrong with his leg?" His left calf is wrapped in a fresh bandage.

"His leg is ulcerated. It can happen when a deep cut gets infected and the immune system isn't working too well. It should be cleaned and wrapped every day. One time when I did that I could see that the ulcer went all the way to the bone. It looked like a red crater with a very white spot at the bottom."

"Will it heal?"

"Eventually it should, with the right care."

She turns to leave. "Remember," I tell her, "to meet me down here a little before noon, so we can wash up. We can stop for some lunch on the way back if you want."

"I'm not very hungry."

"Maybe it's the heat. You feel okay?"

"I feel great!"

"We can just get a coke or a beer."

"That sounds perfect. Now I need to get back upstairs."

As she leaves the silence descends as an unwelcome contrast after Jenny's *elan*, and with it comes a touch of loneliness. I will pass the time by thinking of all the good things I have seen in the streets over the past couple of days.

An open manhole with a rusty six-cylinder engine block placed across it, so no one will fall in. A boy using a stick to roll a bicycle rim along beside him as he sings to himself. A woman of grace carrying over a hundred eggs layered in cardboard squares on her head, her shoulders and spine more erect than those of a ballet dancer, and people careful to step out of her way.

Four men helping a tap-tap driver push his broken vehicle to the side of the road. A group of men playing dominoes at a folding table on the sidewalk, smacking the tiles down hard. A man stepping off the curb to help a woman take an enormous load of plastic tableware off her head.

A goat nibbling contentedly on a pile of garbage. Shirts and pants hanging for sale on a concrete-block wall, warming in the morning sun. Women sitting and talking in front of some baskets of tomatoes and chadeks. A black cooking pot with dough bubbling in oil. Two telephone wires dangling from a pole over the sidewalk, pushed high to be out of reach and danger. Dozens of children with their little book bags and checkered school uniforms jostling each other as they compress themselves into a small bus.

A woman leading a loaded burro, her sandals slapping on the pavement. A man cutting another man's hair, both of them sitting on a broken slab of concrete. On top of a high bank, some boys amusing themselves by throwing clods of dirt down onto the sidewalk. A thin man pushing a wobbly wheelbarrow full of red stalks of sugar cane and a machete to strip them.

People carrying, on their heads: a new queen size mattress, a bound-up bunch of straw brooms, a towering pile of wicker baskets, a chicken-wire box, six chairs laced together to create a perfectly balanced work of art.

Another man assisting an old woman out of a tap-tap, her cloth bag in one of his hands and her elbow supported elegantly by the other. Two men shaking hands and then holding each other's hand loosely as they talk, as though unwilling to lose their connection.

Spirit has everything to do with simple human contact, in the eternal paradox through which spirituality creates and then re-creates itself from the material world.

"We need to create time to be with one another."

That is one part of Michael's philosophy, and it would be no great surprise or disappointment for him to learn that it has been said before. I asked him once what he would do to change the world. When he finished his magnetic, high-pitched laugh, he said he would not do more than he is doing now, but he hoped that other people might do more of it too.

"We're too caught up in speed. We tend to value people for what they do rather than just because they are. Simply to be is to proclaim God's greatness."

It is impossible to talk like that and be pessimistic about the world at the same time. His optimism is the result of its steady development within a religious context. As a student in Catholic schools, he tells me, he studied the lives of the saints. Because he aspired to be a veterinarian, Saint Francis was a favorite.

"I felt a stirring to be of service, so I joined the Franciscans. But I was young and idealistic, so I found them to be watered down. I left, searching. For a while I worked by myself on skid row in San Francisco.

The name, given his choice of a city, must have been following him. In his early 20s he went to Assisi, made famous by Saint Francis. He talked his way into some connections, worked in a guest house, and lived in the spirit of his favorite saint.

"A guest told me about Mother Teresa, who seemed to embody what I was looking for. I found her in Rome, but at that time she wasn't taking Americans as brothers. She sent me to a Trappist monastery in Utah. Eventually I was allowed into the MC order and found what I wanted."

In fact, he was the first American male to be allowed to join. His early assignments as a Missionary of Charity took him to Viet Nam and Cambodia. Later he would work in Los Angeles; eventually he was assigned to Haiti. Over time he would leave the order to begin his work with children from the streets of Port-au-Prince.

He is organizer, an inspiration, a builder. The boys' home has grown from one house to a second, for handicapped children, and to another in a smaller town. He has had disappointments over the years, but they are small in proportion to the successes. When I asked him about the best of those, his answer was more spiritual than specific.

"I'm just thrilled by the work we do here. I try to live in the present moment, to discern what God is saying through what is happening. Some of the boys are really becoming leaders, but that wasn't part of my plan. I didn't have a plan. I like it now that the children are getting involved with the community. They're learning that they need to be of service. They're being transformed by God, and there is so much to celebrate. That's why we're so vibrant here."

The idea of vibrancy caused me to ask him what he thought were the most important words in the language. That slowed him down for a moment, as though he has never taken time to think about important words.

"Acceptance. Service. Simplicity. Mercy. Joy."

By now the neighbors have become accustomed to the acoustical outcomes of a philosophy based on words like vibrant, celebration, and joy. Birthday parties, religious festivals, dart games and the like are nothing if not loud, the voices of children and teenagers and guests nearly overpowering Michael's laughter. The dance shows are even louder and by now have become famous. Most of the boys participate in one way or another, but the most talented of them receive professional training and have performed often in the states. The shows are part of the guest house experience for the many church groups that stay there. Everyone joins in the dance and song at the end of a performance, with Michael's voice almost as loud as the drums. It would not be a welcome experience for persons who are prone to headaches or tend toward melancholy.

Art, and not only that of dance, has become central. In that way Michael has come fully under the influence of Haiti. Art is important here not because the country is lacking in other kinds of achievement but because its people know, with a knowledge born more of pride and passion than of ambition, that creativity is a measure of spiritual progress and that artistic accomplishment is a token of the fullness of life. Even in a country that is thought by its many pessimists to be doomed, it is not possible to doom the impulse of art.

"Earlier I was very austere, but now I am more into beauty, finding God in the arts. We still stress simplicity, and there is no change in the faith or the power of transformation. The only difference is the austerity." He means that they live somewhat better now in terms of food and accommodations, but the point sounds odd coming from a man who owns almost nothing and who often sleeps in a recliner chair.

The emphasis on art over austerity does not diminish the centrality of the spiritual, which can have even its comic side. We found that in a recent visitor. A well-off Haitian, now living in Miami as part of the Haitian diaspora, he was as arrogant as was to be expected from his class. He had most of the answers to the problems of Haiti, none of which seemed to include the idea that the country's government might actually help its people instead of dutifully carrying out the demands of the wealthy.

Michael and I sat with him one evening on the roof terrace of the boys' home, drinking cokes and listening to what was essentially a monologue. I could see that Michael, who rises each day at 5:00 am, was dozing off in the half-light, and I was gradually wandering off myself, as anyone would do while listening to a fool. Then suddenly he won back our attention.

"I have one wish in life," he said in a low whisper that must have been meant as a dramatic counterpart of the darkness around us. "More than anything else, I want someday to take my wife's hand and my hand and touch the hand of Mother Teresa!"

"Then you might be interested in what some people do here in Haiti," Michael said drily. "They work with the dying at her place, Sans Fil."

"Oh?" he said. "I don't know where that is."

The next morning we were being something less than charitable about the waste of a good evening.

"That guy spoke really good English," I said, "except that he apparently never learned our pronouns. The only one he seemed to know was 'I'. He's ever heard of 'you' or 'they' or any of the others."

"You must have enjoyed his big wish about Mother," Michael laughed. Except he doesn't know where Sans Fil is."

"Somehow I wasn't surprised at that."

"Before he gets excited about touching Mother Teresa's hand," Michael said in the way he has of combining the best of religion and poetry, "he ought to go down to Sans Fil and meet Christ on a bed."

Michael is the only person I know who would say something like that.

"Most of the time people don't even know the poor exist," Mother Teresa said. "We look but we don't see."

We should all be so diplomatic.

One of Haiti's great charms is that it offers an endless supply of both the best and the worst of our species. The humanitarians like Michael have come to do something of value; others are in Haiti to enjoy the uniqueness of the culture or sometimes for reasons that are less laudable. The result is an amalgam of idealists, realists, crackpots, religious zealots, drug dealers, sex addicts, people on the run from problems elsewhere, the naive, the lost, the found, some outright scoundrels, some hard-hearted, some soft-hearted, some hard-working, and some just hanging around. Bars and guest houses are the best places to observe them in all their variety.

Lunch at Sans Fil will be served roughly at noon, when a young Haitian orderly appears with a cart carrying red plastic bowls of rice and beans. Then any interest in shaves and massages evaporates. It is time to move on. Together we re-arrange number nine's gown one more time, and he pulls it down over his legs.

"*Na we pita.*" We will see each other later.

"*Na we, m'sieur. Merci.*"

A few minutes ago the metal door swung shut in a draft, causing the air in the room to become as lifeless as some of the men on the cots. A little breeze through the room is welcome, for the cooling effect as well as -- we like to tell ourselves -- a way to blow unwelcome particles away. Anyone who has spent any time in Haiti has been warned about scabies, malaria, hepatitis, typhoid, dengue fever, tuberculosis, and some diseases most people have never heard of. Gowns and masks are available, but most of us go without, since they separate rather than bring people together.

Before coming to Haiti the first time, I asked Michael over the phone if he took pills to prevent malaria. He said no. After I arrived, he informed me that he has had malaria twice.

"But you told me not to bother with malaria pills," I protested.

He laughed the high-pitched laugh. "No, I just told you that I didn't take them. That's all you asked."

"You've got a great sense of humor. Anyway, what was malaria like?"

Michael shrugged. "I had a fever for a few days. You get over it."

Just letting go is a big part of the secret. It is remarkable what you can let go of after spending time in a place like this. By degrees, things that are undreamed of at home become the norm, challenges and discomforts become routine.

What a difference now from my first time in Haiti. It is a difference made more evident by the comfort of so much that is now familiar. It was dark that first time when we landed, because darkness comes early and fast nearer to the equator. I stepped out of the airport into a humid evening and a milling, weaving crowd that pushed up against new arrivals, wanting to carry bags, take people somewhere, or sell something. It was one of those times when patience is just a step away from panic.

"We'll pick you up at the airport," Michael had said over the phone. Uh huh. Just how is that supposed to happen in this chaos? I stood guard over my luggage and kept saying no. I realized that I had no address to give to a driver, and no likelihood of finding a phone. Time slowed, and then it seemed likely that I was doomed to stand forever, tied to my bags and prodded by an urgency not of my making, in that pulsing chaos.

No, I was not doomed to stand there forever. Suddenly three of Michael's smaller boys appeared below my line of vision, which had naturally been directed toward larger adult shapes in the crowd. No wonder I had not seen them. They were popping up and down as though on little springs so that I would eventually notice a small cardboard sign with my name on it. How they knew to recognize me will remain unknown. No matter. They pulled me and my bags to a waiting pickup truck.

The driver of the truck swung us back and forth as he dodged the potholes and the people who crossed casually in front of us, caught in the headlights like silhouettes on a tent. Along what appeared to be a main artery going steadily uphill, people stood in small groups around charcoal firepots. A weak, flickering light from the coals illuminated strange, dark faces that were only feet away from the open window when we slowed or stopped for traffic. Spooky.

Then reality hit in that way it can only when you have become too comfortable with the normal. An hour and a half ago I was in Miami. Now I am in Haiti! Haiti! This is the land of two generations of Duvalier tyranny and its murderous henchmen, the Tonton Macoutes. It is a country of intractable poverty and exotic diseases and recurrent political violence, the land of zombies and the misunderstood rites of voodoo. Thus it is that the imagination can mix legends and stereotypes, myth and misinformation, to give romance that aura -- dreaded and desired at the same time -- of danger.

That whole first week, I left the boys' home only with a companion. Finally, trying to summon the nerve to explore by myself, I confessed my anxieties to Michael.

"They look at me like they're angry. I don't know if I should be in the streets alone."

"They're just curious, that's all," he said. "They don't see a lot of white people in the streets, just in cars. Smile at them and say '*Bon jour*. '"

So I went out alone, all the next day, through the crushing markets and the sweating streets, up into the hills above the city where the air was clearer and the wind became a refreshment. I smiled and said "*Bon jour*." And they smiled back and said the same to me. I was finally in the scene, a lone white among blacks, seeing but largely unseen and certainly not bothered.

Someone opens the door now, bringing new light and a breeze that instantly cools the room by several degrees. A group of four people has come into the room. They survey the men on the beds and then cross the room to our corner. There is a slight southern accent in their voices as we greet each other.

"Is it okay for us to be in here?" He-year.

"Sure. The door blew shut, that's all."

"Are you a doctor on the staff?"

"There aren't normally any doctors here. The sisters are the staff. Some of us are just helping out."

"Where are you from?"

"Western New York. How about you?"

"We're from Tinnissee. How long are you he-year for?"

"A few weeks. We come down during the break between semesters."

"Is this place only for men?" one of the women asks.

Me-yen. We are graced with two-syllables for the effort of one, as though in the belief that a word that had doubled its sound has also enlarged its meaning. In this setting the practice constitutes a small treat, a slow-paced relief from the contractions and elisions of rapid-fire Creole.

"This room is. The women are upstairs. You can go up there if you want to. Go back the way you came in and you'll see some stairs."

"Are all these me-yen dying?"

"Some of them are. Others are just here for a while."

"Do they hey-ev A-yids?"

"We don't always know what they have. There really isn't much diagnostic equipment around here. It's more of a hospice. But no, there isn't that much AIDS here, in spite of what you may have heard. Some have HIV, but they've also got cancers and heart conditions and other problems. Plus a lot of TB. For that matter, this man right here has TB."

"How dew you know?"

"You start to recognize the sound of the cough. It's way down in the chest, and when it starts it's hard for them to control. Besides that, he's been spitting blood."

To their credit, no one of them takes those involuntary two steps backward when I say that.

"Aren't you afree-id of getting TB yourself?" the woman asks.

"Before maybe, but not anymore. The men are usually pretty good about turning away if they start coughing. And I always get a skin test when I get home. So far, so good."

"This is one of Mother Teresa's places, isn't it?"

"Uh huh." I direct their gaze to her picture on the wall at the end of the room. "She's also got another place like this one across town, and a clinic, and a hospital for children."

"Do yew work they-air too?"

"I have, but I like it better here. And there's usually more help over there. You know, everybody likes babies."

"What do you do mostly?" the other woman asks.

"We do pretty basic stuff -- give them shaves, massages, baths. Sometimes we change a dressing or maybe do some simple physical therapy when they're up to it. Their limbs are stiff and they can use some flexing. We help some of them get outside for some fresh air, or to the bathroom. Some of them like to have their heads shaved. Maybe that's cooler for them, and cleaner. And sometimes the sisters have some special projects. But mostly it's basic comfort care and attention."

"You're saying 'we' but it looks like you're alone. Are others working he-year?"

"Not at the moment. Some men from a church left a while ago. A student of mine is working upstairs, with the women. There's lots of people helping out around here. Last year my daughter was here with me."

The undertone in her questions and the glances she exchanges with her husband suggest they might like to do some of this themselves. They come back sometimes, once they have seen.

"How did yew find out about this place?"

"That would be a long story, not really worth telling. It's just a matter of making connections, the way you are doing right now."

"You're doing some good work."

"Well, mostly it's little things. But thanks for saying so."

It is good to have visitors. The men around us seemed to feel a connection even if they could not follow the conversation, and the room deflated almost physically when the visitors left. But not in another sense, because they left something behind. They were on the edge.

No, not an edge. Maybe more like a corner. The idea of turning comes to mind. It is a time-honored theme in literature, philosophy, and religion. Usually it is related thematically to a search. Whether that search is for wisdom, enlightenment, self-knowledge, happiness, peace, new beginnings -- any or all of these under whatever names -- the search has to begin with a turning away from the demands and the distractions, the lures and follies of the immediate material world. Turning away is the first movement of turning toward.

The metaphor of turning, and the stories that develop it, revolves partly around questions of extent: a life can turn a few degrees, or many. A life can also turn only at times, or turn in slow, uncertain steps. Or even turn back. Or it can turn against or around, or turn into something else. If life's path were nothing more than a straight line, we would die of boredom after a hundred steps.

Some people turn very little. There is sufficient reason for that, because life is demanding. If we all went to the woods and lived simply, as bachelor Thoreau famously advised, the human race would be finished in one generation. Or to make the same point less dramatically: the desire for a family and a career, the need for some measure of security, the natural appetite for some of life's pleasures -- all these are reasons that the world is too much with us, as Wordsworth said. But the world cannot be entirely ignored either.

Turning is a highly individual thing, and no one should have to feel bad about never having turned very much. Still, it must be the case that everyone, at some transient time, senses that there is something different, and better. It is a consciousness that comes like a faint scent on the wind or a delicate motion caught in the corner of the eye.

We are reminded daily that we are live in difficult times, with worse perhaps to come. One way to deal with personal angst, anger, frustration or helplessness in difficult times is to turn those feelings into thoughts and then into actions that have positive effects. That is not a complicated idea. It does seem to need more reflection and endless repetition.

Those visitors thought we were doing good things here. That is nice to hear, even if it is not good for the ego. What they don't know is that it's pretty easy to get annoyed with these men. Attention and care can be taken for granted and that can lead to making demands.

"Over here, *blan*," one will call from across the room, wanting my attention next without being very gracious about it.

"You can wait," I'll say with a little edge in my voice. "I'll get to you."

"Give me your watch," another will say. No "please" even.

"No."

"Give me your hat."

"I need it myself."

So there is a need to focus on something else Mother Teresa said. "It's not how much we give, but how much love we put into the giving."

That is all very well. Everyone loves love and loves to talk about love. Haiti's needs are more practical. For example, love could take the form of a solar oven, which is itself a little thing. Sometimes we go up into the mountains for a day trip, maybe to visit an orphanage. The change from the heat and the urban sink of Port-au-Prince is immediate, and we cannot get enough of the cool, clear air and the quiet. Soon the hillsides catch our attention. Some of them show impressive work with terrace-style farming, but others are bare. Not bare earth, but bare rock. It is a first-hand look at one of Haiti's most serious long-term problems, erosion. Erosion is a problem in many parts of the world, but except for environmentalists and geographers not one that is exciting enough to get much attention.

Centuries of Haitians foraging for firewood to turn into charcoal have resulted in Haiti's once-lush mountains and hills being stripped of a major part of its vegetation. When the vegetation is gone, the top soil soon follows. It runs down the gullies during the rainy season, washes into the Caribbean, sinks to the bottom and is lost forever. And when the topsoil is gone, everything is gone. Their source of food and of important export products is under that blue-green water, a lost treasure more valuable than those legendary treasures from sunken ships.

It is at the point now where much of the charcoal used for cooking is imported, costing scarce money and fouling the air when it is burned. All this is happening in a country where the sun beats down on the earth every day.

A simple solar oven can be made from a piece of glass and metal as common as tinfoil. Free cooking, no air pollution, no dependency on anything except that bright, consistent sun.

A solar engineer would point out that a better oven than one made of tinfoil could be designed and manufactured for a few dollars apiece. That would take some organization, which seems in short supply around here. It would also take quite a lot of consciousness-changing to convince the average Haitian to make the switch. It would take another kind of turning.

All that would be easy compared to what it would take to remediate the problems of Haiti. Michael asked me recently to talk to one of the church groups at the guest house. It was a lively crowd of college students led by their minister, doing some project or another outside of town. Sitting among the potted plants on the terrace that evening, they were an attentive audience. What they said, and what I said, was probably not as coherent or well-put as it appears here, but I am remembering what I can of it.

Haiti is like most third world countries, I told them, with a long, sad history of greed and exploitation. That history is so long that it goes all the way back to Columbus, who landed on the island looking for gold. The eventual result was the genocide of the aboriginal Arawak Indians, followed by various wars.

"Haiti ended up as a French colony. That's why you see so much French influence in the architecture and art. For a time it was the richest colony in the Caribbean. Then came a slave rebellion against the French with brutality on both sides that even Hollywood would have trouble imitating."

"And the slaves won, but it took a while, right?" somebody asked.

"Right. It was just a few years after our own war for independence from England. Haiti has the distinction of being the first black republic in the world. Since our own country still had slavery and didn't want to encourage any slave rebellions of our own, we refused to recognize Haiti for 60 years. That is just one example of our misuse of this country, but some other time for that."

"Unfortunately Haiti's early leaders began a pattern of violence and political instability that has never really stopped. Of 50 heads of state in nearly 200 years, 27 have been overthrown by one means or another, five were killed, and one committed suicide. The reason I have those statistics so clear in my head is that I just read them."

"The people seem to be making it, somehow. And they're so... like, kind."

"They are, and you're right to wonder. In a culture of exploitation, the victims of oppression often turn on each other. Some of that goes on here, of course. It's surprising that you don't see more of it."

I stopped to let them think about that.

"Isn't Haiti a democracy?"

"It is, but a fragile one. Even a strong democracy can't always spread the wealth as much as we would like. Here the wealth stays in the fewest hands possible, that is, in the hands of a few rich families. Those who have it here have used the government, the army, the police, private paramilitary groups -- just whatever means are necessary to hang on to their wealth and privilege. The lengths they go to keep things from changing can be pretty imaginative and sometimes even laughable. Except when you see the damage it does, as you have been seeing. Then it's not funny."

A young woman, sitting cross-legged in the front, looked up. "Doesn't the government do anything for the poor in this country?"

"Not if it can help it. The Haitian government gets ranked as one of the most corrupt in the world. Remember, the government is controlled by the rich. They're totally indifferent to anyone outside their own little groups, and most of the time even the poor somehow accept that. Not always though. That's why the country has such a reputation for violence."

"I don't feel afraid."

"Good, and you shouldn't. There's probably more to be afraid of at home. The Haitians taken together are gentle, friendly people -- except when there seems to be some new chance to do something about the economic inequality. Then things can heat up around here. Poverty breeds violence, no question, and it doesn't matter what country you're talking about. First world, third world, any world. Mother Teresa once said that God doesn't create poverty. We do, she said, because we don't share."

"The Bible says that we'll always have the poor with us."

"I know the quote, and I think Christ got it wrong. He should have said that we'd always have the rich with us."

A few of them laughed, and a few others looked like that was playing a little loose with their scripture.

Another warmed to the topic with ideas that he probably got from his minister. "There's different ways to be rich and poor. We see a lot of material poverty in Haiti, but you can find an equal amount of spiritual poverty in affluent countries. Maybe it's true that the more you have of the one, the less you have of the other. We need to find the right balance."

It could be that young people like these will save us all in the end. We old ones have tried everything else. We have tried the huge programs of social and political change, we have tried education and religious movements, and we have seen revolutions whose promises are perverted sooner or later into more of the same, or worse. Here, we are all the way down to shaving dying men and thinking about solar ovens.

There is something seductive about this situation, these efforts to do some little thing. At first it seems impossible -- hot, dirty, depressing, possibly infectious. Once underway it does not seem so at all. In a documentary I sometimes use in class, Mother Teresa speaks about picking up that first dirty and dying beggar from the streets. After you have done that first one, she said, you are able to go on doing it. It begins to grow on the person.

That is a lovely oversimplification. The world is more than the connection between the giver and the receiver. Aside from that, it has to be asked who is helping whom? Brother Andrew, who was for a time in charge of the MC Brothers, had a different take on the whole matter of charity. It is the poor who make us rich, he wrote. The needy raise the whole question of what life is all about. Maybe, he said, we need them more than they need us. The sisters must have talked to him, and that is why we hear them laughing, and sometimes singing, as they go about their work.

"Is that the meaning of life?" a philosopher once teased me, "shaving a dying man?" "Could be," I said. That made me wonder how much time active humanitarians spend thinking about the meaning of life. My guess is that it is very little.

Part of the meaning of life is blind chance: good luck or bad luck. Some of us get lucky with the life we are born into and then live, some of us do not. It is frightening to consider the kind of life you might have had except for good luck. You could have been born in one of the *bidonvilles* -- I do not like the word "slum" -- of Haiti, for example. Or maybe born far better off than that but disabled. Or gotten injured in some terrible accident at age three. Or become the victim of some wasting disease at age twenty. The possibilities are endless for the bad things that can happen through bad luck.

It is doubtful that the men in this room have thought much about luck. Are they even thinking about death? Is their silence a part of some understanding that brings peace just at that point when it no longer matters?

The faint sound of music is coming from somewhere, maybe a radio in the next room. With it comes another memory. That turning first year, I heard a guitar in the corridor. It was being played by a well-formed man with a full head of white hair and a square, white-bearded jaw. He wore a hospital gown, but he seemed anything but sick as he played. He was not a Haitian, judging from his features and skin tone. He talked and sang in Spanish, his ringing falsetto voice going "yi, yi, yi" between Mediterranean melodies and rhythms, with a strong upstroke on the major chords. Probably he was from the neighboring Dominican Republic, and I imagined how the songs he sang that afternoon had been sung in better times to a comely senorita who looked down, hazel-eyed, from a wrought-iron balcony.

With Pierre, a wheelchair-bound man who said he once lived in New York City, I sat outside one afternoon and listened to the old man play. Pierre noticed me watching the graceful movements of his fingers on the strings, thumb picking out the bass melody.

"Can you play it?" he wanted to know.

"A little bit"

Without asking, Pierre took the guitar and handed it to me. Instead of protesting, the old man smiled and nodded his encouragement. Maybe they were both tired of the Spanish music.

"Go ahead," Pierre said, "play something."

"I'm a little afraid to. This thing's not in very good shape."

In fact, it was hard to imagine a functioning guitar in any worse shape. The sound board was warped and cracked and the bridge was partly unglued. Two of the tuning pegs looked ready to pull away from the head.

I strummed and picked a few chords very gently, surprised to find that it was actually in good tune and somehow hung together. It was a perfect symbol of Haiti: on the verge of collapse but making music in spite of that. As I played a few standard folk tunes, Pierre and the old man clapped softly with the rhythm and smiled their enjoyment. I would have played more except for the thought of having to hand back a broken guitar with no hope of fixing it. So I gave it back while it was still intact, and the old man said "*gratias*" and clapped some more, not palm to palm but gently, forefingers to palm like an aristocrat at a symphony.

It was one of those times when jagged edges fit together. It was not a moment of profound revelation, moments of the kind that are reserved for the holy among us. Because of where we were, the moment did have something of that quality of going through life "with one eye fixed firmly on eternity," a remarkable line read somewhere. It said that life would be more harmonious if we did that more regularly, not waiting until the last days.

What comes from this experience is a sense not of life's meaning, but of life's paradoxes. Here there is a feeling of peace in a troubled land, a sense of joy in the midst of suffering, of spiritual wealth created from material poverty, of dignity or even something like divinity to be found in those most on the margins of life. It could be that there is a unique wisdom to be found in the connection of deep poverty and near death, even if both are things most people work hard to avoid.

And then the strongest paradox of all: with all the sickness and dying here, this is a healthy place. If anyone becomes depressed here, he or she is missing an important point.

If one goal of art is to present eternal truths through the human condition, this is the perfect workshop for the artist. We can find eternity in the present, it has been said, if we know how to look. And we can look more clearly when we are lulled into silence in a hushed place. Both life and death reveal themselves more fully to us without the interference of all the noises that we construct and then gradually grow to hate.

Any insights gained in a place for the dying are abetted by the slow and steady process of letting go. These men, in their nearly mute resignation, could be an example for the rest of us. Here, I find myself letting go of my recurring suspicions and doubts and negative judgments about actions on a grand scale. The things that once mattered do not matter as much anymore, as though I am suspended in a vacuum untroubled by values.

In a way, though, I still feel that I have been right all along, even if just saying the same things over and over in slightly different ways. Governments and activism and reform politics are right for some people to engage with, but not for others. They can bring about positive changes, even if those changes do not last long and have to be fought for all over again at another time. But they can never fully and finally end material suffering, and they are not likely to include spiritual growth in their agendas.

Still, that is no reason why people should not try to change the things they think they can change. There is that old idea that the world is perfect as it is, even if we cannot see that. No, the world is not perfect as it is, and those who want to be activists should go ahead and try to make it better. Orwell said that the political life offers no moral guidance. That may be true for some of us, but it is not true for everyone.

Yes, letting go means dropping the judgments. The simple truth is that people differ on what is good for them, and they differ on what happiness means. It is pointless and patronizing, sometimes even downright dangerous, to tell people what they should value and what they should not value.

On the other hand, people generally agree on what is bad -- like sickness, war, poverty, homelessness, lack of opportunity -- and they do what they can to avoid those things that concern themselves and those nearest to them. It would be much better if we could enlarge the circle of our concern.

It must be an advantage for these men, in their own letting go, that life has provided them so little that wants keeping. Until this point, life has at least been preferable to death, even if its pleasures have been few. But that is the problem with those who live their lives only for pleasure: they get the rhythm but they never really hear the music.

Now, with little left of comfort and nothing of hope, the men in this room can confront death with the equanimity of the purified.

"Can you hear that music?" I ask the man on the nearest bed.

He looks up and says something, so I am satisfied that he can.

"It sounds good, doesn't it?"

There is no response this time. A fly buzzed when I died, Emily Dickinson wrote. How could she have known about this place?

"Your food is coming soon," I say to him. "You'll like that, too."

He is looking up as though there is something interesting on the ceiling, something that is making him wonder if life is always preferable to death, or if there may be a kind of superiority in suffering, or whether abandonment is preferable, finally, to struggle. It is probably only out of politeness that he nods -- a slight and slow lowering of his head which I notice only because I am watching him so closely -- as though he has understood me. The movement confirms that some life remains, but there is a definite sense that his spirit, along with what his spirit truly understands, is already in another place.

Chapter Nine

Ken invited me to his sentencing, almost as though it was a graduation ceremony or the marking of some other major life transition. In a way, it was.

I did not attend. That was not because I was upset with him or unwilling to have a part in the final stage of his undoing. I had classes to teach that morning, and he assured me that other friends and supporters would be there.

We did manage one visit before he left. The jail looked familiar in its grey utility, even after a fairly long time away from it. Ken appeared to be reconciled to a long five years in prison, though he spoke hopefully about an appeal of his sentence. I could not help noticing how he talked and joked -- across the tables of the visiting room and in unabashed violation of the rules -- with other inmates. He would be the politician even there.

He wrote soon after arriving at the first of what would become several prisons.

"Well here I am again after nearly ten years of being a free man, now subjected to the life in this desolate, violent and untamed world known as prison. A place where love and compassion are concealed; a place where dreams die and visions become impaired. But then again, Uncle Derek, my dreams of helping youth were conceived here in a place like this. And if not for those past endeavors, I would not have had the great opportunity to have met you or some of my other closest friends and loved ones! Boy do I truly miss you! I love you Uncle Derek! Too bad it is often times that the ones we care for we hurt or disappoint by our foolish actions. But I always remember sitting in your kitchen that day and you conveying the message about your unconditional love and friendship to me. That is what helps me to keep going and has given me the courage to write you despite my behavior and lack of confidence in myself."

He wrote that he was getting support from many people. I wrote back that he deserved whatever support we could give him and more. Letting go is all very well, but it was clear that neither of us was willing to let go of the connection.

Of course he would have to carry activism right into the new environment. He knew his rights, and he had a quick eye and even quicker tongue for any misuse of prison authority. During the first several years, the authorities found it necessary to move him from prison to prison, to the extent that I lost track of the number and sometimes did not know even where he was. "You keep this up long enough," I told him at one point," and they'll run out of prisons to send you to. Then they'll have to let you out."

He wrote about a fist fight and how he disapproved of his own role in it. "I'm not here to prove I'm a bad ass, but here to make an effort to improve myself both at the levels of mental, emotional and spiritual disposition. These men don't understand that kind of philosophy and quite frankly I don't expect them to. The only thing most of them can acknowledge is violence, prescribed and instilled from childhood rearing. I was myself once like the lot, thrived on the act of inflamed impulse, but somehow with the grace of a higher power that mentality has begun to deteriorate."

By court order he was forced to relinquish legal custody of Alicia. His depression over that resulted in a month's stay in a mental health unit. After that, a new prison, another development, along with an odd sense of what constitutes good and bad news.

"Now for the bad news. I'm no longer in general population and I'm now in segregated isolation in protective custody after a near knife attack. I'm okay and the good thing about the whole episode is the fact that the Department of Corrections must now move me to another facility, hopefully nearer home."

"Well, here is some good news! I've been up here in isolation for weeks now and have accomplished many goals. I'm back writing fervently and have completed two chapters of my autobiography. I've been reading a lot and lots of prayer plus meditation. The stillness of solitude has its rewards."

Indeed: he had finally learned that lesson. Another letter, written in red ink, lurched between positives and negatives.

"Today, Uncle Derek, as I sit in this vast wilderness of brick, mortar and steel, I can see with discerning eyes the real hypocrisy of many things in our society. I am but a manifestation of both our ills and bliss, and what affects the rest of the world is also an effect on me directly or indirectly.

"We live in a time when our social ills have become a pendulum of severe mood swings, enormous and extreme. Filled with the quest of pleasure and instant gratification. Then we gravitate to an acerbic tone of discontent for our fellow mankind. And people say don't be concerned!

"My personal quest to make right the wrongs has elicited an endless search for this crazy utopia that I must now admit doesn't exist: a place of unconditional love, understanding, and free from bondage and racial exclusion. This is only a trumped-up illusion of my mind.

Yes, the writing continued to have something of the overblown about it, but that was a good sign to me: the passion and energy had survived it all.

"Even now as I sit idle in a world of chaos, a world of uncertainty, a world of non-existence, I still feel summoned to work for others. Yes, I often question my motives. Are they pure? Do I just want to *feel* needed -- don't we all in some way or another? Or is it a desire to be of service to my fellow man and woman?

"When I was out there in the "free world," some folks would assert that I was too willing to risk myself for another. I can remember jumping in front of this one teenager who was about to shoot another kid down the street from where I lived. As I now reflect how silly that was then, I still like to think that I saved a life that day. That sort of thing set the tone of saving the world, as if I were the last beacon of hope, the great emancipator, a knight fighting the status quo, attacking with iconoclastic views."

I loved that: finally some self-irony and a little humor. Progress.

He wasn't done: "Bold, daring, creative, innovative and steadfast. But I was unable to stand the test of time, and within that six year period I felt myself dwindling in values, in that moral fiber which is the pillar of principals, the chief pulse of character."

"I'm beginning to sound like some cheap poet, but still this is my state of mind, as real as it gets."

That and a lot more. It gave me the chance to be a mentor again. I wrote back that I wanted him to work even more on himself. I reminded him that there was plenty to do for people right around him. And of course I could not let pass the chance to respond to the remark about utopias.

"There is something in many of us that wants to think things *can* be better than they are, even when we know how unlikely that is. I take that as a positive sign about humanity, in spite of all the negative evidence of history and even daily life. *Can* idealist thinking really make any changes? I think so, even if the changes are small and temporary. And in the end, the change may be mostly in oneself, but what's wrong with that?"

Eventually we wrote fewer letters, which is just as well since the reader has probably had enough of this by now. We wrote less often because he was eventually moved to a prison only 45 minutes away, allowing for easier visits. I liked it that he was reading constantly, as well as writing not just more of the long-running autobiography but two other books. Over time he placed three pieces in our local paper's opinion page.

"My days are filled with reading and writing, meditation and prayer – a lot of the latter," he told me during one visit. "Now fighting for peace of mind, I find myself constantly re-evaluating self."

That wasn't just progress. It was the perfect chance.

"Have you ever heard of the oracle at Delphi?"

"I guess maybe."

"I'll spare you the full lecture. The point is that two of the most clear and profound statements in western philosophy were written centuries ago on the Greek temple at Delphi. One of them is the advice to know thyself. That seems simple enough, until you really try it. There's even the question of whether it's possible."

"I'm on it."

"Take your time. I'm twenty years ahead of you and still working on it myself."

After a while it seemed like justice for Afro-Americans would be the next target. During the visits, the conversation came back again and again to lectures on that topic. He would recite parts of the constitution to me, and he liked to develop analogies between slave life on southern plantations and the conditions of life in prison. My mind spun with the statistics he recited, one finger often in the air as though he was testifying before a congressional committee.

"At this rate," I said after another round of data, "we'll put *all* you black guys in prisons. Then we'll have you where we want you."

"Every prison I've been in, I keep meeting friends from the neighborhoods. That guy over there," -- he pointed to a man sitting with his wife and daughter -- "I've known him for years. He used to help me out."

Naturally a new organization was in the making, Judicial Watch. It would showcase how minorities are given unequal legal treatment and expose those who are doing it.

"I've written to a lot of people in the city already," he said. "Told them to be ready, because I'm coming. I'm gonna be an itch they can't scratch."

"One thing for sure. You absolutely can't do a thing that will give them a chance to put you back here, got it? I don't want to hear about you even spitting on the sidewalk."

"I've got better plans than that."

"Okay, do whatever you want as long as it's legal."

"It'll be legal, don't worry."

"But there's something else, and I don't just mean whatever new plan you're hatching. I don't want you getting a reputation as a screwball. People saying 'Oh, that's just that crazy guy who's always doing weird things. 'You do that and pretty soon nobody's listening. You're ignored, wasting your time."

He thought about that for at least two seconds. "Okay, that's a point. But I'll make them listen even if they kill me for it. Somebody's got to speak out. I don't mind being a non-conformist."

"I'm not talking about being a non-conformist, and you can speak out all you want. I just don't want to have to be behind you all the time, pulling you back like some mad dog on a leash."

"Come on. There's just way too much complacency and you know it. I won't be complacent again."

"Are you kidding me? You've never been complacent a day in your life. Actually, a little complacency might just be a good thing for you."

"Now you're the one that's kidding."

"Yeah, but I said that so I could get back to what I was saying about the Delphic oracle. Remember, I said there were two things written there."

"Okay, let's have it."

"It says 'nothing in excess'." In other words, do everything in moderation. You might want to give that a try sometime."

"That's hard for me."

"I know it is. In a way that's to your credit. It's been all or nothing for you, and that's what gave you the energy and drive -- and did I mention commitment? What made you so effective?"

"I can't hold back when I get on to something."

"And a lot of others can't step forward. Just remember that more is not always better."

"Besides, I wanted to make amends."

"I know that, but I wonder just how many amends you think you have to make. You did more on your own in a five-year period than a bunch of agencies and government programs could do in twice the time. That's because you knew to keep it personal. You flew, man, not under the radar but over it."

"And crashed."

"Yeah, flying *too* high and too fast. But I'm starting to think of that whole time as your version of a Buddhist mandala, you know, a beautiful intricate design of colored grains of sand, a zillion hours of devotion and work, and then they pour it into the river and it's gone."

"Because?"

"Because it's about the process, not the result, and because in life nothing lasts."

"Okay, but we're not talking about sand here."

"That's right, and that makes it even harder if you worry too much about where it all went. Hey, I've been teaching for a long time and I can't possibly know how much good effect I've had on how many students. But I *know* I affected some. You gave some of those kids some dignity and hope and maybe a sense of empowerment and someone who would listen to them. How can you know how much of that lasted and maybe even got passed on? So forget about amends. That's all in the past. It's your future I'm thinking about."

"Me too. I'm glad to be back."

"Do you know what brought you back?"

"What brought me back is basically that I never realized that I deserved a chance to live a life. I always felt sincerely that I was undeserving of any of the things that life had to offer. That's why I always felt close to the kids and I always gave them great accolades on their accomplishments even if they were minimal. It took a long time for me as an adult to understand that, sure, we have to go through the fire. Going through the fire purifies us and it helps us to really understand where we're at in life. If I lived in a world that was just purely bliss and I was always happy, I wouldn't know what it was like to suffer. But I do know because I've suffered all my life. Primarily the suffering was caused by me."

He paused. I knew that this was important in a way that only he, knowing at last the possibility of empowerment and flourishing, could understand.

"Keep going."

"Using drugs exacerbated a lot of problems I had coming up as a teenager and finally as an adult, and today realizing all this I understand that I owe myself, first and foremost, to do whatever it is that is healthy for me, spiritually, physically and mentally. And that's where I'm at. I truly feel I deserve this today and I won't allow anything or anyone to tell me different."

Really, it was usually not as heavy as all that. Quite a bit of the time was spent laughing, one of the things we always did best. Often we found ourselves repeating many of the same themes, and we knew it. We also knew that some of it was just talk, nothing more than a way to pass the time. That part of it was happily familiar.

Finally, finally he had learned one other truth, even if it was the hard way and he pretty much had to learn it for himself. He wrote once from prison that a person who loves himself doesn't engage in drug abuse or other harmful activities. "My father loves himself," he said during one last visit. "He's never once been in jail. I'm liking who I am now and someday I'll love myself like that."

"You know that new organization you're talking about?"

"Yeah, what?"

"I'll be a member of your board."

"You *mean* that?"

"Sure. Why wouldn't I?"

An Afterword

Most of what has been told in this book happened some time ago. Of course much has changed over the years: new situations and problems have replaced old ones, people have moved on, contacts broken and sometimes revived only to be lost again.

As for Ken, we spent some good times together after he returned from that five-year sentence, but then we drifted apart. Eventually, I told him that it was best for him to make it on his own, without further help from me. I reminded him that he had often said exactly that about his struggle with addiction. There was no dramatic breakdown of the relationship, just the sense that everything had been said and done that there was to say and do.

Still, it seems that we will have some sort of connection without having to make the arrangements. It was one of those small-world coincidences, the kind more likely to occur in fiction -- or in a place where people have lived for a long time -- that brought us together. I was walking home from the city when I saw a thin black man coming in my direction. He was a hundred yards away and across a street that separated us with five traffic lanes. Even at that distance there was something about his stride -- steps slightly longer than normal and taken with a confident bounce -- and something about the squared-back shoulders that made me think of Ken. No wonder: it *was* Ken.

He saw me then and ran across the street and crushed me in a long hug. We could hardly keep from interrupting each other, trying to compress years into minutes and in the process failing to say all that was most important. He was working for a time in some sort of volunteer legal capacity, he said, and of course we needed to get together. He gave me a phone number. When I called it sometime later, the line had been disconnected.

That does not matter. If we were fated to meet that day and in that way, we will meet again. Call that providence if you will, but it's also the case that we have kept a few people in common. It is more fitting that things not be forced; they should be allowed to play out as they will.

Sometimes I think about the work we did together, the successes and the shortcomings – and not only ours but those of all the people I came to know in that period -- and I remind myself to keep some perspective. We are not talking here about some gigantic struggle between good and evil. To frame these episodes in those terms would be excessive and very much self-serving. The universe is immense beyond the best scientific imaginings, and to dwell on success and failure in any short-term human undertaking – and they are all short-term in the long view -- has about the same value of tracking the flight of a fly on a summer afternoon.

The things that were achieved were noteworthy more as examples than for their results. What *are* results, after all, in a world of constant change? Today's good results can become tomorrow's new problem as easily as they can lead to better things. The drive and energy that impel a person toward benevolent actions can, with that perversity that gently mocks much of life, turn upon themselves. At such times we need to remember that it is not the results that should be judged; it is the intention, the motive.

That is a familiar idea in moral philosophy and it needs to be said one last time: what counts is our *willing* of the good. With that as the foundation, people act, and the examples set by their actions are the only things that are specific and lasting. When they point toward the possibility -- no, when they create the fact -- that people *can* put community and justice and humanity over personal gain and gratification, they should be celebrated.

Yes, we will meet again. And even if it isn't Ken that I meet again, I will see him in young people I often read about or hear about -- young people and older ones too who have felt the compassion and summoned the courage and developed the imagination that have together bought them to places where light drives away darkness as surely as happens with every new dawn, and to times that are more satisfying and more meaningful, clearer and longer-lasting, because they move us that much closer to the infinite power of the good.

MANDATOR
REPAT

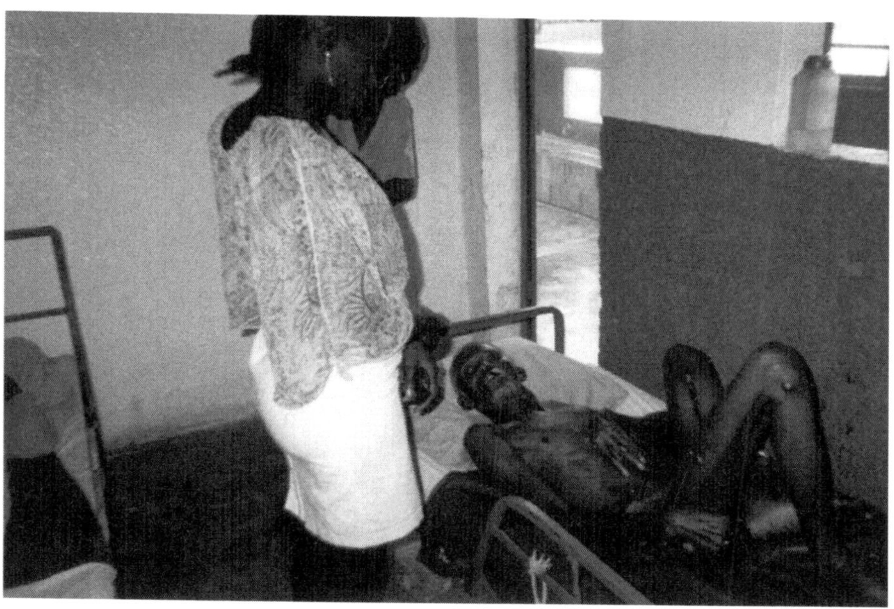

An Acknowledgement

Special thanks are due to those who had the patience to read the manuscript of this book, in the following order: Dr. Rebecca Housel, Reverend James Callan, Dr. Timothy Madigan, Cathleen Hutton, Ken Barksdale and Sandy Culver. Without their suggestions and above all their encouragement, that manuscript would not have become the book you are holding in your hands.

About the author:

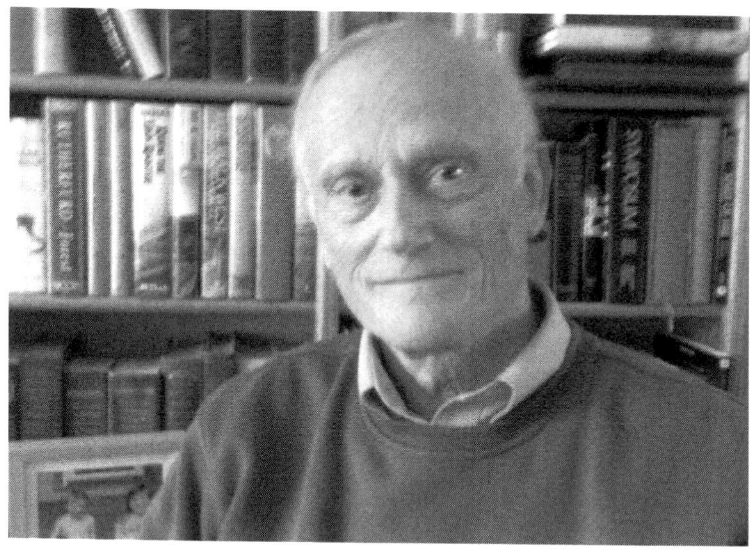

Derek Harrison has taught writing, literature and philosophy at three colleges in Rochester, New York. He is the author of several books for use in college courses and has contributed numerous articles to professional journals. His travels have taken him to more than 60 countries, some of which have played an important part in the development of this book. Those travels have put him in contact with many people of many different and interesting sorts, but the ones he likes best of all are in this country: his daughter, two sons and five granddaughters.

Starry Night Publishing

Everyone has a story...

Don't spend your life trying to get published! Don't tolerate rejection! Don't do all the work and allow the publishing companies reap the rewards!

Millions of independent authors like you, are making money, publishing their stories now. Our technological know-how will take the headaches out of getting published. Let "Starry Night Publishing.Com" take care of the hard parts, so you can focus on writing. You simply send us your Word Document and we do the rest. It really is that simple!

The big companies want to publish only "celebrity authors," not the average book-writer. It's almost impossible for first-time authors to get published today. This has led many authors to go the self-publishing route. Until recently, this was considered "vanity-publishing." You spent large sums of your money, to get twenty copies of your book, to give to relatives at Christmas, just so you could see your name on the cover. Now, however, the self-publishing industry allows authors to get published in a timely fashion, retain the rights to your work, keeping up to ninety-percent of your royalties, instead of the traditional five-percent.

We've opened up the gates, allowing you inside the world of publishing. While others charge you as much as fifteen-thousand dollars for a publishing package, we charge less than five-hundred dollars to cover copyright, ISBN, and distribution costs. Do you really want to spend all your time formatting, converting, designing a cover, and then promoting your book, because no one else will?

Our editors are professionals, able to create a top-notch book that you will be proud of. Becoming a published author is supposed to be fun, not a hassle.

At Starry Night Publishing, you submit your work, we create a professional-looking cover, a table of contents, compile your text and images into the appropriate format, convert your files for eReaders, take care of copyright information, assign an ISBN, allow you to keep one-hundred-percent of your rights, distribute your story worldwide on Amazon, Barnes & Noble and many other retailers, and write you a check for your royalties. There are no other hidden fees involved! You don't pay extra for a cover, or to keep your book in print. We promise! Everything is included! You even get a free copy of your book and unlimited half-price copies.

In four short years, we've published more than fifteen-hundred books, compared to the major publishing houses which only add an average of six new titles per year. We will publish your fiction, or non-fiction books about anything, and look forward to reading your stories and sharing them with the world.

We sincerely hope that you will join the growing Starry Night Publishing family, become a published author and gain the world-wide exposure that you deserve. You deserve to succeed. Success comes to those who make opportunities happen, not those who wait for opportunities to happen. You just have to try. Thanks for joining us on our journey.

www.starrynightpublishing.com

www.facebook.com/starrynightpublishing/

30109821R00208

Made in the USA
Middletown, DE
13 March 2016